SOTHEBY'S
CONCISE ENCYCLOPEDIA OF
PORCELAIN

SOTHEBY'S
CONCISE ENCYCLOPEDIA OF
PORCELAIN

GENERAL EDITOR · DAVID BATTIE

conran
OCTOPUS

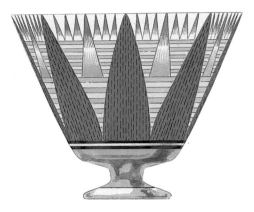

First published in 1990 by
Conran Octopus Limited
a part of Octpous Publishing Group
2–4 Heron Quays
London E14 4JP

This paperback edition published in 1994 by
Conran Octopus Limited. Reprinted 1995, 1999

British Library Cataloguing in Publication Data
A catalogue record for this book is available from the British Library

ISBN 1 85029 648 0

Series Editor Polly Powell
Art Editor Helen Lewis
Picture Researcher Nadine Bazar
Copy Editor Sandy Shepherd
Editorial Assistant Christine Rickerby
Assistant Art Editor Mike Snell
Picture Research Assistant Virginia Winder
Illustrators Richard Natkiel Associates, Coral Mula
Production Julia Golding

Typeset by Servis Filmsetting Ltd. Printed in China

Special photography
The publisher would like to thank Roy L. Davids, Leticia Roberts, Elizabeth White,
Philip Howell, Lynn Pearson, Anne Pollen, Tessa Aldridge, Katie Klitgaard and the ceramics
department at Sotheby's in London, New York and Billinghurst for their help with this book.

ILLUSTRATIONS ON PAGES 1–12

Page 1: Russian 'Seamstress' plate, 1924
Page 2: Display of Chinese blue-and-white porcelain (mostly Kangxi), Beningbrough Hall, Yorkshire
Page 4: Royal Doulton design for a vase, Christopher Dresser, 1867
Page 5: A group of Chinese ceramics, including examples of Qianlong, Kangxi, Yongle,
Zhengde, Xuande and Yongzheng porcelain
Page 6: Lithograph from the 1862 Paris exhibition
Page 9: German vases displayed at the Great Exhibition, 1851
Page 10: Miles Mason tea and coffee sets, 1805–10
Page 12: German canes with porcelain handles, 18th century

CONTENTS

DAVID BATTIE
Fakes and Forgeries

David Battie joined Sotheby's in London in 1967 and worked in various departments until becoming a director in 1976, having headed the Ceramics and Oriental Works of Art Department at Sotheby's Belgravia since its inception in 1971 (now closed). He is a founding contributor to the BBC's The Antiques Roadshow and has taken part in numerous other radio and television programmes. He has written the price guides to both nineteenth-century British porcelain and pottery as well as contributing to various other publications. He has lectured widely in many countries.

ANTHONY DU BOULAY
*Early Continental Porcelain
(excluding Medici and Sèvres)*

Anthony du Boulay was educated at Winchester and Geneva University. He joined Christie's in 1949 and became head of the newly created Ceramics Department in 1956. He became president of Christie's, Geneva in 1967. He retired in 1980 since when he has been a part-time honorary adviser on ceramics to the National Trust of England and Wales. He has lectured world-wide on porcelain as well as writing a number of articles and two books on Chinese porcelain. He has appeared in the BBC's programmes Going for a Song and The Antiques Roadshow.

GEOFFREY GODDEN
Chinese Export Porcelain

Geoffrey Godden is the Managing Director of a family firm of antique dealers, founded in Worthing in 1900. A collector since his school days, he now lectures and has written over twenty-five reference books, including his widely researched *Oriental Export Market Porcelains*. For more than forty years he has dealt in Chinese and Japanese export porcelains, and many examples in leading collections have passed through his hands. He is engaged in research on the English East India Company.

OLIVER IMPEY
Japanese Porcelain (excluding later Japanese)

Dr. Oliver Impey is Senior Assistant Keeper in the Department of Eastern Art, the Ashmolean Museum, Oxford and a Fellow of Green College. His research has concentrated on the export arts of Japan, especially porcelain and lacquer on which he has published widely. He has also written on the effects of those and other oriental arts in Europe (*Chinoiserie*, 1977). He is currently working on a book on the kiln-sites of Arita and porcelain manufacture before the export period.

JIMMY JONES
Welsh Porcelain 1780 to 1820

Jimmy Jones is an acknowledged authority on Welsh porcelain. He is a well-known lecturer on the subject and an Honorary Life Member of the National Association of Decorative and Fine Arts. With his co-author Sir Leslie Joseph, he recently published a comprehensive and definitive work on Swansea porcelain.

JOAN JONES
Minton 1820 to present

A life-long Minton enthusiast and collector, Joan Jones studied ceramics under the late Reginald G. Haggar, the painter, designer and former Minton Art Director. Joining Minton in 1977, she was appointed Curator of the Minton Museum in 1979 and has spent the last ten years researching, lecturing and writing on all aspects of the porcelain.

GORDON LANG
The Discovery of Porcelain

Gordon Lang has been at Sotheby's since 1974, and is the Senior Tutor and Deputy Director of the Sotheby's Educational Department. He is the author of two important exhibition catalogues, *The Wrestling Boys*, Chinese and Japanese porcelain at Burghley House and *The Powell-Cotton Collection of Chinese Ceramics*.

TERENCE LOCKETT
English Porcelain 1780 to 1820

Terence Lockett is a freelance lecturer and writer. Author of books on Rockingham, Davenport and Victorian tiles, he has also written numerous articles for academic and collectors' magazines. He is founder Chairman of the Northern Ceramic Society, Fellow of the Royal Society of Arts and a member of many ceramic history societies. He regularly appears on the BBC's The Antiques Roadshow.

MARK NEWSTEAD
*Continental Porcelain 1780 to 1930
(excluding Sèvres)*

Mark Newstead is an expert at Sotheby's in nineteenth- and twentieth-century European ceramics. He has written several articles and is currently working on a book about sang-de-boeuf techniques.

TAMARA PRÈAUD
Sèvres

An archivist and palaeographer, Tamara Prèaud has been the archivist of the Sèvres Factory since 1969. She is the author of numerous articles, catalogues of exhibitions, a book on the Sèvres Factory as well as one on ceramics in the twentieth century. She has translated several books on ceramics and lectured at many conferences for the International Ceramic Fair and at seminars of the French Porcelain Society.

DAVID PRIESTLEY
Qing Imperial Porcelain

David Priestley was educated at New College, Oxford. He read Chinese, and, in his final year, studied Chinese ceramics under Mary Tregear, the Keeper of Eastern Art at the Ashmolean Museum. He joined Sotheby's Chinese Department in 1984 and now travels frequently to Hong Kong, where he is a Director of Sotheby's Hong Kong. He is also a Deputy Director of the Chinese Department in Sotheby's London.

Henry Sandon
Later English Porcelain

Henry Sandon was originally a professional musician, but the chance discovery of Medieval and Roman pottery in his Worcester garden led to a passion for ceramics. He was curator of Royal Worcester and the Dyson Perrins Museum for 17 years, has written half a dozen major books on porcelain and pottery and is now well known for his appearances on television programmes such as The Antiques Roadshow.

Simon Spero
Early English Porcelain

Simon Spero is an antiques dealer with a shop in Kensington Church Street, London, specializing in eighteenth-century English porcelain and enamels. He has been a regular contributor to various magazines over the past twenty years and his books include *The Price Guide to 18th Century English Porcelain* (1970) and *Worcester Porcelain, The Klepser Collection* (1984). He has lectured widely in America and Britain.

Garrison Stradling
American Porcelain

Garrison Stradling is an author, lecturer and antiques dealer in partnership with his wife, Diana, based in New York. Specializing in early ceramics and glass, The Stradlings are the country's foremost dealers in American porcelain. Mr Stradling's most widely quoted article concerning American porcelain, *American Ceramics and the Philadelphia Centennial*, was published in the July 1976 bicentennial issue of the magazine *Antiques*.

Lars Tharp
Later Japanese and Medici Porcelain

Conducted from an early age through the Nationalmuseum, Copenhagen, where his grandfather was Keeper of Antiquities, Lars Tharp was educated at Gonville and Caius College, Cambridge. In 1977, he joined Sotheby's as a cataloguer of ceramics. Currently a Director of Sotheby's in Sussex, where he lives with his wife and daughter, he also writes, lectures and appears on the television.

FOREWORD

*P*orcelain has been produced in vast quantities over the centuries, in every decorative style. The aesthetic range is enormous, from a plain Song bowl, whose appeal lies in its glaze and with the perfection of a simple form, to the most elaborately enamelled and flower-encrusted centrepiece produced at Meissen or in Victorian England. The present value of porcelain is as wide-ranging as its aesthetic appeal, offering to collectors whose means may be large or small the opportunity to form a collection of the greatest interest. This encyclopedia has been designed to give a tempting and informative introduction to the whole spectrum of this fascinating field.

JULIAN THOMPSON

INTRODUCTION

*D*espite their apparent fragility, ceramics are great survivors. They were the first entirely man-made objects and almost every primitive society produced them from readily available ingredients. They could be used for food storage, cooking and for transporting water. Their presence enables archaeologists to date precisely when a site was occupied by using the thermoluminescence test which can pin-point when the pots were fired.

In China, several thousand years of ceramic tradition and experimentation led eventually to the intermixing of china stone and china clay to produce a new material — true porcelain. It was strong, did not chip or crack easily, would take moulded or incised patterns, could be potted to almost miraculous thinness and, strangest of all, was translucent. Half a millennium of further development led to the discovery that cobalt under the glaze produced a strong blue. Within a few hundred years, vases and dishes had migrated from China to Europe to become objects of wonder, valued more highly than gold.

The constant research in Europe to produce true porcelain was not successful until a thousand years had passed since its discovery in China. Softer bodies had been made earlier — in Italy and France — but to Germany falls the honour of the first production of European hard-paste porcelain.

This book, which pulls together the work of fifteen authors, each a specialist in his or her field, recounts the story of porcelain in every country in which it was made, from its earliest beginnings until the twentieth century. It explains the factors that led to the success and failure of different factories: the trade, the scientific experimentation, the artists and the styles. The photographs that accompany the text have been selected to epitomise the enormous diversity of the long history of porcelain.

THE DISCOVERY OF
PORCELAIN

---

*T*o the Chinese go the laurels for the discovery of porcelain. It was no sudden accidental coming together of the right ingredients, but a slow evolution over millennia.

Like almost all primitive societies the prehistoric Chinese developed pottery for storing and cooking food and for water. Indeed, the existence of pottery is one characteristic of a settled society, for even the most primitive pot needs skill in the preparation of the clay, levigation and firing. If pottery developed to help people live in many societies — including the Chinese — it was also there at their death. Funerals developed during the Han and Tang dynasties into the extraordinary burials of miniature pottery animals, servants, grooms and soldiers, interred to serve the deceased in the afterlife. It was the skills developed in forming these that would eventually lead to a strong, white, translucent material: porcelain.

DETAIL OF MING JAR, JIAJING MARK AND PERIOD, 1522–1566

This polychrome jar is painted in the wucai *palette. The bold, if somewhat crude, brushwork is typical of the late Ming period.*

*There was a long process of experimentation and
refinement before Chinese potters were able to
construct the kind of kilns capable of achieving the
high temperatures necessary for producing true
porcelain.*

EARTHENWARES

AND POTTERY

The evolution of porcelain, a sub-species of earthenware or pottery, starts in China during the late Neolithic cultures of the north. The earliest examples have been unearthed in an area that stretches from the Shandong peninsula in the northeast, westwards along the plains on either side of the Huangho river into the Gansu corridor. These very early earthenwares, which date from the fifth or fourth millennium BC, are basic utilitarian vessels for storage, cooking or carrying water. They were hand-made, created with coils of clay that were then squashed together by hand or patted with a wooden spatula, which ensured that the seams did not leak. Sometimes the pot was decorated with simple repeated motifs that were either gouged into the clay or tapped into it with a sharp tool.

Not all Neolithic pottery was functional in the general domestic sense: some remarkable funerary vessels exist from the Yang-shao culture in Gansu province. Many of these generous red-bodied vessels are painted in black or dark brown slip with geometric or stylized zoomorphic designs. This pottery, which dates from the third millennium, shows a great advance in skill, for although it is coiled, the sides have been smoothed so carefully that the surface undulates only slightly.

The other major Chinese Neolithic culture, the Long-shan, which was centred in the Shandong peninsula, bequeathed us the fast-turning wheel. This machine, developed by the third or second millennium BC, made possible crisply profiled and burnished pottery vessels of elegant form. However, this does not imply that the wheel was used exclusively from then on, for there are many examples from subsequent periods to contradict that argument. In fact the wheel was often used only to finish off the rim or foot of a 'coiled' vessel.

Further significant developments took place during the Shang dynasty (*c.*1600–1028 BC), the earliest historic period of China. The first was the construction of kilns suitable for firing ceramics at high temperatures. This idea was probably borrowed from the technically advanced bronze industry, where extreme heat was necessary for smelting metals. The second was the use of glaze, which perhaps evolved from the casual dressing of wood-ash; this was precipitated during the firing onto the upper surfaces of the vessel. If originally the glaze effect was accidental, it was soon regulated to produce an even, overall

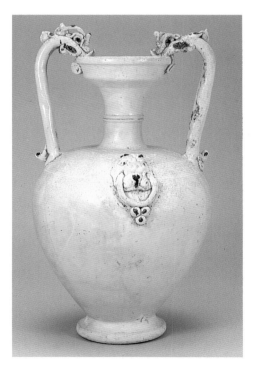

WHITE EARTHENWARE FUNERARY
URN, TANG DYNASTY, 618–906
(36.9cm/14½in)

*The high-shouldered body of this piece is
surmounted by a slender trumpet neck.*

covering. It meant that previously low-fired porous earthenware could be made impervious by glaze. Although the Shang dynasty was a period of technological innovation, its pottery played a secondary role to that of bronze, as the many ceramic copies of that material confirm.

The next development took place during the Zhou dynasty (1027–771 BC) when pottery was fired to a temperature of around 1200°C (2192°F); the Chinese potters had thus achieved the lowest temperatures at which stoneware can be fired. The material from which stoneware clay is composed is semi-fluxed in the firing, which makes it impervious to liquids, even without a glaze.

Later, in the Han dynasty (206 BC–AD 221) lead-silicate glazes appear; these are usually green but occasionally have misfired and have become a deep straw colour. Most of these glazes have partially broken down into strata creating an iridescent effect.

THE BEGINNINGS OF PORCELAIN

The first porcelain was probably made during the Sui (AD 581–617) or early Tang (AD 618–906) dynasties. It almost certainly evolved from the high-fired northern white wares that appeared in the fifth or sixth century, and which were produced in the kilns of Hebei, Henan, Shaanxi and Anhui provinces, to the north of the Yangtze river.

As a material, the early porcelain does not seem to conform to the usual Western view of porcelain or 'china'. (The latter was the name by which it was generally known in England in the seventeenth century and which has remained in colloquial usage up to the present.) The slightly coarse and granular chalky body and the rather creamy parchment-coloured glaze contrast with the slick and unctuous porcelains of Meissen, Sèvres or Spode. Most examples of early 'china' are relatively

DING YAO DISH, NORTHERN SONG DYNASTY, 960–1127
(16.1cm/6⅜in)

The centre of this shallow form is carved with lotus blossom; its unglazed rim is bound with copper.

simple in form, and include dishes, bowls, wine pots, storage jars and even bird-feeders. All of these types of porcelain adhere to the vocabulary of forms current in the seventh, eighth or ninth centuries and borrow from metalwork, lacquer or other types of earthenware.

By the time of the Tang dynasty it is clear that production was on a vast scale, catering for every stratum of society. Li Zhen, a notable writer of the period, commented 'The white cups of Neiju (a species of this northern porcellaneous ware called Xing) are used everywhere by rich and poor alike'. By 'everywhere' the writer probably meant metropolitan China, but examples of this early ware were excavated by German archaeologists at Samarra, a city on the Tigris, where the Abbasid caliphate built a palace, and which was occupied between AD 836 and 883.

Another account of early porcelain in a different region of China occurs in the treatise entitled *Ahbar as-sin wa l'hind*, 'The History of China and India', a compilation of traveller's recollections by an unidentified Arab writer in AD 851. In a description of Canton, where there had been a long-established colony of Muslim merchants, who presumably shipped their commodities to Samarra and Fostat, the writer states: 'here (the Cantonese) have pottery of excellent quality, of which bowls are made as fine as glass drinking cups, the sparkle of water can be seen through it although it is pottery'. As pottery does not allow light through it, the material must have been porcellaneous.

These early wares were usually undecorated, save the occasional piece which has a little carving to the rim but no moulding or painted embellishment.

NORTHERN WHITE WARES AND DING YAO

The porcellaneous white wares of the northern Liao dynasty (AD 907–1125) are generally small in scale, of simple form, and with little or no decoration. The majority of the production, like the Ding Yao wares, was of dishes and bowls. Bowls were typically conical with straight or slightly rounded sides that flared from a narrow foot, the latter measuring less than one third of the rim diameter. The foot itself is quite shallow, probably no more than 2–2.8 mm ($\frac{1}{16}$–$\frac{1}{8}$ in) in height. The granular off-white paste is covered in an irregular glaze of greyish tone with the merest suggestion of blue. The glaze is dotted with tiny brownish flecks, and tends to run in tears and also to gather more towards the rim where its colour is slightly yellowish. The throwing contours on the sides of the vessel are quite prominent.

The porcellaneous body of Ding Yao wares is close-grained and white; in fact it is very close to that of the other northern white wares. The most distinctive feature of this group is the creamy glaze. It is a translucent, yellowish-ivory colour but takes on a brownish or olive hue where it has been applied too generously or where it has gathered in angles or crevices. On deep bowls and vases the glaze occasionally dribbles in streaks down the vertical walls of the vessel. The glaze is not very glassy but has a fine muslin-like texture, the surface dimpled with the minutest craters.

Ding Yao wares were decorated either with carving or with moulded designs; the latter method was unknown before the twelfth century. The first technique was done with fluid strokes and on a generous scale, relative to the size of the vessel. Early specimens, which date from the tenth or eleventh century, are generally very strongly carved compared with the subtle treatment of the twelfth and thirteenth centuries. Themes are invariably natural: lotus or peony sprays, fish swimming among waterweeds, or fowl on a river-bank. Moulded designs, on either dishes or bowls, are much more intricate. Again, they are usually naturalistic, some perhaps borrowed from contemporary textiles. The glaze on the moulded group softens the contours of the design, leaving a more even appearance than on the carved pieces, which have an irregular effect where the depth of each incision governs the tonal intensity of the glaze.

Bowls or dishes made up the majority of the Ding Yao output; vases, bottles and other forms were rare. They were fired on clay pads whereas most flatware was fired upside down in 'saggars' which could hold ten or a dozen plates or bowls. This clever and economical way of firing did have one serious drawback, however, which was that the rims of the pieces had to be left unglazed. Once cooled, the bowl or dish had to be bound with a thin sheath of copper or some other metal.

As the Sinan Treasure has proved, Ding-type wares were produced not only in the north of China but also in the south, well into the fourteenth century. This southern group has a slightly greyer appearance, even if the designs were similar to those of the northern types.

CHINESE CELADON

The ancestry of Chinese celadon ware, of both northern and southern types, can be traced back to the olive-glazed wares of the Warring States period and the Yue wares of the Han dynasty. The northern type, termed Yaozhou, is composed of a greyish stoneware, related to Junyao and to other local northern ware. The southern type, from Zhejiang province, is composed of fine

ZHEJIANG CELADON VASES, SONG OR YUAN DYNASTY, 13TH OR 14TH CENTURY (tallest: 37.5cm/14¾in)

Sinuous shapes and relief decoration based on flower or vegetable forms are characteristic of this period.

porcelain stone which has been slightly adulterated with iron, allegedly to improve the depth of colour of the glaze. Northern celadon has a rich olive-green glaze over a granular grey clay which, when exposed, tends to burn a dark rust-brown in the firing. Decoration on this type of celadon is found either carved or moulded with dense floral patterns.

The southern type is a colder blue-green colour; the most sought-after tone is termed *kinuta* (Japanese for mallet), so-called after a number of mallet-shaped bottles. A superb example is in the Bisha-mondo Temple in Kyoto. The later Zhe-jiang wares of the Yuan (1280–1368) or early Ming (1368–1644) tend to appear somewhat warmer or yellow-green in colour, although fine examples of the more refined *kinuta* glaze can be dated to the fourteenth century.

The early wares of the southern Song dynasty (1128–1279) are of classic simplicity, in keeping with the taste of the Song court. Forms are predominantly flower-inspired, such as lotus bowls and vases, or are based on archaic bronzes with little additional embellishment except, occasionally, some subtle carved motif.

Yuan and Ming celadons are altogether grander and more complex. Firstly, improvements in the clay composition and technology meant that it was possible to make very large pieces, for example dishes measuring 61 cm (24 in) in diameter. (In contrast, Song pieces are relatively small; few pieces are more than 33 cm (13 in) wide). Secondly, surface decoration became more crowded and sculptural. Often, the whole vessel or dish was carved or moulded with vegetal or animal subjects, following the trends of the underglaze painted porcelain of Jingdezhen.

Although celadon continued to be produced during the fifteenth century, its heyday was past, replaced in general affection by the colourful porcelains of Jingdezhen. Production and standards declined, obeying the natural laws of the market-place. Very little celadon of any note was made after the fifteenth century.

QINGBAI, THE SOUTHERN PORCELAIN OF JINGDEZHEN

Qingbai, sometimes known as Yingqing (which translates as 'cloudy, misty or shadow blue'), was produced during the Song period (960–1279) and is probably the porcelain described by Marco Polo on his travels through the China of Jenghiz Khan. He observed that 'bowls the colour of azure' could be obtained very cheaply: 'One may buy two or three bowls for a single Venetian groat'. The Qingbai glaze is, at its greatest intensity, a rich sky-blue colour. Normally, the thin and translucent glaze is either pale green or blue but appears much deeper toned where it has pooled. Where the glaze has been rubbed or is thin, it suffers from rust-coloured speckles and suffusions (a fault also seen on early Bow porcelains).

The body or paste of Qingbai ware is a grey-white that generally oxidizes to a strong red colour in the kiln in just the same way as the Jingdezhen blue-and-white porcelains of the Yuan and Ming dynasties.

QINGBAI PORCELAIN, SOUTHERN SONG OR YUAN DYNASTY, 13TH OR 14TH CENTURY

These three pieces demonstrate the diversity of Qingbai porcelain. (ABOVE)

QINGBAI DISH, SONG OR YUAN DYNASTY, 13TH OR 14TH CENTURY
(14cm/5½in)

The pale green glaze terminates immediately below the rim. (LEFT)

The most common Qingbai wares are bowls or dishes with either plain or petal-form rims, the latter shape effected by cutting several small notches. Bowls and dishes were mostly fired upside down, but with a marginally wider unglazed border around the rim than that of the Ding Yao group. Wares include bottles, ewers and vases, often with 10 or 15 prominent lobes running vertically up the vessel. Commonly egg-shaped, these tall vessels are surmounted by long trumpet-shaped necks and are set on short, slightly splayed feet, sometimes carved with gadroons or simple grooves. They were fired on circular clay collars or three or more small clay pads. The spouts on ewers are very tall and gently tapered, rising from the shoulder of the main body to terminate level with the top of the vessel. The thinly made handles are also long and elegant, often based on metal prototypes. The decoration is carved, depicting flowers such as peony or lotus among scrolling foliage. The early wares are decorated with more restraint than those of the Yuan dynasty (AD 1280–1368) which can be complex and crowded and not necessarily harmonious. On certain Yuan pieces, such as the Gaignières Fonthill bottle in the National Museum, Dublin, there is a tendency to over-elaboration.

SHU-FU WARES

The Shu-fu wares, also from Jingdezhen, are similar in feel to Qingbai porcelain. More heavily potted, they have a dense green or blue glaze which is opaque and generally duller than Qingbai. Bowls and dishes, the former often with ridged sides, are set on a thick square-cut foot. The unglazed base is pointed like a shallow cone and the exposed biscuit tends to burn red in the firing. Some pieces are moulded with tiers of overlapping petals, after contemporary silver shapes, or with scrolling foliage. A few specimens are moulded with characters such as *ji*, *lu*, *shu* or *fu*; the latter two, meaning 'privy council' and 'prosperity', give this group of porcelain wares its name.

BLUE-AND-WHITE *GUAN*, YUAN DYNASTY, 1280–1368 (27.3cm/10¾in)

The generous, bulbous body of this jar is painted with a narrative subject, probably an episode from the Yuan drama, 'The Romance of the Western Chamber'. Encircling the base is a frieze of non-contiguous petal panels. The shoulders are decorated with a floral meander below the short neck embellished with a wave pattern. (LEFT)

OTHER WARES

Among the Qingbai and Shu-fu porcelains of the later Yuan period is an unusual group of objects, mainly of a smaller size. It comprises globular oil jars, with or without tiny lugs flanking the neck, *guan*-shaped or truncated jars, pear-shaped bottles with tall trumpet necks, cuboid jars, bowls, dishes and a curious assembly of human figures and animals. These wares are either left plain or decorated in underglaze iron, copper or cobalt. This technique, already known on Cizhou stoneware of the thirteenth century, was introduced onto porcelain early in the fourteenth century. Underglaze iron was simply splashed on in a series of spots whereas underglaze copper-red or cobalt-blue were used to paint flowers, birds, animals or humans. By far the most commonly encountered themes are floral, usually chrysanthemums with straggling stems and short spiky leaves. On larger vessels, the border patterns are usually pointed lotus-petal panels with pendant lobed leaves around the base and a very carelessly rendered classic scroll. Whatever the subject, the painting was always executed in an energetic but cursory manner. This group, which seems to have been exported almost exclusively to southeast Asia, for it has been unearthed there in some quantity, particularly from burial chambers in the Philippines and Indonesia, is a counterpoint to the massive Yuan blue-and-white jars and dishes found in India, the Middle and Near East.

UNDERGLAZE BLUE SAUCER DISH AND BLUE-AND-WHITE EWER, YUAN DYNASTY, 1280–1368 (ewer: 26.7cm/10½in)

In comparison with earlier pieces, the saucer dish shown here seems almost casual in its decorative composition, with all the elements in the design appearing to jostle for space. The ewer is divided into eight horizontal decorative elements, the overall design tending to conflict with the natural profile of the vessel. (BELOW)

SECOND HALF OF THE FOURTEENTH CENTURY

In the Percival David Foundation in London, there is a pair of temple vases that bears the date AD 1351 and an extensive inscription dedicated to a Daoist temple about 120 km (75 miles) from Jingdezhen. Nearly 60 cm (2 ft) high and modelled after a bronze form, they are the most important evidence of the development of blue-and-white. The main body, shaped like a slender egg, is surmounted by a tall trumpet neck with a galleried rim, and sits on a high splayed foot. On either side of the neck is an elephant's head and trunk, which forms the support for two loose porcelain ring handles (which are now missing). Apart from the main theme

THE GAIGNIÈRES FONTHILL VASE, *c.1300*

This is the earliest documented example of Chinese porcelain in Europe and was given as a gift in 1381 to Charles III of Durazzo in Italy by King Louis the Great of Hungary. The complexity of the design, using carved and applied motifs, and the emphasis on the horizontal orders which tends to break up the natural lines of the vessel, are characteristic of this period. (RIGHT)

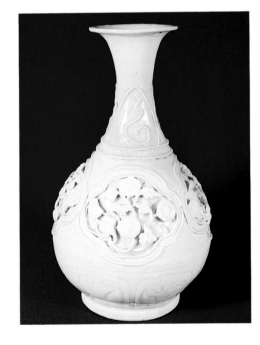

PAIR OF BLUE-AND-WHITE TEMPLE VASES, DATED 1351

Painted with four-clawed dragons cavorting above crashing waves, the seven ancillary decorative bands comprise almost the entire canon of minor ornamentation found on underglaze cobalt porcelain dating from the middle of the fourteenth century. (OPPOSITE)

of the design – a sinuous, four-clawed dragon prowling among highly stylized cloud clusters – there are seven ancillary bands of decoration on each of the vases.

It is worth dwelling on these minor elements, because they are representative of the late Yuan, and at least one or two of them appear on most jars or dishes of the period. The basal frieze is made up of pointed petals, slightly separate from each other and containing Daoist precious objects. (Buddhist or Daoist objects in leaf panels are frequently found on both painted and moulded porcelains of the fourteenth century). Above the base frieze, on the sloping section of the foot is a band of peony meander with detailed or modelled flower-heads among large and small spiky leaves. There are two other flower borders on the

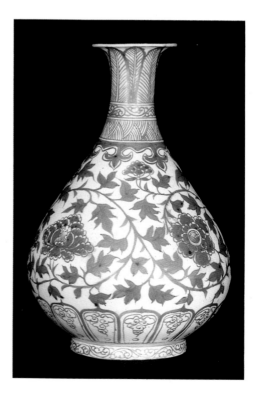

JINGDEZHEN BOTTLE, LATE 14TH CENTURY (32cm/12⅝in)

Difficulty in obtaining cobalt ore forced the potters of Jingdezhen to use copper as a substitute.

David vases: one has chrysanthemums with cross-hatched centres, similar to those on the so-called southeast Asian export type, with leaves resembling a short, fat, tapered fern; the second band depicts lotuses whose lobed leaves are again tapered, but with little spikes jutting out from the base of the leaf. These three bands are unquestionably the most common floral patterns of the late Yuan and early Ming periods.

A wave pattern was also extremely popular, mainly on the perimeter of dishes or on the neck of a jar. In the curious early form of this pattern the crest of the wave looks like a hump-backed squirrel. By the early fifteenth century this wild water has become conventionalized and regular.

Other border patterns of the Yuan and early Ming include the 'thundercloud' and the trellis. The first is a squared scroll similar to the Greek key-fret pattern; it is mono-cellular around the middle of the fourteenth century, double-celled towards the end of the century, and is often continuous in the fifteenth century. The trellis is a series of repeating lozenges, shaped like the diamond on playing cards. Each lozenge is decorated with small dashes projecting inwards from the middle of each side to meet in the centre of the lozenge.

DECORATION AND FORM

The main decorative themes of the second half of the fourteenth century are scrolling lotus, peony or chrysanthemums; two mandarin ducks on a lotus pond; mythical beasts such as the kylin in fenced gardens; fish swimming among eel grass and water-weeds; and, rarely, figure subjects. Whatever the design, there is a sense of energy in the image that outweighs the organizational skills of the painting.

The most common forms of this period are dishes with flat rims that are either plain or barbed; bowls with a small foot, rounded sides and a sharply everted lip; bottles of a generous pear shape with a tall narrow neck that flares outwards at the top; baluster vases with high shoulders and very small constricted necks (*meiping*). Almost all of

these wares are heavily potted with clearly visible luting seams. The foot-rim on the dishes is low and wedge-shaped, whereas on the bottles the profile is more varied, sometimes tall and undercut, and at other times low and wedge-shaped. In this period the base is left unglazed, which allows the porcelain to burn red in the firing.

EARLY MING

Hongwu, the first emperor of the Ming dynasty (reigned from 1368 to 1398), promulgated a ban which prevented the Chinese from travelling beyond the frontiers of the country, an edict which had dramatic consequences for trade. Cobalt, the essential ingredient in blue-and-white porcelain, and which was probably mined near Kashan in Persia, became difficult to obtain. It was often substituted by copper ore, a more readily available raw material. The result was an underglaze red of unpredictable tones, ranging from a clean pinkish-red to an unappealing liverish colour or even silvery-grey. The glaze on many late fourteenth-century porcelains has a waxy feel and can be much glassier than the earlier wares. Thematically, there is little change from the decorative canon of the Yuan: natural subjects with flowers predominate and occasionally a mythical beast or a human being appears.

The decoration of the Hongwu period, while still dynamic, appears a degree more orderly and has a more sensitive use of space than in the preceding period. On jars, vases or bottles there is less emphasis on the horizontal placement of the design that was typical of the mid-fourteenth century. Instead, the main theme begins to occupy a greater proportion of the vessel; the minor elements are gradually reduced in scale, and banished to the upper and lower margins. Another aspect of the decoration is a greater harmony between the main and secondary themes, a striking change from the irreconcilable patterns of the late Yuan.

Between 1350 and 1400 the forms of ewers, vases, bowls or dishes undergo little detectable change.

THE EARLY

FIFTEENTH CENTURY

The establishment of kilns in the fourteenth century to provide porcelain for the imperial capital marks a turning point. From this period there is a remarkable change in the quality not only of the material but also of the potting and decoration. To many authorities, the porcelains made during the reigns of Yongle (1403–1425) and Xuande (1426–1435) are, quite simply, the best. They may not possess the elegant and feminine appeal of the Chenghua period that followed but they are manifestly more powerful and robust in character.

The wares of the early fifteenth century show a perfect balance between the design and the space it occupies. Flowers or foliage are not squashed up against the boundaries of the dish and there is no sense of crowding such as there is in the late Yuan, or for that matter in that period of decline, the sixteenth century. The layout of design and decoration on these pieces has been carefully planned but it is not rigid, nor does it lack a certain energy.

BLUE-AND-WHITE BOWL, EARLY 15TH CENTURY (13.2cm/5⅛in)

Painted in underglaze cobalt blue with a somewhat blurred appearance typical of the early Ming reigns of Yongle and Xuande, this bowl is unusual in that it bears an Arabic inscription. (ABOVE)

BLUE-AND-WHITE WINE CUP OR BOWL, YONGLE MARK AND PERIOD, 1403–1425 (9.2cm/3⅝in)

The interior of this dish bears the archaic four-character mark of the emperor Yongle. Underglaze reign marks, usually composed of six characters, first appeared in the early fifteenth century. (TOP LEFT)

STEM CUP WITH UNDERGLAZE RED DECORATION, EARLY 15TH CENTURY (W11.7cm/4½in)

Stem cups are ritual vessels which first appeared during the Tang dynasty. Underglaze red was used extensively in the late fourteenth century. However, it proved difficult to stabilise and consequently fell into abeyance. (ABOVE LEFT)

STEM CUP, XUANDE MARK AND PERIOD, 1426–1435 (H10.5cm/4⅛in)

This cup is painted with five-clawed dragons in underglaze blue and copper-red. (LEFT)

The most common designs in this period are vegetal: scrolling lotus or chrysanthemum; combinations of seasonal flowers; flowers and shrubs emblematic of the 12 months, fruiting gourd or bunches of grapes. Other subjects include birds perched among blossoming branches, dragons hurtling among clouds, and the male and female phoenix balanced perfectly in circular motion. The human figure is rare on early fifteenth-century porcelain and the few figure subjects that do appear are probably drawn from contemporary pattern books. The uniformity of almost all the decorative themes of this period suggests the use of such sources. Few specimens are without a comparable counterpart.

Border patterns are conventional and standardized; the classic scroll no longer meanders informally along the foot-rim or mouth but proceeds in a neat and predictable manner. The petal panel, too, has undergone a more radical change; while the outline still resembles a pointed arch, the interior has been simplified. The pendant curly scroll has been replaced by a more defined motif, sometimes painted in reverse, that is, reversed in white on a solid blue ground. The panels are also smaller relative to the vessel and are, with a few exceptions, contiguous. As for the thundercloud pattern, it is in a transitional phase: while there are many double-celled versions, there are also continuous arrangements. Other border motifs include the stiff or pointed leaf or plantain and the 'wave-and rock' pattern, both continuations of fourteenth-century prototypes.

The characteristic glaze of the early fifteenth century is thick, bluish or greenish, and saturated with bubbles that create minute depressions in the surface. This has been likened to the skin of an orange, although the 'craters' in the glaze are much smaller than those on an orange. This textured surface distorts the underglaze decoration, blurring it and giving it a subtle soft appearance.

On Yongle and Xuande porcelains there are small areas of brown-black discoloration in the cobalt blue. This is a typical

MING BLUE-AND-WHITE BALUSTER *MEIPING*, YONGLE PERIOD, 1403–1425 (36.5cm/14¼in)

Painted in slightly blurred underglaze blue with groups of seasonal fruits and flowers, the careful spacing and almost botanical accuracy of this vase's decoration demonstrate the salient features of the early fifteenth century. (LEFT)

MING BOWL, XUANDE MARK AND PERIOD, 1426–1435 (28.9cm/11⅜in)

This heavily potted bowl is characteristic of early fifteenth century blue-and-white wares. The measured spacing and organization of the main theme — a continuous floral meander — is a perfect example from this period. (BELOW)

defect of the period, caused by superfluous cobalt floating up to the surface of the glaze and being burnt during the firing.

A considerable number of new forms, some of Middle Eastern origin, are seen in the early fifteenth century including moon flasks, which as the name implies, are disc-shaped vessels with a pair of handles flanking the short straight neck. A variant of this has a somewhat larger swollen neck resembling a garlic bulb; the strap handles are grooved and have heart-shaped terminals of cloud-collar or *ruyi*-head type. This latter vessel is based on an Islamic metal flask of which there is a thirteenth-century Mamluk example in the Freer Gallery in the Smithsonian Institution, Washington D.C. Other non-Chinese forms that appear are a bulbous-bodied tankard with a straight but faceted neck, probably derived from Ottoman silver, and deep basins with straight vertical sides and flat rims, borrowed from Syrian or Egyptian glass or brass shapes.

The native innovations of this period are

SECOND HALF OF THE FIFTEENTH CENTURY

The period between the end of the reign of the emperor Xuande, in 1435, and the reign of the emperor Chenghua (1465–1487) was an interregnum in which the scale of porcelain production was slowed down. Following the interregnum, the kilns at Jingdezhen increased their production to meet the growing demand, once more fulfilling large orders for the imperial court and the government. Porcelain had, in the meanwhile, undergone a substantial transformation in style: its decoration had evolved, perhaps in a less obvious manner, and a variety of new shapes had appeared and old forms were subtly changed.

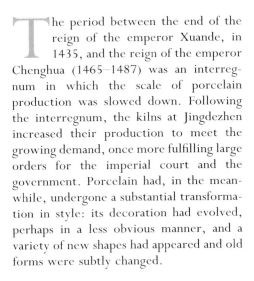

WINE CUP PAINTED IN *DOUCAI* **PALETTE, CHENGHUA MARK AND PERIOD, 1465–1487 (H5.4cm/2⅛in)**

The technique of painting porcelain with overglaze enamels was at first confined to small objects, probably because of the difficulty of firing in suitably controlled conditions. (ABOVE)

BLUE-AND-WHITE FLASK, EARLY 15TH CENTURY (30.7cm/12⅛in)

This flask is based on a Middle-Eastern metal form of a slightly earlier date. (TOP)

the small bowls with deep convex sides that rise from a very small foot, termed *lianzu* or lotus-shape; they indeed resemble a half-opened lotus. Also of Chinese inspiration are the bowls with lobed sides and correspondingly lobed footrings, a most unusual feature. Other examples of new forms include truncated jars (*guan*) with high shoulders and rounded sides; ovoid vases with trumpet necks; and shallow bowls with short double-ribbed concave sides.

In the early fifteenth century, following the establishment of the imperial kilns, reign marks first appear. On some extremely fine white wares the reign mark of the emperor Yongle is engraved in archaic script. Although the same type of script was also used on underglaze blue pieces, such specimens are very rare. During the subsequent reign of Xuande, six, or more rarely four, character marks were used regularly. Most often they were written in two columns on the base of the object but occasionally they occur written horizontally below the rim of a bowl or on the shoulder of a jar or tankard.

In contrast to the greenish thickly bubbled glaze and the rather blurred and dark-speckled underglaze blue of Yongle and Xuande porcelain, the glaze of the Chenghua period is clearer and a little more glassy, but with a curious smoky ivory appearance. The best way to discern this characteristic is by juxtaposing a Chenghua piece with either an earlier or a later piece. The British Museum and the Percival David Foundation in London have such comparative displays. The underglaze cobalt-blue of Chenghua is a shade greyer than its predecessor but generally does not suffer from its oxidized black speckling. The underglaze design is also more sharply focused but nonetheless remains perceptibly on the 'soft' side, compared, for example, with the blue-and-white decoration from the Kangxi period (1662–1722).

The brushwork of this reign is executed in a delicate, almost tentative, hand and, although well balanced, lacks the bolder feel of early fifteenth-century blue-and-white. There is also a noticeable loss of detail and a greater sense of space. This is particularly evident in the more linear, less painterly treatment of flowers and foliage. On the whole, subjects are painted in a more 'feminine' manner.

Although the general appearance and subject matter of Chenghua porcelain is little different from earlier fifteenth-century ware, there are a couple of notable exceptions. Firstly, there is a group of beautifully potted flared bowls sensitively painted with meandering flowers, such as lotus or hibiscus. These are termed 'palace bowls' and are brilliant examples of the prevalent court style. The second group consists of wares of diverse forms – *meiping* vases, *guan* jars and dishes – painted in an informal style with figure subjects, scholars, officials and attendants in a semi-desert landscape with the suggestion of a breeze tugging at their loose garments. This type has been classified as the 'windswept scholar' group and probably evolved during the interregnum period.

A development of the fifteenth century was the use of overglaze enamels on porcelain, a technique first applied to the northern Chinese cizhou stonewares in the thirteenth century. By the time of the Chenghua reign, porcelains painted in a combination of underglaze blue and overglaze had reached a very high standard. The term used for this palette is *doucai*, which translates as 'contrasting or contending colours'. Apart from underglaze cobalt blue, other colours include a soft manganese-brown, copper-green, yellow and black. Here the entire design is outlined in underglaze blue. A second, lower tempera-

ture firing is required for the overglaze enamel colours which complete the decoration. Almost all wares decorated in this range of colours are small in scale, usually measuring no more than a few inches at their greatest dimension. Within this extremely rare group, stem cups and wine cups are the usual forms. The latter are sometimes painted with a chicken, rooster and chicks pecking at grain scattered on the ground. These tiny 'chicken cups', which are among the most sought-after and costly porcelains ever made, were copied with

great accuracy along with the Chenghua reign mark during the early Qing dynasty (1644–1912). Other enamel wares of this and the subsequent reign of Hongzhi (1488–1505) fall into two categories. The first group is straightforward glazed porcelain painted in overglaze enamels only, without underglaze blue. The second, but more distinctive type, is unglazed but fired porcelain, decorated by painting the enamels directly onto the biscuit. This latter type is termed *fahua* and in appearance closely resembles contemporary Chinese

MIDDLE MING
DRAGON BOWL,
ZHENGDE PERIOD,
1506–1521 (20cm/7⅞in)

The dragon is engraved while the porcelain is in the unglazed state. The design is then coated with wax to prevent the glaze adhering to it while the bowl is glazed. After firing, enamel is applied and the bowl is then fired again. (LEFT)

BLUE-AND-WHITE
JAR AND COVER,
CHENGHUA MARK
AND PERIOD,
1465–1487
(14cm/5½in)

The truncated body of this jar is painted in underglaze blue with a frieze of different trailing flowers. (ABOVE)

BLUE-AND-WHITE PALACE BOWL,
CHENGHUA MARK (SIX CHARACTER)
AND PERIOD, 1465–1487 (15.3cm/6in)

The Chenghua underglaze blue decoration appears more sharply defined than early fifteenth-century blue and white. (LEFT)

cloisonné. The bold designs are executed in up to six colours if we include the white that is simply a clear glaze on the biscuit. The dominant colours are a rich purple, cobalt-blue and turquoise, although yellow, manganese-purple and green are also used but invariably in a minor role. Whatever the subject of decoration, whether floral, avian or figurative, every element of the design is outlined in slightly raised threads of slip that prevent the colours from merging. In contrast to the diminutive and delicate *doucai* porcelains, the *fahua* group is generally large in scale with a generous baroque appeal.

Occupying a position between the glazed and unglazed wares is a group with an unglazed design incised into the biscuit, usually a five-clawed dragon, surrounded by a glazed surface. Sometimes, the vessel or dish was fired without any further treatment, allowing the unprotected unglazed area to burn to a russet colour due to the presence of iron in the porcelain body. Generally, though, the unglazed design was painted in green enamel, the glazed area either left plain, or itself dressed in a yellow lead-silicate wash. Most surviving specimens of this type are saucer dishes or leys jars. This technique was not an innovation, simply a variation of Yuan development.

THE SIXTEENTH CENTURY

Most authorities agree that the classical period of Ming porcelain ended with the reign of Zhengde (1506–1521). Although there is little change in the body or glaze, there is a noticeable difference in the quality of the brushwork and the organization of the design. The painting is executed with a light touch, a far cry from the heavily 'modelled' peonies, chrysanthemums or lotuses of the fourteenth and early fifteenth

LATE MING SAUCER DISH, WANLI MARK AND PERIOD, 1573–1619 (19.2cm/7⅜in)

Figure subjects are rare on porcelain before the sixteenth century but, by the reign of Jiajing (1522–1566), there is an increased use of small-scale figures.

centuries. In fact flowers, especially lotus, are rendered in a rather schematic manner, unlike the more naturalistic treatment of their ancestors. The surrounding foliage, too, is flat or linear with tightly curled outline-and-wash leaves, resembling a fleur-de-lys. The foliage meanders about the porcelain filling space like an organism rather than a carefully planned arrangement. In this respect the decoration resembles the slightly bolder but equally random scrolling foliage found in 'cloud collars' on mid-fourteenth century blue-and-white ware.

The conventional imperial wares, whether saucer dishes, leys jars or vases, are all painted in the same crowded manner. The imperial five-clawed dragon ensnared among dense foliage is more like a centipede, an effete descendant of the potent dragons of Xuande, and perhaps a reflection of the weak emperor and his luxurious court. Some examples with the four-character mark of Zhengde, such as the tall baluster vase in the Percival David Foundation, are quite poorly potted and painted. Indeed, such pieces are not too far away from contemporary non-imperial and export wares in quality, presaging the inevitable decline in all porcelains in the second half of the sixteenth and early seventeenth centuries.

The porcelains produced at Jaozhou in northern Jiangxi during the fifteenth century are the finest of the Ming dynasty, and whatever followed is recognized as an inferior descendant. However, even if there is a noticeable decline in standards, this does not mean that the sixteenth century is a period devoid of interest. On the contrary, the majority of the porcelains of this century are arguably more varied and complex in many ways than those of the preceding century. There are, of course, conventional well-known types such as the saucer dishes painted with a central spray of hibiscus within a border composed of four separate sprays of vine, peach, pomegranate and lotus. This pattern, painted in underglaze blue with or without a yellow ground, was produced in the reigns of the Xuande, Chenghua, Hongzhi and Zhengde emperors. This sequence confirms the conservative backbone of the Chinese potter and patron. However, foreign influences were soon to manifest themselves on Chinese porcelain in the second, third and fourth quarters of the sixteenth century.

The early sixteenth-century porcelains are bluer in appearance than the late fifteenth-century wares. The glaze is thick and suffused with minute bubbles, lending a 'soft focus' look to the underglaze cobalt which is, at its best, a clean almost sky-blue tone with little or no black oxidization.

An unusual group of blue-and-white, painted with either Arabic or Persian inscriptions, appears during the Zhengde reign. The majority are small objects for the writing table, such as brush-rests, table-screens, pen-boxes and ink-slabs; dishes and bowls are more rarely encountered. The inscriptions can be mundane, spiritual or philosophical; a pen-rest in the

BLUE-AND-WHITE BRUSH-REST, ZHENGDE MARK AND PERIOD, 1506–1521 (D13.2cm/5⅜in)

During this reign Muslim eunuchs, who made up the imperial bureaucracy, commissioned many porcelain writing objects. (RIGHT)

MING POLYCHROME JAR, JIAJING MARK AND PERIOD, 1522–1566 (34.2cm/13½in)

By the sixteenth century, large pieces, such as this jar commissioned by the Emperor, began to be painted in coloured enamels using the wucai palette. Here, cobalt blue has been used under the glaze to render part of the design, the remainder having been completed in overglaze enamels of iron-red, green and yellow. (RIGHT)

MING BLUE-AND-WHITE JAR, JIAJING MARK AND PERIOD, 1522–1566 (25.3cm/10in)

The high-shouldered body, which is characteristic of the mid-sixteenth century, is painted with pendant beads supporting the Eight Buddhist Emblems. (ABOVE)

Percival David Foundation boasts the helpful description 'pen-rest' in Persian; another reads 'I was loitering in a deserted place when suddenly I found a treasure'. These pieces were probably commissioned by Islamic eunuchs, who enjoyed great privilege and power in the imperial bureaucracy. The production of these so-called 'Mohammedan' wares ceased with the accession of the emperor Jiajing (1522–1566), a ruler who was intolerant of Islam and, latterly, Buddhism. He simply got rid of the Muslim officials and with them their expensive toys.

The porcelains of the Jiajing reign, while not beautiful in the classical fifteenth-century sense, can be dynamic and full-blooded. The material is generally less well refined, the potting sometimes clumsy and warped, and the painting too frequently casual and indefinite. Fortunately there are compensations: the greater variety in decorative themes, particularly figure subjects, and the rich purple-cobalt blue that was frequently used.

The paste of Jiajing wares is rarely free of flaws (most of these are iron-spots) and it has a tendency to burn red where exposed in the firing. The glaze is brilliant and glassy and blue or green in tone. The smooth surface contrasts with the marginally duller glazes of the immediately preceding reigns. The cobalt, termed 'Mohammedan' blue because it was imported from the Middle East, probably from near Kashan in Persia, is of an unprecedented colour. It is a warm, almost purple-blue, distinctive among the grey-blues of the Zhengde and the late fifteenth-century reigns. Details of the design are often lost in the wet-looking cobalt, indicating that it might have proved difficult to control.

As far as decoration is concerned, there are a number of new elements that characterize this reign. There is an increase in figure subjects: children playing (a favourite theme), narrative subjects, and fairly wooden scholars and dignitaries, perhaps drawn from printed books. Confirming the imperial obsession with Daoism is the large number of pieces, both marked and unmarked, painted with pine, *lingzhi* fungus, the crane and the deer. These Daoist emblems of longevity are occasionally accompanied by Laotze, the Daoist immortal, an ancient with an enormous cranium. Some pieces are curiously painted with a *shou* (Chinese symbol for longevity) formed by the twisted trunk of a tree. Daoist themes remained especially popular as decorative motifs on *kraak-porselein* until the end of the Ming dynasty.

It was during this period that Europeans first commissioned porcelain from the Chinese. The Portuguese were the first Europeans to round the Cape of Good Hope in 1497 and open up the trade routes to India, southeast Asia, China and Japan. Although they arrived in Chinese waters in the second decade of the sixteenth century, it was not until the middle of the century that a formal trade agreement was signed between the countries. There are a number of pieces of porcelain from this period that include European devices and armorial bearings in their decoration.

THE EARLY SEVENTEENTH CENTURY

By the end of the third quarter of the sixteenth century there was a marked change in the organization of the decoration of porcelain. The middle of the century was characterized by a somewhat disjointed nature in the motifs, best exemplified by the 'Jorge Alvares' bottle dated 1552, in the Victoria and Albert Museum. By the 1570s, however, the designs were no longer simply isolated but

MING *WUCAI* BRUSH BOX AND COVER, WANLI MARK AND PERIOD, 1573–1619 (30cm/11¾in)

This rare box is decorated with a five-clawed red dragon, leaping in pursuit of a phoenix.

MING JAR, c.1570
(39.3cm/15½in)

The central theme of pavilioned, rocky islets has a disjointed, 'cut and paste' look, characteristic of the second half of the sixteenth century. The minor bands — meandering foliage on the short neck, scrolling lotus and horses on the shoulder frieze, rocks and wave patterns encircling the base — are all common forms of decoration from this period.

MING JAR, WANLI PERIOD, 1573–1619
(36.3cm/14¼in)

In contrast to the more sinuous profile of earlier porcelain, a heavy, truncated form is typical of late Ming jars. The regimented nature of the decoration — floral reserves on a trellis ground, interrupted by vertical and horizontal straps — is confirmation of the emphasis on mass-production.

separated by lines that formed small compartments. This device enabled the untrained artisan or child, forced by the corvée system to work in the potteries at Jingdezhen, to concentrate on some small element of the design where skill was not of paramount importance.

The border panels of the so-called *klapmuts* dishes of this period are typical. All are invariably painted in the same slipshod manner with flowers, Buddhist emblems or precious objects. These dishes, along with other similarly decorated porcelains, were shipped in their hundreds and thousands, first by the Portuguese and latterly by the Dutch. This type of ware was termed 'kraak-porselein' by the Dutch, because it was originally brought to Europe on board Portuguese vessels called carracks, or 'kraak' in Dutch. Two of these Portuguese carracks, the Santa Caterina and the San Yago, were captured by the Dutch in 1602 and 1604 and brought back to Holland. Their cargoes were auctioned in Amsterdam and Middelburg. The sale of more than 150,000 pieces proved to be a sensation among the royal, the rich and the fashionable. Among the purchasers were Henry IV of France and James I of England, the latter adding to the extensive collection already accumulated by Elizabeth I.

These relatively humble wares had caused such excitement that the newly formed Dutch East India Company (founded in 1602) began to include porcelain in their cargoes of pepper, nutmeg and other exotic commodities. Although third rate by comparison with other Chinese porcelains, it had immense appeal for the Dutch, as evidenced by the number of *kraak-porselein* bowls, dishes and vessels in still-life studies. Every prominent Dutch still-life artist of the seventeenth century — Breughel, de Heem, Claesz, Heda, Van Rostraeten, Beert and Luttichuys — included late Ming exportware in at least some of their works. *Kraak-porselein* dishes or bowls crammed with oysters or fruit are displayed alongside *façon-de-Venise* wineglasses, silver-gilt goblets and other accoutrements of status.

Shortly after the Dutch had established a permanent trading station in Formosa in 1624, a different type of porcelain appeared on the market. Whether it was an independent Chinese development, or brought about by pressure from the Dutch, or simply a straightforward evolution, is difficult to determine. As a contrast to the mechanical *kraak-porselein* with its predictable motifs, this new porcelain is fresh and accomplished. This group has been termed 'Transitional Period' porcelain because it straddles the end of the Ming Dynasty and the beginning of the Manchu or Qing dynasty. 'Transitional' porcelain did not supplant *kraak-porselein* but complemented it. Both of these types were manufactured at Jingdezhen and exported via Nanjing.

The most salient feature of Transitional porcelain is the decoration. Here repetitive motifs are eschewed in favour of more naturalistic themes of flowers and beasts, but above all, of figure subjects. There were figure subjects on Yuan blue-and-white, perhaps depicting an episode from the 'Romance of the West Chamber'. Such pieces, however, were very rare. In the Jiajing, Longqing and Wanli reigns, pieces with figure subjects were not uncommon but they were not obviously narrative, merely figures at an endless convention. In 'Transitional' porcelain, however, figure subjects are more frequently narrative, abstracted from a drama, a romance or a novel. They seem more human than the somewhat wooden figures of the sixteenth century: they are natural, at ease among friends, examining scroll paintings or simply reclining in a sequestered, cloud-wrapped, mountain garden. Whatever the theme, the sense of gentlemanly informality and conversational intimacy is predominant, encouraging us to intrude.

Even if the story varies, the backgrounds are remarkably uniform and include the depiction of a banana plantain and grass rendered with a series of crescent-shaped brush-strokes, the latter technique being unknown in other periods. The neck and sometimes the base of some vessels are incised with narrow bands of barely perceptible patterns, a revival of the early Ming *anhua* or secret decoration. This type of embellishment is most often found on brushpots, rollwagons (tall cylindrical vases with a constricted neck) and other tall vessels, most of which have flat and unglazed bases or a channel foot-rim found mostly on dishes.

Coincidental with the Transitional wares is the introduction of new forms, many of North European origin. There are utilitarian objects such as mustard pots, salts, candlesticks, tankards (*schnelle*), oviform ewers (*enghalskrug*) and decorative vessels, bulbous jars with flat covers, tall bladder-shaped bottles and rollwagons.

BLUE-AND-WHITE DISH, TIANQI
PERIOD, 1621–1627 (21cm/8¼in)

This form of decoration was termed ko-sometsuke, ('old blue and white') by the Japanese. The theme on the dish is of a bamboo raft breaking up in a river. (BELOW LEFT)

KRAAK-PORSELEIN DISH, c.1600
(BELOW)

BLUE-AND-WHITE TRANSITIONAL
BRUSHPOT, c.1635 (20cm/7⅞in)

EARLY CHINESE
EXPORTWARE

Many hundreds of years before the establishment of the sea routes to the western world, Chinese ceramics were being transported to southeast Asia, India, the Persian Gulf, and even to Egypt. Ceramics of the Tang dynasty (618–906) and porcellaneous wares have been recorded in all these places. In Samarra, where the Abbasid caliphate built a palace (evacuated 883), excavations carried out in the early years of this century unearthed large quantities of northern Chinese porcellaneous wares; these were found side-by-side with locally made copies, albeit in earthenware.

Transporting such fragile objects over land made large-scale trade difficult. Therefore, relatively few ceramics reached the Mediterranean world before the sixteenth century. Records on contemporary accounts suggest that these isolated specimens would have been very costly or even beyond price, given as a tribute gift or token of friendship from one ruler or potentate to another. There are several recorded examples of porcelain gifts in fifteenth-century Europe.

Italy features prominently as a beneficiary of such treasures whether by gift or trade, or as a douceur to encourage commerce. For example, the earliest documentary piece of Chinese porcelain in Europe, the so-called Gaignieres-Fonthill bottle of *Qingbai* porcelain was presented by Louis the Great of Hungary to Charles III of Durazzo in 1381. Pasquale Malipiero, the Doge of Venice, received a gift of porcelain in 1461, as did Lorenzo de' Medici in 1487, who was given some 20

DANIEL MAROT ILLUSTRATION, c.1690

Marot created a number of designs which incorporated Oriental porcelains as part of an interior display. This illustration shows a fireplace festooned with porcelain in such close order that it is difficult to distinguish the pieces from the moulded surround, providing a good example of the extremes to which 'Chinamania' was taken in the late Baroque. (ABOVE)

pieces of porcelain, including vases from Abulfel Hamet, Sultan of Egypt.

Venetian and Genoese merchants virtually controlled the market in Eastern exotica and, therefore, it would be surprising if the occasional piece of Chinese porcelain did not figure among the shipments of silks and spices. Our earliest record of porcelain in England is that of the three pieces which arrived at Southampton for the newly crowned king, Henry VIII. Within a decade or so of this gift, porcelain became more available, but at a price and via Portuguese middlemen.

In 1497 Vasco da Gama rounded the

sported must have been considerable.

As a result of the expansion of this enterprise, there were by the end of the century about 10 shops in Lisbon dealing solely in porcelain. From Lisbon, it must be assumed that at least some of this porcelain, along with other exotic commodities, was then shipped to the northern European ports of Antwerp, Hamburg and London.

Whatever did reach the Netherlands and England seems to have had an impact on the fashionable world. However, none of the pottery produced in these areas during this period reflects Oriental influence, indicating that, at least, there were no large

(Over 150,000 pieces, roughly commensurate with the retrieved cargo of the Dutch East Indiaman, *Geldermalsen*, were auctioned in 1986.) The excitement caused by the sale of the porcelain resulted, shortly afterwards, in the Dutch dispatching vessels of their East India Company to purchase porcelain for themselves. (The Dutch East India Company had been established in 1602, just two years after their English rivals formed their own.) For most of the seventeenth century the Dutch competed with the Portuguese and the English for the lion's share of the China trade, or the 'Big Melon' as it was later known.

Cape of Good Hope and, with the aid of an Indian pilot, reached Bombay. By 1514 Portuguese ships had entered Chinese waters and opened the way for direct trade between China and the West.

In about 1520 the King of Portugal stipulated that at least one third of the cargo of homeward-bound vessels should consist of porcelain. Some of these Portuguese trading vessels, called carracks, were of the order of 1,000 and 1,500 tons. By the standards of the day, the volume tran-

retailing outlets to encourage copyists. This situation was to change – Spanish and Portuguese shipping represented lucrative targets for English and Dutch privateers.

Several Iberian vessels were taken as prizes, with porcelain itemized among their fabulous cargoes. Undeniably the most important was the capture of the Portuguese carracks, the San Yago and the Santa Caterina, in 1602 and 1604. The porcelain from these vessels was sold by auction in Middelburg and Amsterdam.

BLUE-AND-WHITE COVERED VESSEL, SECOND QUARTER OF THE 17TH CENTURY (26cm/10⅛in)

This delightful vessel exemplifies the spirit of informality inherent in ko-sometsuke. (ABOVE LEFT)

THREE VASES, KANGXI PERIOD, 1662–1722 (centre vase: 45cm/17¾in)

The outer pair of yen-yen vases is painted with figure subjects deriving from printed sources; the central rouleau *vase has decoration executed in gilding on a* bleu soufflé *ground.* (ABOVE)

KOREAN PORCELAIN

In 1938, 84 fragments of white porcelain were discovered together with typical Koryu celadons in a Koryu kiln site on the west coast of Korea. Some were plain and others carved or incised, while the remainder were inlaid with designs of willow, crane or peony, in typical Korean style. The sherds included pieces of bowls, vases, dishes, and cups with their recessed stands, covered either in pale green or blue Qingbai glaze, or a yellow-ivory glaze

KOREAN
CELADON BOWL,
12TH CENTURY
(16.5cm/6½in)

The flared sides of this bowl are crisply carved on the exterior with overlapping lotus petals.

resembling that of the northern Chinese Dingyao porcellaneous wares. These early porcelains are thought to date from the twelfth century when porcelain was first manufactured in Korea. Many of the early porcelains are very fine, and compare favourably with contemporary Chinese wares. There are relatively few specimens in Western collections; most are found in Japan, China and, of course, Korea.

CELADON

Celadon-type wares have been produced in most southeast Asian countries proximate to China including Korea, Annam (present-day Vietnam) and Thailand. Korea was the first to manufacture this green-glazed stoneware, as early as the tenth century. At

first, Koryo dynasty (918–1392) celadon was influenced largely by the Yue wares of northern Zhejiang province in China, but later evolved a distinctive native style. Although some Korean celadons are similar in form and glaze to their contemporary Chinese counterparts from the kilns of Longquan, also in Zhejiang, such pieces are the exception. On close inspection the subtlety of Korean celadon becomes apparent. The glaze, for example, is generally an elusive greyish green, a fraction more bluish than the best *kinuta* pieces. Forms, as well, are more dynamic. The profile, particularly of hollow wares, is more sinuous, and vessels appear disproportionately tall and liable to topple. This contrasts with the more predictable and stable Chinese celadon ware. To summarize, Korean celadons lack conventionality, and, as such, are immensely appealing.

The grey stoneware body of Korean celadon is covered in a bluish-green glaze, although it can vary from a mis-fired yellowish green to a pale greyish sea-green colour. The best examples have a 'glassy' and translucent glaze which is generally crackled, unlike Longquan which is thick, opaque and does not usually crackle.

Almost all of the Koryo period wares of the twelfth century are based on flower or vegetal forms such as the melon-shaped ewer, the bowl carved with overlapping

lotus petals on the exterior, or the bud-shaped cup. On bowls and dishes the floral effect of a half-opened flower is heightened by the slightly notched rim.

Korean celadons are decorated by moulding, incising, carving or by inlay. The first three techniques are self-explanatory, but inlay, at least in terms of celadon, is peculiar to Korea, and requires some clarification. Using this technique the potter carves channels in the 'leather-hard' clay following his chosen design. The channels or grooves are then filled with contrasting coloured strips of clay and the surface then smoothed off.

Decorative themes on the Koryo celadons, like the vast majority of Song ceramics, are mainly natural subjects such as plants, especially chrysanthemums, lotus, peony or bamboo. Bird, animal or human subjects are much less common.

Korean celadons are fired on three or more spurs which leave rather untidy protuberances encrusted with kiln-grit, each approximately 9.5–19 mm ($\frac{3}{8}$–$\frac{3}{4}$ in) across, depending on the size of the subject. The bases of dishes, bowls, waterpots and similar objects are convex and covered in glaze with the exception of the spur marks.

EARLY PORCELAIN

Fine China clay, suitable for the manufacture of high-quality white porcelain, is found in ample supply throughout Korea and a high proportion of the ceramic industry was involved with its production. For example, in the census of 1424/5, out of a total of 321 listed potteries some 136 were engaged in porcelain manufacture.

In 1466 King Sejo promulgated a ban on the manufacture of white porcelain except for the royal household. It is impossible to know if any clandestine production of white porcelain was conducted but certainly porcelains decorated in underglaze iron and copper continued to be made for the middle orders of society.

The first attempts to produce blue-and-white porcelain were made in the middle of the fifteenth century. The earliest mention of this type of porcelain occurs in the *Sejong Sillok*, or Annals of the Reign of King Sejong (1419–50). It is recorded here that in 1428 the king received a gift from China of five large and five small dishes decorated in blue. Two years later he was given a further gift which included blue-and-white dragon dishes. These gifts almost certainly inspired Korean potters to emulate the Chinese wares, for in 1456 King Sejo (reigned 1456–68) requested some blue-and-white porcelain from his own potters.

These early wares were probably made with cobalt imported from China, as fifteenth-century histories suggest that native cobalt ore of the right grade was extremely hard to find. Admittedly, cobalt was discovered in the south of Korea in 1464, and was refined and used to decorate a piece presented to King Sejo. This, however, proved to be an isolated and short-lived success and although prizes were offered in 1469 for further discoveries of cobalt, there is no record of any having been made. The only surviving piece of documentary blue-and-white from this period is a flared bowl painted in cobalt with blossoming plum branches and inscribed with the two characters Chung Shik, the name of a man who has been identified as a successful candidate in the National Examinations of 1432 and who later rose to a position of eminence in the government.

Because of the difficulties in obtaining even Chinese cobalt, the manufacture of blue-and-white porcelain was severely restricted. As a consequence King Sejo issued a decree whereby all blue-and-white was to be made exclusively for the royal household and the military caste. This restrictive edict remained in force until the reign of Myongjong (1546–67).

The production of blue-and-white, as well as other ceramics, received an almost fatal blow following the campaign of the Japanese under Hideyoshi in the 1590s, when the country was overrun, the potteries left in a shambles and most of its workmen carried off to Japan. Settled on the easternmost Japanese island of Kyushu, these unwilling immigrants were instru-

KOREAN CELADON BOTTLE, 12TH CENTURY (34.6cm/13⅝in)

The globular body of this piece and its tall, tubular neck are inlaid with willow and floral medallions in white and black on a celadon ground. (LEFT)

KOREAN JAR, 17TH CENTURY (34.6cm/13⅝in)

This high-shouldered vessel is painted in underglaze iron-black with an energetically rendered dragon among clouds. (BELOW)

mental in setting up the first porcelain-manufacturing kilns in and around the town of Arita. Their presence is confirmed by much of the early ware from this area, which has a pronounced Korean feel.

There was a further set-back as a result of the Manchurian invasion in 1636, and it was not until the beginning of the eighteenth century that the Korean industry was once again stable. An official factory was established in 1718 at Punwon, near Seoul, which produced blue-and-white for an expanding market that by then included customers outside official circles. The Punwon factory lost its imprimatur in 1883 but continued to manufacture blue-and-white in competition with provincial potteries throughout Korea, although by that time most of the porcelain being produced

was second-rate. The lack of skill and finesse was noted in 1876 by a Japanese visitor who commented that Korean blue-and-white was 'thickly-potted and poorly made . . .'. Ironically, following the introduction of Japanese potters and their modern mass-production techniques to the kilns of Punwon, the great tradition of Yi porcelain was forgotten.

FORM AND DECORATION

From large, heavily potted storage jars to small water droppers for the scholar's table, Korean porcelains are highly distinctive. Nearly every piece manifests a sense of informality, whether in the potting of the vessel or in the artist's brushwork. Evidence of the men who made the jars or

KOREAN INLAID
CELADON BOX,
12TH CENTURY
(D8.3cm/3¼in)

*The celadon ground of
the box is inlaid with
a circlet of flowers in
white and black clay
within grooved
borders.* (LEFT)

KOREAN WHITE PORCELAIN BRUSH-
HOLDER, 18TH CENTURY (H14cm/5½in)

*The side of this cylindrical piece is delicately
carved with a fruit vine.* (ABOVE)

KOREAN FACETED JAR, 16TH OR 17TH
CENTURY (H19.1cm/7⅝in)

*This small jar is painted in underglaze copper red
with medallions and blade-shaped lappets.* (RIGHT)

though they were thinly potted from a fine, closed-grained clay, they are prone to glaze flaking or peeling. The use of inlay in these wares, a technique translated from celadon, was a much favoured type of decoration peculiar to Korea. For obvious reasons the inlaid clay had to be a contrasting colour, and grey celadon clay was used. The later wares are left plain, moulded in relief, carved or painted in underglaze cobalt-blue, copper-red or iron-brown. A few pieces are decorated with a combination of relief or carving and underglaze painting.

A catalogue of the potter's repertoire includes: high-shouldered inverted baluster jars; bulbous jars with slightly angular rather than globular sides; storage jars with generous egg-shaped bodies, called *chochin tsubo* ('folding paper lantern') by the Japanese, who were avid collectors of Korean ceramics; wine bottles, some of bladder shape, others more pear-shaped, but all with tall, tube-like necks with thick mouth-rims; medium-sized faceted jars, hand-built, with anything from eight to possibly a dozen facets; brush-pots, frequently pierced; water-droppers, often naturalistic in form, such as a peach on a twig stand; incense burners; pipe-rests; square bottles; water pots that look like teapots but are for pouring hot water onto tea-leaves already placed in the cup; models of the Holy Mountain, usually a rocky islet with pavilions, sages, animals and birds,

brushpots is everywhere – from a casually knife-pared foot to the fingermarks left by a glazer 400 years ago. Perhaps, of all the Oriental porcelains, Korean reveals the true art of the potter. Some Arita porcelains come close in feeling, but most Chinese ware seems conservative and unemotional in comparison.

The body of Korean porcelain is coarse-grained and greyish and appears to lack plasticity because most of the vessels are relatively thickly potted. This thickness meant that many of the larger vessels tended to collapse or become lop-sided in the firing. The unglazed foot-rim has, with time, become greyish and dirty-looking, possibly because the paste is a little porous, like some English soft-paste porcelains.

The foot-rims and bases of many of the larger jars, particularly of the sixteenth and

seventeenth centuries, are spattered with coarse kiln-grit. The throwing contours are quite pronounced on the inside of most larger pieces but less so on the exterior. Unglazed areas are burnt to a wet-looking, pale rusty red in the heat of the kiln. The glaze is bluish or greenish, somewhere between the greyness of Shu-fu and the azure intensity of Quingbai, both Jingdezhen wares. The surface is liberally pitted and pock-marked, indicating a lack of care in the refining process. On many large storage vessels the central zone develops a strangely regular and almost rectangular rust-coloured crackle, whereas the lower and upper portions remain relatively clear.

The white porcelain of the earliest phase, whatever the colour of the glaze, tends to craze, either with long but isolated cracks or with a dense network. Even

reminiscent of the Daoist-inspired brush-rests of the late Ming period in China.

The painting of porcelain in underglaze colours is invariably bold and quickly executed. The most popular image is the large and usually four-clawed dragon, often depicted alone patrolling his fictile domain. Other painted animals and birds include the tiger, tortoise (or turtle) and the crane. The range of flowers includes the peony, lotus, chrysanthemum, bamboo or reeds. Clumps of finger-citron or Buddha's-hand citron appear, sometimes together with symbols of longevity and bats, mainly on the late Li dynasty wares.

Another favourite theme is the use of overlapping circles enclosing grasses and scrolling clouds, which appear regularly on faceted and high-shouldered jars, either in underglaze copper-red or cobalt-blue, but very infrequently in iron-brown.

Figure subjects before the eighteenth or nineteenth centuries are extremely rare. Border patterns are limited but include a stiff leaf rather like a Roman sword, but of varied length, arranged around the base or neck; a type of key-fret, composed of linked but alternately inverted 'T's; and a trefoil, similar to a shamrock and probably based on the Chinese *ruyi* head. Moulded or pierced wares are not uncommon, but their themes are taken from the vocabulary detailed above. Pierced work is particularly fine on cylindrical brushpots, carved through with contemplative subjects such as peony, bamboo, or the phoenix, the bird of a happy augury, or Buddhist emblems.

ANNAMESE
PORCELAIN

The term Annam refers to the northern region of present-day Vietnam, which is centred on the city of Hanoi and occupies an area that forms an irregular circle with a radius of approximately 100 km (62.5 miles). The Chinese who occupied this area between 1407 and 1428

called it 'Annam', meaning 'the pacified south' (although the Vietnamese themselves would never have employed such a derogatory title). Under French control, from the beginning of the nineteenth century until the middle of the twentieth century, it was known as Tongking and had the southern city of Hué as its capital. This region contains large deposits of the materials used in the production of porcellaneous wares, namely kaolin and feldspar. However, even with the right ingredients, it appears that the kilns were incapable of reaching a sufficiently high temperature to achieve only a semi-vitrified stoneware.

Almost all Annamese wares are neatly potted with short, square-cut foot-rims. For example a 7 cm (3 in) diameter oil jar will be supported on a foot-rim measuring between 1.5 and 1.3 mm ($\frac{1}{16}$ and $\frac{1}{8}$ in) in height and about 4 mm ($\frac{3}{16}$ in) in section. By comparison, a Chinese vessel of the same dimensions would have a foot-rim perhaps twice as high but of slightly thinner section. Annamese ware has a smooth, refined and generally grey or pale buff appearance, but it is neither translucent nor does it 'ring' like Chinese porcelain.

In order to make the ware look white (like Chinese porcelain), it was necessary to cover the greyish clay in a thin white slip. The marriage of the glaze to the underlying surface was not always very satisfactory and there is a tendency for the

ANNAMESE WATER DROPPER, PROBABLY 15TH CENTURY (L8cm/3⅛in)

Modelled in the form of a kneeling, caparisoned elephant, this piece is painted in native underglaze blue. (ABOVE)

ANNAMESE *KENDI*, PROBABLY 15TH CENTURY (H10.8cm/4¼in)

The compressed, globular sides of this kendi *are painted in imported cobalt blue with scrolling peony blossoms.* (ABOVE LEFT)

glaze to flake. Finally, the rim of large dishes and bowls is invariably unglazed, a feature that has no obvious explanation. Despite the influence of Chinese potters on most Annamese wares, there are exceptions particularly with regard to shape.

TYPES OF ANNAMESE WARE

Annamese porcellaneous wares can be grouped into the following categories: white, green or brown monochromes; underglaze iron-black (which is often brown rather than black) and cobalt-blue; and the enamelled wares, usually painted in green and red, often in combination with underglaze blue.

The earliest group, and a relatively rare one, is the monochromes; these show an

ANNAMESE BLUE-
AND-WHITE
SAUCER DISH,
15TH CENTURY
(26cm/10 6/16 in)

*This saucer dish is
painted in native-
mined cobalt with
traditional
chrysanthemum and
foliage patterns.*

affinity with the Chinese wares of the southern Song and Yuan dynasties both in form and decoration, and are derived from Qingbai and Shu-fu porcelains or even Zhejiang celadons.

Among the vessels in this small group are carved or plain beakers with slightly bellied, barrel-like sides that are sharply chamfered towards the flat footless base; small deep bowls or wine cups with out-curved rims, carved on the exterior with chrysanthemum petals; cosmetic boxes of a flattened form; compressed globular oil jars with between six and eight vertical lobes; and tall pear-shaped bottles of Chinese *yuhuchun* form. The somewhat primitive firing technique of this early group is obvious in the spur-pontil marks or a biscuit (i.e. unglazed) ring on the interior where the vessel has been stacked for firing. These 'blemishes' are found only on beakers, bowls or saucer-dishes and, as they do not occur on the later and more accomplished blue-and-white wares, probably indicate a pre-fifteenth century date.

The underglaze iron-black group comprises mainly bowls, saucer-dishes with plain or occasionally petal-shaped rims, beakers, oil jars, covered boxes, zoomorphic ewers and pear-shaped bottles. Almost all are painted in a bold, cursive manner with flowers and foliage, and are redolent of Chinese underglaze blue or red wares. The larger hollow wares like the high-shouldered jars (*guan*) or the pear-shaped bottles are perhaps the best examples of this group.

The decoration on a typical *yuhuchun* specimen is laid out in horizontal bands that, working upwards from the base, are arranged as follows: a basal frieze of lotus panels, the outline resembling a pointed arch and enclosing a pendant ribbon-like scroll; a band of scrolling lotus, peony or chrysanthemum occupies the widest part of the vessel; a further frieze of lotus panels with Buddhist emblems is situated on the sloping shoulders up as far as the narrowest section of the trumpet neck; and finally a collar of upright plantain leaves encircles the widely flared mouth. This arrangement, where all the design bands are of equal height and divide the vessel into four decorative zones, is very similar to the way the Chinese painted their early underglaze

porcelains. In other words, a large number of elements went to complete the design, rather than only one theme predominating, as happened in the fifteenth century. The use of underglaze iron as a decorative medium seems to have ceased with the introduction of cobalt blue at the beginning of the fifteenth century.

Wares decorated in underglaze cobalt blue comprise the most important and largest group of Annamese ceramics. Two types of cobalt ore were used. The first was an indigenous cobalt with a high manganese content, which fired in the kiln to a somewhat greyish blue. It was applied in relatively thick strokes that left a rather clumsy and mechanical impression. The second type of cobalt ore, probably imported from the Middle East, had a low manganese content, which resulted in a clean blue that varies in intensity from a pale cerulean to a decidedly purplish hue. This latter cobalt seems to have been employed solely on more refined pieces, and was painted on with thinner strokes that give a more definite but daintier effect.

The most common forms in this group are small globular oil jars, which are sometimes lobed, and average around 7.5 to 10 cm (3–4 in) in diameter. Next come boxes and covers with convex sides and flat covers, again with comparable dimensions to the oil jars. Other forms include: pouring vessels, often zoomorphic, taking the shape of elephants, dogs, tortoises and ducks (usually in pairs); kendi (ritual ewers); bottles, either with a compressed globular body and a tall tubular neck, or with a generous egg-shaped body, narrow neck and flared rim; wine cups; bowls; and saucer-dishes.

The bases of the saucer-dishes and other generally larger items are sometimes dressed in an iron-brown wash. The reason for this colouring is the source of much speculation, one theory being that such items were reserved for ritualistic purposes, although there is little to substantiate this idea. Another possible explanation is that it was done to pass off these Annamese wares in the export market as the more highly regarded Chinese porcelains, the bases of which burnt to a characteristic iron-red or russet colour in the firing. However, there should be no confusion between the two species as the Annamese is a decidedly bitter-chocolate colour whereas the Chinese variety is red-brown. The decoration of blue-and-white is mainly floral with the occasional appearance of a bird or animal on the more important specimens, and the human form is rarely, if ever, seen. Whatever the theme, almost all are derived from earlier Chinese porcelains of the Yuan (1280–1368) or early Ming (1368–1644) dynasties.

Border or ancillary decorative elements too are transmogrifications of Chinese motifs. Border patterns include trellis, the classic scroll, basket-weave, cash (coin) and wave designs. The Annamese wave pattern differs from the Chinese version in that it is broken up into small isolated scalloped-edged groups rather than being continuous. Furthermore, on large dishes it appears on the cavetto that encloses the main theme, whereas on Chinese dishes it is used to embellish the flat outermost rim. The wave and the trellis motif are also regularly used as a diaper or filler pattern for the rectangular panels on vessels.

DATING

The fairly limited repertoire of designs used by Annamese potters over a considerable period makes the dating of these wares highly problematical. The absence of Chinese-style reign marks and cogent archaeological material makes accurate dating impossible. The 'borrowed' Chinese designs at least provide us with a *terminus a quo* but they must be treated with great caution, as the famous dated Annamese bottle in Istanbul's Topkapi Sarayi warns. The inscription on this piece informs us that it was painted by an artisan called Bui of Nam Sach Chau in the eighth year of King Dai Hoa (1443–1454), a date corresponding to 1450. Yet the main theme that occupies the central zone, of peony flowers set among bold scrolling stems and broad

spiky leaves, is painted very much in the style of late Yuan blue-and-white, that is, about the middle or third quarter of the fourteenth century. The basal frieze of petal panels enclosing cloud scrolls is also from the same source. Both these elements together with the classic scroll are used extensively on Annamese wares throughout the fifteenth century although they were outmoded by decades, if not a century, in China. It is surprising that little attempt was made to introduce the more up-to-date styles of Yongle (1403–1425) or Xuande (1426–1435) into the canon of Annamese porcelain. This, the only dated piece of fifteenth-century Annamese porcelain, remains of immense importance in establishing the chronology of other wares.

Only two other pieces of dated Annamese blue-and-white are extant: a temple vase dated 1575, and a censer bearing the date 1665. Together with the bottle in the Topkapi collection, these documentary pieces confirm the long history of Annamese blue-and-white: the industry enjoyed periodic 'booms' such as the one during the so-called 'ceramic interregnum' in China,

ANNAMESE ENAMELLED BOTTLE, 16TH CENTURY (H18.8cm/7⅜in)

This sturdy bottle is painted in iron-red and green enamel with panels of geometric patterns and stylized vegetal motifs. (LEFT)

TWO ANNAMESE GLOBULAR JARS, 16TH CENTURY (taller:5.4cm/2⅛in)

Typically, these jars are painted in native cobalt with panels of trellis and foliage. (BELOW)

between 1436 and 1465, and again while China was embroiled in the Ming-Manchu wars of the seventeenth century. During the latter turbulent campaign, the lack of Jingdezhen porcelain, especially from c.1650–1680, allowed the Annamese to make good at least part of the shortfall. The newly established kilns in Arita (Japan) were the main beneficiaries.

Annam, which for centuries had been supplying the markets of southeast Asia, especially Indonesia and the Philippines, received a great boost from this gap in the market. For example, one junk from Annam carried a cargo which included 10,000 porcelain bowls. It has been estimated that in the period from 1663–1682 the Dutch East India Company imported nearly one-and-one-half million pieces of Annamese porcelain to Batavia (Jakarta) alone. But this did not last long. In the late seventeenth century the resumption and streamlining of production at Jingdezhen combined with the additional competition from the Japanese producers, signalled the start of a decline in the quality and demand for Annamese ware.

QING IMPERIAL PORCELAIN

---

*T*he history of porcelain-making in China goes back nearly a millennium and passes through three major dynasties before it reaches the conquering Manchus, whose Qing dynasty came to power in 1644. At its broadest this history can be characterized as a progressive union between primal vigour and spontaneity on the one hand, and sophistication of technique on the other. By the middle of the eighteenth century the process had reached an advanced stage, when some wares produced for imperial appreciation were of such refinement that only fastidious taste on the part of The Emperor kept them on this side of meretricious.

The history of Qing porcelain for court use, taken in isolation, follows a similar course to that of Chinese porcelain as a whole. It passes from the innovations of the Kangxi period (1662–1722), through the aesthetic perfectionism of the Yongzheng period (1723–1735) and the tightly controlled decorativeness of the Qianlong period (1735–1795) to the sometimes rather studied or over-decorated styles of the Jiaqing (1796–1820) and Daoguang (1821–1850) periods. From there it moves downhill through the reigns of the second half of the nineteenth century and first decade of the twentieth century, when mechanical copies and ill-conceived designs abounded.

These typifications are, of course, very general. It is possible, however, to follow the train of change rather neatly by examining a series of wares of the same pattern through the different reign periods. Such series of wares are very common, and represent 'repeat orders' to the imperial kilns in Jingdezhen for items of daily court use.

QING PORCELAIN WITH STORAGE BOXES

The Chinese collector did not display his collection on open shelves. Each piece was kept in a fitted box, lined with silk on the inside and covered with plain cotton or brocade on the outside. Traditionally, a collector might show his pieces to a fellow connoisseur one by one from their special labelled boxes.

DECORATION

A typical example of a series of wares of the same pattern is that of *wucai* 'dragon and phoenix' bowls. *Wucai* refers to a popular decorative technique, introduced during the Ming dynasty, whereby part of the design is rendered in cobalt blue beneath the glaze and, after firing, the remainder is added in coloured enamels. The whole is then refired at a lower temperature. The pattern always consists of a red and a green dragon divided by a pair of swooping phoenix, but the execution of the pattern varies from reign to reign, although it usually remains similar within each reign.

The Kangxi dragon is lean and long-bodied. The front quarters are somewhat painfully contorted, so that the belly, outlined in underglaze blue, appears as the shoulders, and the clawing forelegs execute a kind of backstroke through the flickering flames and obstructing foliage. In addition the three-tufted streaming mane conceals an implied coil in the neck. Overall it exhibits a rawness and a powerful determination in its energetic pursuit of the elusive 'flaming pearl'.

The Qianlong dragon, by contrast, is more simplified. The loops in the neck have disappeared, so that the raised foreleg is as one would expect, the left one. The body is shorter and sleeker, better-fed looking; its countenance is one of majestic glee. The Daoguang dragon seems closer to the Qianlong than to the Kangxi one, but much of the vigour of its movement has been dissipated by the lowering of the left foreleg. It is now trotting, no longer swimming or flying.

The colouring too changes from one period to the next. The Kangxi iron-red is dark and dry and swiftly applied, clearly set off by the underglaze blue line of the belly. The Qianlong iron-red is richer, more orange, and the underglaze blue has vanished on the body of the dragon. The green enamel has a pronounced bluish tint. The Daoguang iron-red is similarly orange, but like the Kangxi version it is swiftly applied, giving it a scratchy look in places.

WUCAI 'DRAGON AND PHOENIX' BOWL, KANGXI MARK AND PERIOD, 1662–1722 (13.2cm/5¼in)

The painting is raw and vigorous. Notice the contorted shoulders and the use of underglaze-blue to line the belly.

WUCAI 'DRAGON AND PHOENIX' BOWL, QIANLONG MARK AND PERIOD, 1735–1795 (15.4cm/6⅛in)

A few decades later, the dragon looks confident, but less purposeful. The bowl gives the suggestion of majesty rather than of vigour.

WUCAI 'DRAGON AND PHOENIX' BOWL, DAOGUANG MARK AND PERIOD, 1821–1850 (14.9cm/5⅞in)

Daoguang potters made copies in the earlier styles, but their version lacks movement.

IDENTIFICATION

By practising this type of comparison it becomes possible to recognize which wares from a series are from which reign periods, without relying on marks on the base. This is a skill which can be of great use when deciding if something is 'of the period',

that is, of the period indicated by the reign mark. There are a great number of wares confusingly painted with reign marks which suggest an earlier date of manufacture than is really the case.

Study by continual comparison serves a further, more general, purpose in the appreciation of Qing imperial porcelain. It makes it easier to distinguish conscious or unconscious (largely the former) quotation from, and reinterpretation of, earlier wares. Applying it, about half the repertory of Qing wares can be divided into those that take their inspiration largely from Ming prototypes, and those that take it from either pre-Ming wares or other areas of Chinese art, notably archaic bronzes and lacquer. The other half of the Qing repertory consists of wares which are more or less of pure Qing inspiration. By far the largest group is that of the well-known *famille-rose* wares that came into being when pink enamel derived from colloidal gold was introduced from Europe, near the beginning of the eighteenth century. They subsequently evolved in their own, very Chinese fashion. In the following sections in this chapter, each category will be considered separately.

QING WARES INSPIRED BY MING PROTOTYPES

The favourite wares selected by the Qing potters for copying or drawing inspiration from are those of the early Ming reigns of Yongle (1403–1425) and Xuande (1426–1435), and the later fifteenth-century reign of Chenghua (1465–1487). Wares made during these 'classic' reign periods have beauty about them which the Qing potters tried very hard to capture both in their direct copies, sometimes so accurate it is difficult to believe they were not intended to deceive, and in those wares that only quote various decorative motifs from the Ming repertory. The idea of going to great pains to copy a style already several centuries old is deeply bound up with the nature of Chinese art in general, which is highly reflexive, and has always had a strong tendency to antiquarianism. In the case of imperial porcelain it seems likely that the Qing rulers also

wanted to validate their status as sovereigns of China – it was part of the general desire for sinification that has historically always affected those who have successfully conquered the larger and more cultured land.

During the Kangxi and Yongzheng periods, many *doucai* wares were made in imitation of Chenghua originals. *Doucai* decoration, a rather superior relative of the *wucai* decoration described earlier, was introduced during the Chenghua period. Its identifying feature is that all the enamels over the glaze are outlined in cobalt-blue under the glaze, with few if any solitary areas of cobalt-blue. The effect is one of depth and delicacy, and is well described by the name *doucai*, which means literally 'dove-tailed colours'. Genuine Chenghua examples of this technique are among the most sought-after of all Chinese ceramics, and command enormous prices despite their usually diminutive proportions. Qing copies are often uncannily accurate, down to the Chenghua reign mark inscribed in Chenghua-style calligraphy. In fact, there are few people in the world who can reliably tell them apart. Side by side, though, there are distinct differences, most obviously in the colour of the blue, which is softer on the originals, and in the tone of the glaze, which in the originals has a curious but very pleasing warm ivory tint that the Qing potters could never capture. The copies themselves, however, are highly prized, and if they declare their true origin by a Kangxi or a Yongzheng reign mark, can be very expensive indeed.

Produced concurrently with these close copies was a body of *doucai* wares based more loosely on Chenghua patterns. Mostly bowls and dishes, they form a series like the *wucai* 'dragon-and-phoenix' bowls, which continues down through the reign periods. The best examples, usually Yongzheng, are among the most technically brilliant creations of the Qing dynasty, with glittering translucent enamels precisely set off by underglaze blue outlines, giving an impression of great fragility and preciousness. Later examples, even into the middle of the nineteenth century, can be highly satisfying

DOUCAI STEMCUP, KANGXI MARK AND PERIOD, 1662–1722 (8.2cm/3¼in)

The decoration closely follows that of a Chenghua period stemcup. Chenghua doucai pieces have always been held in enormous esteem. This Kangxi copy is in part homage to the earlier reign, but is also an assertion that the Qing potter could make a piece, in its own way, as fine.

objects, though there is a tendency in the Qianlong period and after to add opaque *famille-rose* enamels in a mistaken attempt to enrich the decorative effect.

Much the largest group of Ming-inspired Qing wares are blue and white. The situation is complicated by the fact that, unlike Ming *doucai* wares, which were made almost exclusively in the Chenghua period, with a brief revival during the Wanli period, the evolution of blue-and-white porcelain continued through all the Ming reigns, and through the Transitional period between the Ming and Qing dynasties, into the early Qing. As a result there is a large number of early Qing blue-and-white wares that are only Ming inspired insofar as they are the descendants of Ming wares. Many of these show a marked similarity to Qing export blue-and-white wares: the blue is applied in bright washes, the glaze is thin and very clear, and the

subject matter is often of sages in landscapes and other genre scenes. Some have reign marks, though they are usually inscribed in a freer hand than those on more obviously imperial wares. The market for these was principally among the ruling scholar elite rather than the imperial household itself.

These apart, however, there is an easily discernible group of high-quality wares which take their model directly from fifteenth-century prototypes. As with the *doucai* wares they fall more or less into two groups: highly ambitious, often close, copies, which either bear their correct reign marks, or have no reign marks (Yongle wares are very rarely marked); and more simply decorative wares, adapting fifteenth-century patterns, that form series.

An obvious characteristic of Qing copies is that the Qing potters were unable directly to capture the subtle, and only partly intentional, effect known by its Chinese name of 'heaping and piling'. This refers to the uneven, painterly way in which the cobalt-blue was applied, which resulted in small areas of highly concentrated pigment which after firing produced dark spots near or at the surface of the glaze. When the effect is fortuitous these small 'heaped and piled' areas can set off the painting to advantage, much in the same way as the groups of modelling dots and short strokes used by Chinese landscapists emphasize and enrich the scene. The cobalt-blue used in the Qing dynasty was more highly refined and did not give this effect even when a similar painting style was adopted. The solution the porcelain painters hit on was to add small dots.

This simulated 'heaped and piled' effect can also be seen on the series of less grand court wares, and the way in which it is applied is a useful indication of date. On Yongzheng and Qianlong wares the groups of dots are usually compact and well placed, but on later nineteenth-century wares they become increasingly mechanical-looking.

Ming underglaze red decorated wares, which used copper instead of cobalt as the colouring agent, were also copied during the Qing dynasty, though less commonly.

'TEA-DUST'
GLAZED VASE,
QIANLONG MARK
AND PERIOD,
1735–1795
(33.5cm/13¼in)

This vase copies a Song Dynasty (960–1279) stoneware copy of an archaic bronze vessel called a hu. The 'tea-dust' glaze gives an effect like the patination of the surface of an archaic bronze, although similar vases in other colours also exist.
(RIGHT)

'ROBIN'S-EGG'
GLAZED VASE,
QIANLONG MARK
AND PERIOD,
1735–1795
(27.7cm/10⅞in)

A good example of Chinese antiquarian taste, this vase is adapted from a Song dynasty (960–1279) type which, in turn, uses a Neolithic jade cong as its inspiration. The cong is said to be a symbol of the earth. Here, it is further embellished with the eight magical trigrams. The glaze, though, is a Qing innovation. (RIGHT)

THE INFLUENCE OF PRE-MING AND OTHER AREAS OF CHINESE ART

Pride of place among all Chinese ceramics is given, by common consent, to the finest Song dynasty (960–1279) porcelains and stonewares, and among these to the Song official wares, Ruyao and *guanyao*, though others follow close behind.

Song ceramics, with their finely articulated shapes and subtle glaze effects, were perfect materials for copying. In addition, many of the Song ceramics themselves were inspired by earlier archaic bronze or jade shapes. The Qing copyist could therefore impart antiquarian flavour and at the same time experiment with the monochrome glaze techniques that were becoming an increasingly popular form of decoration during the eighteenth century.

CORAL-GLAZED CHRYSANTHEMUM
DISH, QIANLONG MARK AND PERIOD,
1735–1795 (16.5cm/6½in)

This dish follows a contemporary Fujian lacquer type, and very nearly matches it for delicacy. The poem in the centre is composed by the Qianlong emperor in its praise.

QING DYNASTY INNOVATIONS

Enamoured though they may have been with the past, the Kangxi, Yongzheng and Qianlong emperors were equally keen that their dynasty should be seen to be able to develop great art in its own right. To this end the imperial kilns were completely reorganized at the end of the seventeenth century and a superintendent was appointed to take charge of production who was more or less directly answerable to the Emperor.

DECORATION

Following this was the introduction of rose enamel from Europe, somewhere around the beginning of the eighteenth century. At first the new enamel, which could be opacified to any desired tint of pink, was used primarily on metal bodies, and it was at this stage that most of the experimental work was done with the help of the Jesuit

fathers at the court. It was only a short time before the first true *famille-rose* porcelain wares appeared.

The earliest group of *famille-rose* porcelains are known collectively as Kangxi *yuzhi* wares after the four character marks *Kangxi yuzhi* (Imperially made in the years of the Kangxi period) enamelled on their bases. These early wares were enamelled in the palace rather than in the imperial kilns and porcelain blanks, unglazed on the exterior, were sent up for this purpose. As seems often to be the case when new mediums are introduced, the earliest examples are among the best despite the technical difficulties that are experienced.

It is interesting to note that until very recently this family of bowls was mistakenly attributed by western scholars to the late eighteenth or nineteenth century. With hindsight it is hard to see how this misconception occurred. Most likely it was because the evolution of *famille-rose* wares which were not enamelled in the palace followed a rather different course. In their

case the rose enamel appeared first very near the end of the Kangxi period on wares that in other respects more closely resembled *famille-verte* wares. These wares were similar to *wucai* wares but with blue enamel replacing the underglaze blue, and they were rarely (though with important exceptions) of imperial quality. The disparity between these and the palace-enamelled wares perhaps led to the conclusion that both types could not be of the period.

Palace-enamelled wares continued to evolve beyond the *yuzhi* bowls, and during the Yongzheng and Qianlong periods there appeared a family of wares of exceptional quality. The porcelain itself has an adamantine brilliance and the enamels are minutely shaded with great subtlety. The subjects are usually flowers, or birds and flowers, though figures and landscapes are also found. One of the characteristics of this type is that the painting, of a quality equal to any court painting on silk, begins as a masterfully controlled confusion of foliage, rocks and tree-trunks near the base, which

is gradually resolved towards the top, leaving a large area of white on which a couplet is inscribed in black enamel, appropriate to the subject. The pieces with more unusual subjects are similarly inscribed with poems, and all have a number of small mock seals in pink enamel.

This family of wares generally goes by the name *Guyue Xuan* ('Old Moon Pavilion'). Not all palace-enamelled wares belong to this group. Technically *Guyue Xuan* is a misnomer because it refers in fact to a non-imperial Peking glass-enamelling workshop of the late eighteenth and early nineteenth centuries. However, for better or worse the name has stuck.

The range of *famille-rose* wares enamelled in Jingdezhen rather than in the palace is very great; though they can often be grouped into families it is rare to be able to follow a series down through the reign period as with many of the wares described earlier in the chapter.

Into the nineteenth century it is still possible to find *famille-rose* wares of high

FAMILLE-ROSE BRUSHPOT, QIANLONG MARK AND PERIOD, 1735–1795 (12.1cm/4¾in)

It is rare to find Europeans depicted on a piece designed for the home market. The quality of the enamelling, and the traditional Chinese form clearly show it was never intended for anywhere other than the palace. (ABOVE)

FAMILLE-ROSE TEA POEM TRAY, JIAQING MARK AND PERIOD, 1796–1820 (W15.9cm/6¼in)

Famille-rose wares of high quality continued into the nineteenth century. The long poem in the centre is in praise of tea, and is attributed to the Jiaqing emperor. (BELOW)

'PEACH-BLOOM' GLAZED CHRYSAN-THEMUM VASE, KANGXI MARK AND PERIOD, 1662–1722 (21.5cm/8½in)

A fine example of 'peach-bloom' glaze, one of the most beautiful of the innovatory Qing monochrome glazes. Wares decorated with this glaze come only in a small number of shapes, for scholarly use. (BELOW)

quality, though as time goes on they become fewer. In the Jiaqing period they are still plentiful, however. There are, for instance, a number of types of these small dishes, usually of oval or of barbed oval form known as 'tea poem' trays. All are inscribed in the central panel with a long poem in praise of tea, usually attributed to the Jiaqing emperor and dated to 1797. The dishes themselves, of course, are later in date than the composition of the poem, but the quality of the enamelling in the inscription gives lie to the simplistic notion that exceptionally fine wares were not produced after the Qianlong period.

MONOCHROME WARES

Famille-rose wares apart, the most important advances made during the Qing dynasty were in the field of monochrome wares. Having successfully managed to simulate most Song and Ming monochrome glazes, the Qing potters, or at least the chemists

working alongside them, greatly expanded the repertory of colours both by introducing new materials and by re-employing the more common ones – copper, cobalt and iron – in imaginative ways. One of the best known of these is the Kangxi 'peach-bloom' glaze, based on copper, which, depending on the firing cycle could fire to a velvety peach-red colour or transmute in places to a shade of sage-green.

There are many discussions concerning which particular colour is most desirable. The great variability of this glaze is cleverly set off by its limited use, reserved for a small range of fine scholarly items, water-pots, brushwashers, seal boxes and small vases, within each group of which all are of identical shape and size. The extraordinary fickleness of this new glaze probably dictated that the shapes be standardized, in order to reduce the overall number of variables involved and so that the interaction between the glaze and their particular geometries could be thoroughly and completely understood.

CHINESE EXPORT PORCELAIN

*I*t would be impossible to overstate the importance of the Chinese export trade in ceramics, particularly in the seventeenth and eighteenth centuries, or to gauge the enormous amount of useful and ornamental porcelain that flooded into Europe from the Orient. The far-reaching influence of these imports into Europe continues even to present-day pottery and porcelain designs. The tin-glazed earthenware (delft) that was made in England before and after the English began to make their own porcelain in the mid-1740s sought to reproduce the Chinese blue-and-white patterns that had monopolized the market. It may have been less expensive to produce than importing the Chinese porcelain, partly because there were no government taxes to pay on it, but it was neither as durable or pleasant to use, nor as visually attractive as the Chinese originals were.

Chinaware (the original term for imported Chinese porcelain) made up only a small part of the home-coming cargo, probably less than 10 percent in quantity and also in value. Tea was the main cargo, and the fashion for tea-drinking was partly responsible for the popularity of chinaware. The numerous eighteenth-century oil paintings that show families at the tea-table – a social occasion thought to be worthy of being recorded for posterity – all depict Chinese (not European) porcelain tea wares.

Oriental porcelain still exists in vast quantities. Not all of it is of museum quality or of great historical interest, but even the humblest pieces were well made. They had an attractive white body that did not stain and a smooth, pleasing glazed surface that did not, with the exception of huashi, craze or crackle. The objects were usually well formed, light in weight, semi-translucent, and very fit for their purpose.

GROUP OF CHINESE EXPORT ANIMALS, QIANLONG PERIOD, 1735–1795

Large quantities of these figures were made for the European market.

THE EAST INDIA COMPANIES

The English East India Company, originating in 1600, had vast commercial interests, which were mainly centred on the Indian continent. Trade to and from China represented only a very small and relatively late part of the Company's business. Many of the Company's vessels never traded with China at all; the goods were shipped first to India, and from there to Europe. The Company enjoyed a state monopoly in the trade to and from India and the East. However, this privilege simultaneously entailed restrictions on the methods of sale of imports, and fixed quotas of British goods shipped out to the East in the East Indiamen.

Most European nations had their own trading companies. The Dutch East India Company was particularly important in the trade in Chinese (and Japanese) porcelains, but the French, Swedish, Danish, Spanish and Portuguese were also large importers, and intertrading often took place between the companies.

The Chinese did not distinguish between the various European nations – they were all 'Foreign Devils' – and much the same types of porcelain were made for all the Europeans and stocked by the Chinese merchants in the port of Canton, the main and official trading centre with Europe.

THE EAST INDIAMEN'S IMPORTS

The porcelain carried back by the East Indiamen was divided into two groups. The first comprised the official imports of the East India Company, which were usually ordered in bulk lots, such as 30 tons. These bulk purchases were often of a very mundane character and might be repeated year after year. The need was for standard lines that would pack tightly in the hold, such as plates and dishes, etc.

The second type of import was extremely important to the British – this was the officially permitted private trade. It covered the private investments of the ship's crew (of about 100 men) and the Supra-Cargoes (now generally called Super-Cargoes) who acted for the Directors of the Company and were responsible solely for the commercial success of the voyage. They sold the outward cargo and purchased Chinese goods at the most advantageous prices. Of necessity they had a wide knowledge of what was required, but no special understanding of porcelain and bought largely what was available.

All the special designs were private trade and tended to be of a far higher quality, and more individual in form and pattern, than the Company bulk purchases. They included armorial, crested and initialled

FAMILLE-ROSE TEAPOT, c.1730 (11.5cm/4½in)

The decoration is taken from the Dutch East India Company's new coinage of 1728.

BLUE-AND-WHITE TEAPOT c.1730–40 (11.5cm/4½in)

The teapot is painted in underglaze blue with figures in a garden. The silver mounts are European.

serving to make the vessel seaworthy. These were a commercial cargo, not merely ballast to be dumped when the vessel arrived in China. Most English vessels took flint to China, sometimes carrying as much as 100 tons. There it was sold for up to £10 a ton, a sum which represented a massive profit margin. It is not known to what use it was put, but it was probably a component of basic porcelain mix, or perhaps of the glaze.

Apart from flints, the lower hold would have held iron, tin and slabs of lead. Other cargo included glassware, lanterns, clocks, mirrors, rabbit skins, pistols, swords, spectacles, window glass, brass wire and cutlery. Mechanical toys or very intricate clocks were used as gifts to open the way for profitable trading.

Although cargo was undoubtedly bartered, the main trade was carried out in the conventional manner with coin or with internationally accepted silver or gold.

On the return journey, the profitable but bulky 100 tons of tea and 30 tons of silks had to be stowed above the waterline to keep them dry during the long voyage in the leaky wooden vessels. But, since china is heavy and waterproof, it could be stowed just above the ballast in the hold to make the vessel stable. It therefore formed a vital, but not necessarily profitable, part of every cargo.

The vessel took whatever was available because it had to sail at the prescribed period to take advantage of the northeast monsoons. If these were missed, it would be delayed a whole year. A typical 'non-instruction' to a Supra-Cargo at this early date reads:

'We do not particularise the colours, sizes nor the several species of china ware but leave that to your management and fancy as being upon the place and therefore best able to know what sorts are procurable . . .'

(This order was dated November 11th, 1699 and related to a vessel, the *Wentworth*, bound for Canton.)

Some orders were, however, more detailed as to the quantity of goods required. The following represents part of

ENGRAVING OF THE PORT OF CANTON, 18TH CENTURY

BLUE-AND-WHITE PLATE, KANGXI PERIOD, 1662–1722 (20.3cm/8in)

Made to commemorate the Rotterdam Riots of 1690, this plate confusingly bears the mark of Chenghua (1465–1487). The scene is copied from a silver medallion and shows the demolition of the bailiff's house.

porcelains and those that depicted East India Company vessels and European figures. Most were ordered by the Supra-Cargoes and captains, who acted for themselves or on commission from London dealers or individuals. The crew, on the other hand, bought standard wares. The Company took its cut of the private trade, based on its value when submitted for sale in the Company's auctions.

THE EAST INDIAMEN'S CARGOES

The import of Chinese export market porcelain is but part of the story of East–West trade. The round voyages of the East Indiamen were extremely profitable because the vessels sailed to China or other destinations with a full cargo of British goods. Low down in the hold would have been heavy, waterproof goods such as flints

an order drawn up in January 1709:

'Forty tons China ware, of the sorts undermentioned, or if the quantity should amount to more yet bring it as being heavy goods.
50,000 teacups of the several patterns
50,000 saucers to ditto
5,000 teapots with straight spouts
5,000 small deep plates for the teapots
8,000 milk pots
12,000 boats for the teaspoons
2,000 small tea cannisters
3,000 sugar dishes
3,000 bowls about three pints
All being for tea equipage let there be a number of each sort made of one figure and pattern in proportion to the number above mentioned.'

This order also registered:

'8,000 small cups with one handle, fit for coffee or chocolate
10,000 coarse coffee cups
10,000 small coarse bowls or porringers
3,000 bowles of a pint
3,000 ditto dishes
3,000 bowles of a quart
3,000 ditto dishes
1,000 bowles of three quarts for punch
1,000 bowles of a gallon for ditto
200 bowles of six quarts
3,000 small deep plates to bake in.'

This particular order ·for the 1710–1711 season totalled 234,000 articles, all of the wares for use on the table. It is not known what types of patterns were shipped because the surviving sale catalogues do not describe the decoration, only the basic articles themselves. However, it is almost certain that approximately two-thirds of each consignment would have been decorated in underglaze blue sometimes depicting representations of quite simple landscape scenes or floral designs.

In the 1751–1752 season there were at least 16 European vessels at the Whampoa anchorage down river from Canton. The combined European vessels might have carried 3,200,000 porcelain articles weighing 3,200 tons. This does not take account of the Spanish and Portuguese vessels that traded from Macao rather than from Canton, nor of the so-called 'country ships' which took cargoes of goods to India for re-shipment to other markets. The scale of importation into Europe of Chinese goods was therefore enormous.

THE QUALITY OF EXPORT PORCELAIN

The typical decoration and vast scale of 'ordinary' imported porcelain was revealed when the cargo of the Dutch East Indiaman *Geldermalsen* was salvaged, in 1985. *Geldermalsen* sank on her homeward journey from Canton on 3 January 1752, carrying 223,303 pieces of Chinese porcelain with a total weight of 220 tons, costing in China the equivalent of £9,000. Of this cargo (which also included gold ingots and tea) more than 150,000 pieces of porcelain were salvaged and were in good enough state to be sold by auction in Amsterdam in 1986.

Considering the large number of pieces carried in the 203 chests, *Geldermalsen's* cargo was surprisingly mundane and limited in its blue-and-white patterns. Another unexpected feature was the relatively large number of pieces decorated partly in underglaze blue and partly in overglaze colours and gilding. This Imari style of decoration does not show up on the very basic British orders or sale descriptions but it was undoubtedly imported in large amounts as evidenced by the number of surviving specimens. British manufacturers, particularly those at Bow, Vauxhall, Worcester and Liverpool were also producing similar mixed designs.

The *Geldermalsen* carried quantities of 'Batavia' or 'Batavian' wares, named after the Dutch Company's headquarters in Java. Batavian ware is rather broadly painted in blue and white, but the outside of the bowls and saucers was coated with a brown wash. The pieces are mainly tea wares of rather ordinary quality. Most examples now found in Europe seem to pre-date the period of the *Geldermalsen's* sinking. Masses of 'Brown teacups' feature in the sale records from the early 1700s. Of all the different types of Chinese porcelain decoration, Batavian ware is the only one not copied on English porcelain although it was imitated in pearlware and at Meissen.

The unremarkable quality of much of the *Geldermalsen's* cargo came as a surprise to some present-day collectors, because they tend to base their ideas on special and above-average quality wares that are perhaps displayed in museums or illustrated in reference books. These are clearly not a fair sample of the bulk of porcelain that was produced. Some years before the *Geldermalsen* foundered, the English had cause to complain about the quality of their bulk porcelain purchases:

'. . . The China ware brought home for two or three years past has been very coarse and ordinary, hardly superior to Delft. You must be very careful that what you have now ordered is of a better sort if procurable and let the merchants know that in future you will buy no more of such ordinary sorts . . .'
Supra-Cargo's orders which are dated 21 December 1748.

THE SALE OF EXPORT PORCELAIN

As part of its charter, all Company imports had to be sold by auction. When the porcelain arrived in England, it was sold in very large and mixed lots, not as single items. In this way the Company was able to dispose of its bulk imports with the minimum of cost and trouble. The buyers also had to take their purchases with all faults. Even lots made up of broken porcelain were included in the sales and found buyers. From the auction price the government was able to take its cut or duty via the customs service.

The wholesale lots were described in a most rudimentary manner. Often the numbers of cups and saucers did not match, as in the example of two lots imported on

the *Dashwood* and auctioned in April 1703:

'1330 *tea cups*
1480 *saucers*
2760 *tea cups*
2420 *saucers*'.

The articles here described as 'tea cups' were probably the traditional Chinese handleless cups that we now usually call 'tea bowls'.

Most of the bulk lots were purchased by Chinamen, or dealers, who then divided them up to re-sell in smaller quantities, as required by their customers. Thus a single lot of perhaps 100 teapots could be divided between 100 different buyers, changing hands several times within the trade and being widely distributed throughout the British Isles. As far as the early imports into England were concerned, it was extremely rare to find complete tea or dinner services included in the orders or in subsequent sales. These were made up later by the dealers. By about 1765, however, complete services were being supplied. Individual private trade orders for, for example, armorial services, which were supplied complete, had been ordered since about 1690.

FAMILLE-ROSE PLATE IN MEISSEN STYLE, QIANLONG PERIOD, 1735–1795 (23cm/9in) (ABOVE)

FAMILLE-VERTE DISH, KANGXI PERIOD, 1662–1722 (34cm/13¼in) (ABOVE LEFT)

BLUE-AND-WHITE PORCELAIN, MOSTLY KANGXI PERIOD, c.1700

This collection is displayed as it might have been in the eighteenth century.

THE COST OF EXPORT PORCELAIN

It is difficult to be precise about the original cost of any given article, such as a tea bowl and saucer, a teapot, or even a plate, but on the whole Chinese porcelain was relatively inexpensive. But there was then, as now, no fixed price. The price has always depended on the amount or quality of the decoration, where the item was purchased and how many middlemen took their profit. A recommended mark-up suggested by a London wholesaler to a retailer in Bath in the late 1700s was 33 percent and the wholesaler had already added his margin of profit to the cost at the auction. An enamelled cup probably cost about 50 percent more than a simple blue-and-white one, and it would appear that a Chinese set was less expensive than a comparable English one. On the other hand Japanese porcelains were more highly valued than the more plentiful Chinese porcelain wares.

The law of supply and demand applied as much to Chinese porcelain as to other articles. Sometimes the market was glutted generally or with a given article that had been ordered in too large quantities. At the time that the *Geldermalsen* was en route to Canton, for example, the English market seems to have been saturated with Chinese porcelain. At other times there was a shortage, perhaps because vessels had been lost or delayed, and prices were consequently increased.

Some of the original priced orders show that the cost of the porcelain in Canton was very low. For example, in 1755 10,236 blue-and-white plates cost £112. At the English wholesale auctions the reserve was between eight pence and one shilling, but taxes, commissions and profit margins, etc. greatly increased the prime cost. The resultant figure was perhaps a shilling upwards for a perfect Chinese blue-and-white plate of average quality. Chipped or cracked examples commanded smaller

FAMILLE-ROSE DINNER PLATE AND BLUE-AND-WHITE SOUP PLATE, MID 18TH CENTURY (23.2cm/9⅛in)

prices, but were still extremely saleable.

Even if the Chinese imports had been more expensive than the Bow or other English contemporary blue-and-white plates the buyer would almost certainly have preferred the Oriental wares. They were technically more competent and more pleasing to use: they did not warp and the glaze was not disfigured by small bubbles or black spots.

CELADONS AND SWATOW

Chief among the other types and styles of porcelain exported from China were the celadon wares. The earliest celadons, a development of Yueh, go back to the Song dynasty and are known to have been sent to India, Persia and Egypt. But the celadons perhaps most familiar to Western eyes are those made in the vicinity of Longquan and Hangzhou in Zhejiang province during the Southern Song, Yuan and Ming dynasties. These wares were exported throughout southern Asia, to

Africa and the Mediterranean area as well as to Japan and the Philippines.

The Longquan celadons were heavily potted (this perhaps accounts for the large number that have survived intact) and fired at a high temperature (1280–1350°C) (2354–2462°F). The green glaze is thick and usually covers the base, apart from a characteristic central unglazed ring that burns to a strong orange colour in the firing. Beautifully formed dishes (some of a diameter in excess of 50 cm/20 in), bowls and vases were produced, many with moulded or carved designs of fish, dragons or flower sprays.

The celadons were also produced on a smaller scale at Jingdezhen until at least the end of the fourteenth century when manufacture ceased in favour of the blue-and-white wares. They were produced again, however, during the Qing dynasty when the glaze of these pieces was typically a fine transparent olive-green through which the whole body is clearly visible. Very fine copies of the earlier celadons were, however, also made and exported and can deceive even the most expert eyes.

Swatow wares were probably made in Fujian province and are known to have been widely exported from the sixteenth century onwards to Japan, Indonesia, Malaysia, India and the Near East, while some pieces are known to have been made specifically for the European markets. The decoration of these pieces was primarily in underglaze blue though some are decorated with overglaze red, green and turquoise. Subjects include landscapes and (more commonly) animals, birds and fish, including deer, cranes, phoenixes, kylins and dragons. They are mostly loosely drawn with a spontaneity which particularly appeals to modern eyes, and the decoration often covers the whole area of the pieces. However, the glaze is usually heavily applied and often crackled, which tends to obscure the decoration. Large jars with lugged handles on the shoulders, bowls, lidded cups and oil-pots were made for everyday use, but in Europe at least, the pieces most commonly found are the large dishes, sometimes with wavy rims, with a central panel indistinctly depicting either a crane or a phoenix.

LATE MING
AND EARLY QING
EXPORT PORCELAIN

There are extensive records of Chinese porcelains in overseas countries prior to the reign of the Ming emperor Wanli (1573–1619), but it was not until that period that there were any substantial imports into Europe.

The Wanli porcelains were largely decorated in underglaze blue and reflected Chinese rather than European taste in their shapes and forms of decoration. The quality of the blue tends to deteriorate in the latter part of the reign, when it becomes paler and often has a greyish hue. The pieces produced included bowls, caudle cups, ewers, kendis (sometimes in the form of elephants and frogs and frequently adapted in the Middle and Near East for use as hookahs),

and wine pots. But perhaps the most common form is the dish with alternating wide and narrow panels that radiate from a central hexagonal medallion, and decorated with flowers and rockery, often with birds and sometimes with crickets or animals. The glazed bases of these dishes frequently show radial 'chatter' marks and sometimes have sand on their foot-rims. These characteristics are unlikely to be found on later Chinese copies or on the similarly decorated Arita (Japanese) pieces made from the late sixteenth century, which are usually distinguishable by the spur marks on the base. Such imports were typical of what has become known as *kraak-porselein*.

The decoration on Wanli wares mainly follows that of the earlier Ming reigns although there is a greater emphasis on the human form and fabulous animals as well as Daoist and Buddhist emblems and symbols. Some polychrome wares were also exported, mainly decorated either in the three-colour (*sancai*) or the five-colour (*wucai*) palettes in use at that time.

The period from the death of the Wanli emperor, in 1619, to the accession of the Qing emperor Kangxi, in 1662, is customarily referred to as the 'Transitional'. During this turbulent period, when the Ming rulers were ousted by the Manchu and subsequently attempted rebellions against them, the porcelain-producing centres had no imperial patronage. Some were even more seriously affected – in 1675 the kilns at Jingdezhen were destroyed by fire. The factories sought to make up for the lack of imperial orders by adapting designs and shapes to meet overseas requirements, and large quantities of porcelain continued to be exported.

The range of objects produced was also considerably widened to appeal to foreign taste – for example, spouted jugs, tankards, candlesticks and mustard pots. Blue-and-white dominated as before, but the blue was deeper with perhaps a slightly violet or purple tint, on a clear white porcelain. (This has been likened by one authority to 'violets in milk'.) In the 1640s and 1650s, this body was often speckled or of a greyish

colour, the result of what appears to have been a kiln fault which allowed a fine dust or sand to settle on the glaze during the firing process. The earlier vases, bottles, ewers and similar pieces commonly had flat unglazed bases which were roughly cut with a knife, whereas from perhaps about 1645 they were more neatly trimmed on the wheel. Another innovation was the treatment of rims with brown slip, perhaps as a strengthener. With the rare exception of the soft-paste *huashi*, all Chinese porcelain is hard paste.

Exports to Europe were largely under the control of the Dutch, who were established in Batavia, and a stylized tulip often appears on bowls and other pieces. During the latter part of the seventeenth century the extensive use of many Chinese shapes and designs on delftware is evidence of the high esteem in which Chinese imports were held in Holland. There was also a substantial trade between China and Japan, with many hundreds of different designs in both blue-and-white and polychrome being made specifically for the Japanese market, and also with Malaysia, Indonesia and the Middle East generally. In this context, the salvaging by Captain

Hatcher in 1983/4 of the cargo of a trading vessel sunk in the South China Sea in about 1645 is of particular interest and value: the Chinese porcelain aboard the ship included shapes not previously associated with the Transitional and of a kind not normally exported to Europe. In addition to the usual *kraak*-type dishes, bottles and bowls and the ubiquitous kendis, there were cricket-cages, betel-nut boxes, fruit shapes, straight-spouted teapots, and many other objects for everyday use.

The 60-year reign of the second Qing emperor, Kangxi, runs from 1662 to 1722 but, as already mentioned, about the first 20 years can more appropriately be included in the Transitional period. Court patronage and control were resumed in 1683 with the appointment of a director of the factory at Jingdezhen and the finest pieces were once more made for imperial use. In spite of this, many of the pieces exported were of a quality not seen before in the West. Indeed, to some eyes the Kangxi blue-and-white porcelains reached a level of technical brilliance which has not since been surpassed or even equalled.

Exports to the West multiplied at the turn of the seventeenth century, when the port of Canton was opened to foreign trade. The English Company was permitted to establish its own trading post on the mainland in 1715. Initially, the bulk of the orders was for porcelains decorated in underglaze blue. Decoration in a *famille-verte* palette, which derived from the earlier Wanli *wucai*, but with an overglaze blue enamel instead of the traditional Ming underglaze blue, came into prominence in the last decade of the seventeenth century. These pieces were almost wholly produced in the private factories of Jingdezhen.

Other innovations of the period and also exported in some quantity were pieces decorated in powder blue (*bleu soufflé*), sometimes gilded and sometimes with panels in underglaze blue or *famille verte*; *famille noire*, with its black enamel overlaid with a translucent green glaze; and, at the very end of the reign, the *famille-rose* palette, which included a dominant pink

FAMILLE-VERTE TUREEN, KANGXI PERIOD, 1662–1722 (33cm/13in)

This tureen has been based on a European silver shape, possibly a smaller object such as a porringer.

derived from gold chloride and introduced from Europe. Various monochromes were also produced, including greens, much-admired yellows, *clair de lune*, peach bloom, *sang de boeuf*, and mirror black. Another innovation was the so-called 'egg and spinach' form of decoration made up of a mottled yellow, green and aubergine.

Every conceivable form of object that could be reproduced in porcelain and for which there was an overseas demand was made at Jingdezhen. These were primarily, of course, pieces for everyday use: plates with a condiment flange, tea bowls and cups and saucers, teapots and, rarely, coffee and chocolate pots, chamber pots, salts, mustard pots, candlesticks, tankards, casters, ewers and basins, garnitures of three or five vases and beakers, and bowls. But perhaps the most admired of all objects were the vases of cylindrical and baluster form and the ginger and other lidded jars so splendidly decorated with court and hunting scenes, the Precious Objects, the Eight Immortals and their attributes, the 'long elizas', flowering prunus sprays and blossoms, and scenes from the Romances.

TANKARD, *c.*1785–95 (22.2cm/8in)

The Fitzhugh underglaze-blue borders enclose a famille-rose palette crest, which was painted in Canton on this Jingdezhen-potted tankard. The entwined strap handle is typical of the period.

EIGHTEENTH-CENTURY EXPORT PORCELAIN

The emperor Kangxi was succeeded in 1722 by his fourth son, Yong-zheng, whose reign was to last until 1735. During this period, exports of *famille-verte* porcelains dwindled and were replaced by those decorated in the *famille-rose* palette. Blue-and-white continued to be produced, although perhaps in smaller quantities and without any innovation of shape or decoration. The *famille rose*, on the other hand, was generally of a very high quality unsurpassed in later periods. Noteworthy are the dishes and bowls of almost egg-shell fineness, superbly decorated with simple but harmonious scenes of birds in branches, long-tailed pheasants, flowering plants and fruiting branches, family scenes with adults and children, and the like. Many were painted in the so-called Chinese taste, some had a background of ruby-red and others a ruby reverse. The porcelain had a clear white body which made an ideal surface for the fine paintings. Also of note are the multi-bordered plates, but their decoration, still of the finest quality, tends to be more crowded and more suited to Western tastes.

Garnitures continued to be exported during this period, although the shape of the beakers tended to change and the number of pieces was sometimes increased from five to seven. Foot-rims are usually more spreading than those of the Kangxi period and frequently bear a wide band of diaper – a form of embellishment which appears with much greater frequency in the Yongzheng period than in the Kangxi when the bands were usually much narrower.

During this period other East India Companies were permitted to establish their own trading posts on the mainland: the French, in 1728, the Dutch in 1729, the Danes in 1731 and the Swedes the following year. Canton continued to be the prime

GRISAILLE-DECORATED PLATE, *c*.1750 (23cm/9in)

A superb plate, the decoration of which is taken from an engraving by C.J. Visscher after a drawing by Abraham Bloemaert.

port of shipment. Some of the porcelains made at Jingdezhen in this reign were sent to the port, where there was already a sizeable industry for the enamelling of metal objects, for decoration and re-firing in the muffle kilns. This applied particularly to the *famille-rose* pieces because those in underglaze blue and in the *famille-verte* and Imari palettes (see page 52) continued to be decorated at their place of manufacture.

The emperor Qianlong succeeded to the throne in 1735 and, like his grandfather Kangxi, was to reign for 60 years. This was a period of increasing European influence and also, as the reign progressed, of steady deterioration in the standard of the porcelain exported. Nevertheless, porcelain continued to be exported in vast quantities and, on account of its relative cheapness and durability, continued to dominate overseas markets well into the latter part of the eighteenth century, even though by that time home industries were established.

The *famille-rose* palette was dominant although underglaze blue came a close second, particularly in the field of large tea and dinner services. The rose enamels

tended to lose their early translucency and their harmony was disturbed by the increasing use of an overglaze iron-red.

It was not a period of great innovation, although the flambé glazes reached their peak at this time with shades ranging from turquoise and purple to a rich red and deep crimson. (The glaze is often lightly crackled and the foot-rim is ground where the glaze has run.) Other monochromes include turquoise blue, a variety of greens, coral red and sapphire blue.

It was during this reign that the East India Companies were first permitted to set up their 'factories' (*hongs*) in China. The first of these was established shortly after 1749 (the Americans set up their own in 1784, following the War of Independence); they were burned down in 1822, re-built and then once again destroyed by fire in 1855, after which they were not re-built.

The Jiaqing reign follows that of Qianlong and runs from 1796 to 1820. Trade with Europe continued to dwindle, partly as a result of the Napoleonic Wars, but also due to the establishment of local porcelain factories in Europe.

THE MANUFACTURING CENTRES

Pre-eminent among these centres was the vast complex of Jingdezhen in Jiangxi Province. It was ideally situated with a good system of inland waterways and in close proximity to the raw materials used in the manufacture of porcelain. Various descriptions of the factories have been handed down, but perhaps the fullest and most valuable come from the letters of Père d'Entrecolles, a French Jesuit missionary who went to China at the end of the seventeenth century and died in Beijing in 1741. In his much-quoted letters of 1712 and 1722, he refers to the 'vast sheds where one sees in row after row, a great number of jars of earth. In these enclosures there live and work a large number of workers who each have their appointed task. One piece of porcelain . . . passes through the hands of more than twenty people . . . It is said that one piece of fired porcelain passes through the hands of seventy workers.' He also observes that there were 3,000 porcelain kilns and that at night it was as if the town, illuminated by the flames of the kilns, was itself alight.

Jingdezhen was governed by an imperial officer and its prime purpose was to supply porcelains of the finest quality for the emperor, his family, and the court circles. There were also innumerable smaller privately owned kilns (or factories), some of which, though also the recipients of imperial orders, were free to accept private commissions – it was these kilns that supplied the bulk of the porcelains exported overseas.

Dehua, in the province of Fujian, was the centre for the manufacture of the so-called *blanc de Chine* wares (although blue-and-white was also made) which had probably been produced for several centuries before they were first exported to the West in the course of the seventeenth century. They were much admired (examples are in the Johanneum collection in Saxony) and were copied by Meissen, by the French at St. Cloud, Chantilly and Vincennes, and by the English at Bow, Bristol and Chelsea.

The body of these wares is usually creamy white, glassy and exceptionally translucent. The glossy and brilliant glaze appears in a variety of tones of white with

Two *BLANC DE CHINE* FIGURES OF EUROPEANS, *c.*1700–10
(larger: 31.8cm/12½in)

sometimes a hint of yellow or blue or even pink. Firing cracks are frequently found, particularly in the larger figures and groups, as are smaller stress faults, kendis, wine-pots, vases, teapots, incense-burners, ewers and a host of other objects were manufactured in *blanc de Chine*, but perhaps the objects most familiar to Western eyes, apart from the so-called libation cups, are the figures and groups: replicas of the Buddha, the Daoist Immortals, Guanyin and a host of other deities as well as human beings (a pair familiarly known as Adam and Eve is quite well known), animals, serpents and birds abound. Most amusing are the single figures or family groups of Europeans with their improbable features.

STYLES OF DECORATION

A group of porcelains which was exported to Europe throughout the eighteenth century from the Yongzheng reign onwards was *encre de Chine*. This ware (alternatively known as *en grisaille* and at one time referred to as 'Jesuit-ware') is named after its predominant shades of grey and black, but it may have gilt embellishment or flesh tints. It was used to reproduce prints and engravings, and is frequently found on tea wares, plates, bowls and vases. It was used to paint armorials and any number of different subjects. Some of the paintings display considerable expertise; others have an amusing naïveté.

Also dating from the Yongzheng period is enamelling in *bianco sopra bianco*. In this technique pieces are partly or wholly decorated in white enamel over the glaze. The lotus design with its concentric bands of finely drawn overlapping petals occurs frequently, usually in a pure rose colour. In contrast to this restrained decoration are the tobacco-leaf patterns, with their exuberant floral designs (which sometimes include figures) in deep underglaze blue and bright enamels covering most of the surface. Many services are known in this pattern which must have had an electrifying appearance when set out on a table. Also popular from the late eighteenth century was the 'FitzHugh' pattern, commonly painted in underglaze blue but also found in orange, green, yellow and other colours.

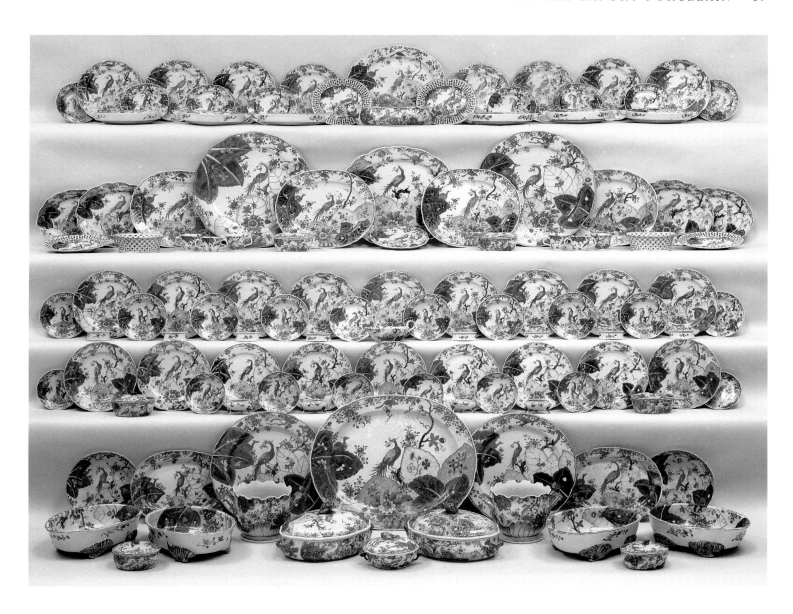

'TOBACCO LEAF'
DINNER SERVICE,
QIANLONG
PERIOD, 1735–1795
(ABOVE)

GRISAILLE-
DECORATED
PUNCH BOWL,
QIANLONG
PERIOD, 1735–1795
(29cm/11½in)
(RIGHT)

THE PRIVATE TRADE

A set of instructions in 1741 includes the request: '500 Sauce boats like the Stone Patterns No. 15 may be bespoke for another year.' These patterns referred to in the instructions are probably salt-glazed English sauceboats, which would have been sent to China as examples to be copied. The order makes clear that new shapes could not be produced in time for the current season and were ordered for delivery the next year.

FAMILLE-ROSE TUREEN, COVER AND STAND, QIANLONG PERIOD, 1735–1795 (43.2cm/17in)

This Rococo tureen has been based on a Continental faience original and would have been ordered by Supra-Cargoes of the French, Scandinavian or Dutch East India Companies.

Once the English stone ware patterns or samples had been forwarded to Jingdezhen, deep inside China, and copied by the Chinese potters, they would hardly confine production to the 500 examples ordered. It is likely that many more were made, which would then be available in Canton for purchase by any other country, there being no copyright restrictions at that time.

Other surviving orders from England contain requests for porcelain decorated with the patterns and in the forms used for metal wares, such as silver, and glass wares. By at least 1710 the Company was employing Joshua Bagshaw to produce 'wood patterns for china ware'.

It is believed that the choice of painted decoration on the Company's bulk purchases was mostly left to the Chinese because the British favoured Chinese rather than European designs. The private trade requirements, especially for the one-off armorial services, the crested or initialled articles, or those painted with European scenes such as fox-hunting, were the exception. In the last case, European prints or book illustrations were undoubtedly sent out to China. It is often immediately obvious that the Chinese painstakingly copied every straight line of the original engraver's shading or cross-hatching where a simple brush-stroke would have been more apt.

The use of book-plates, drawings or paintings of European armorial bearings

was a regular practice. Some armorial services commissioned from China were brought home only for the owner to find his instructions copied too literally. Where an owner had helpfully written the colouring instructions – for red, yellow, and so on – in the appropriate part of the arms, the Chinese painter had merely repeated these words, which were of course meaningless to him. In another example the owner had written across the bottom of the bookplate 'Our coat of arms', and this too was faithfully copied by the Chinese painter.

For the most ornately decorated Chinese armorial service ever made – that for Leake Okeover in the early 1740s – a celebrated artist of the period, Devis, was employed to paint the family arms and mantling. This painting is inscribed 'The arms of Leak Oakover (sic) Esq of Oakover . . . a pattern for China plates, pattern to be returned'. It was in fact returned and is on display at the family seat together with Devis's bill 'for furnishing a pattern plate £1–1–0'. Obviously not every family would go to this trouble and expense, but in every case some sort of print, drawing or painting had to be sent out to China to form a pattern for the Chinese painters who were unfamiliar with the European alphabet, a fact that led to several curious errors.

Little is known about the manner in which the orders for armorial or other special orders were placed with the

captains or Supra-Cargoes. The leading china dealers, all of whom stocked Chinese porcelains, must have established lines of communication with such Supra-Cargoes, and orders would have been placed with these dealers in the same way that one might place an order for an English set. Other orders were probably handed over at London coffee-houses that were the meeting places of the captains and where the official notices of the Company's sales and other activities were also posted. Garraway's Coffee House was one of the earliest retail sources for tea (where tea wares were also available), and this establishment is mentioned many times in the Company's revealing records:

'4,000 coffee cups with a blue flower at the bottom, with inside and blue rims also within and without such as are used in Garraways coffee house.'

It would seem likely that the leading Chinamen, who might have taken orders for special services, would also have had available samples of fashionable shapes, borders, styles of mantling, positions of the arms or crest, and the like. Various late eighteenth-century Chinese pattern plates have survived which have sections of borders and a selection of types of shield or cartouche for the owner's initials.

After about 1720, the overglaze enamel decoration would have been added at one of the decorating establishments at Canton. In 1769 Captain Hickey in Canton related:

'We were shown the different processes used in finishing the China ware. In one long gallery we found upwards of a hundred persons at work in sketching or finishing the various ornaments upon each particular piece of ware, some parts being executed by men of very advanced age and others by children even as young as six or seven years . . .'

The Chinese were extremely good copyists and any drawing, print or painting could be adapted to fit a porcelain blank. The Dutch sent to China both drawings and their delftware, to be copied in hard-paste porcelain. Among them were coloured drawings by Cornelis Pronk, 'Painter and Drawing Master' in Amsterdam. His

SAUCER AND
MILK JUG, dated
1762 (jug:
13cm/5⅛in)

*The crowned 'FR'
monogram is that of
Frederick the Great of
Prussia with his sword
and sceptre.*

Most of the private trade purchases depicted the crest of the family rather than the full arms although in some cases the full bearings appear on the larger, more important, pieces and the crest alone on the smaller items. After about 1770 initials are incorporated in the design, sometimes within a shield or mantling bearing some resemblance to an armorial.

It is surprising that many orders had to be sent out to China when the English factories were flourishing. Even London livery companies, which might have been expected to support home industries, sent to China for their special punch bowls and the like. One explanation could be that the presentation pieces had a certain cachet if they had been made in China rather than in England. It is also true, with regard to the punch bowls, that the Chinese potters could produce larger and better potted examples than their English counterparts could. Price was not the main consideration as the difference was not great and any saving was offset by the delay between sending the order to China and the return of the goods.

The subject matter of chinaware commissioned by Europeans covered a wide

designs were mainly figure subjects such as La Dame au Parasol and La Visite des Docteurs within complex borders, and probably proved too expensive to be a commercial success.

The main private trade market was for services decorated with the armorial bearings of European families, and some 2,900 different services have been traced. The approximate date of production can be gauged from changes in the armorial bearings as families married (and marriage dates are, by and large, easily verifiable). By comparing the various borders or styles of decoration much non-armorial porcelain can be roughly dated.

PAIR OF PLATES
PAINTED WITH
'LA VISITE DES
DOCTEURS',
AFTER CORNELIS
PRONK,
YONGZHENG
PERIOD, 1723–
1735 (23.1cm/9⅛in)
(ABOVE)

FAMILLE-ROSE
MARRIAGE PLATE,
dated 20 December
1750 (22.2cm/8¾in)
(RIGHT)

range – marriage services, mugs for Scottish bankers or for Kent inns, and even political subjects. At least one tea service bears minutely copied engravings from a mid-eighteenth century medical book – hardly subjects for a refined drawing-room. Nor were erotic subjects excluded, hidden away under a bowl or inside a snuff box.

Private trade pieces were usually well decorated and appear not only in *encre de Chine* but more frequently in the *famille-rose* palette and, to a lesser extent, in iron-red and gold. The subjects cover a vast range: those most commonly found include the Judgement of Paris, the Cherry Pickers, the Seamstress, and Juno with her attendant peacock. Then there are pastoral scenes after Boucher and Watteau, and mythological subjects such as Neptune, Venus, Europa and the Bull, and Apollo and Diana. Others depict Don Quixote, harvest and hunting scenes, kilted Scotsmen, and buildings such as the London Mansion House, Ironmongers' Hall and Burghley House.

Some pieces were specially ordered to commemorate local events. One example is the Rotterdam riots, which occurred in the late seventeenth century. Others include a series of six plates decorated in Italian Comedy style, which satirizes speculation in 'John Law's Company of the Indies and the London South Sea Company'; the Treaty of Fredericksburg signed in 1720 between Denmark and Sweden; and the unveiling of an equestrian statue of King Joseph of Portugal in Lisbon in 1775. There is also a large punch bowl decorated after an engraving of 1783 known as 'The Aerostick Stage Balloon', which satirically portrays a group of men (politicians of the day?) and

their ladies about to ascend (or be cut loose) in a balloon inscribed 'VANITY'.

Another popular form of decoration included the depiction of shipping subjects. It was customary for the captain of a vessel to have his ship portrayed on a bowl or sometimes on a plate or dish.

There are numerous biblical and religious subjects and portraits of religious figures such as Martin Luther and the Dutch cleric Pieter Boudaan. Masonic devices and the arms of some of the lodges are common. Sporting subjects are also known, including golf, cricket and a skating lesson after a mezzotint by Cornelis Dusart.

The European factories, or *hongs*, on the Chinese mainland sometimes appear, particularly on the larger diameter bowls. The presence or absence of national flags on the buildings can be used to date objects.

FIGURES

Great numbers of figures were made from the seventeenth to the nineteenth century, those specifically for export being in *blanc de Chine* or decorated in *famille verte* and more commonly in the *famille rose* range of colours.

Figures associated with Oriental religion had a ready market in Europe as did willowy maidens and 'smiling boys'. Westerners were depicted, including a couple (sometimes dancing) frequently referred to as the Dutch Governor Duff and his wife, and another couple usually associated with Louis XIV and Madame de Montespan (or de Maintenon). There are also very many figures and groups which derive from Chinese legends and folklore.

FIGURE OF A DUTCHMAN, QIANLONG
PERIOD, 1735–1795 (44.8cm/17¾in)

*The popular English identification of this figure as
'General Duff' is unlikely.*

COCK TUREEN,
COVER AND
STAND, *c.*1770–80
(stand: H48.9cm/19⅝in)

*This is an example of
the richness and
quality of the best
export pieces. The
arms are those of
Bermudez of Galicia
in north-west Spain.*

Animal models were exported in large numbers: cows, monkeys, elephants, goats, ducks, cocks, cranes, parrots, hawks, phoenixes, owls, quails, pheasants and many others. Dogs appear frequently as recumbent pugs, often supporting incense or joss-stick holders (elephant figures were also made for this function). Buddhist lions appear in pairs (those in *famille verte* being most impressive), as do lions modelled as wine ewers; small frog jardinieres and cats modelled as night-lights were also produced. Dragons, which appear so frequently as a form of decoration on Chinese porcelain, are conspicuous by their absence as isolated figures. Tureens were also made in the shape of ox- and boar-heads, chickens, tortoises, partridges and geese; there is even one example known modelled as a dormouse with young.

EXPORTS TO
NON-EUROPEAN
COUNTRIES

The activities of the English East India Company contributed to the loss of the North American Colonies when the Company sought to press for the repayment of its losses (£7,532–9s–3d) that had resulted from the 'Boston Tea Party' in 1773.

Once the War of Independence ended, in 1776, the Americans lost remarkably little time setting up a trade with China to import directly the goods that previously had been imported from Europe. British records report that American vessels were trading at Canton from 1784 onwards and by the early nineteenth century America had replaced Europe as the dominant market for Chinese porcelain.

The Americans commissioned new and appropriate decoration – the American eagle motif was much favoured as were the arms of various states. A service with the arms of the Order of Cincinnati shipped in 1784/5 and owned by George Washington is one of the best known. Pieces with these designs are now expensive and reproductions or forgeries have been made, some of which are now antique in their own right.

A standard pattern of underglaze blue landscapes within a stylized border dating from the late eighteenth and early nineteenth centuries is known in America as 'Canton'. In Europe 'Canton' describes the colourful flower- and figure-panelled

PART OF A LARGE SERVICE, c.1770

The design is a far removed variation on what is commonly known as the willow pattern and has a lady in a wheeled carriage pushed by a servant. Large numbers of these services were exported to Europe and to America where the pattern is known as 'Canton'.

from ceramic objects. But the Mughals who invaded India in the sixteenth and seventeenth centuries brought with them an appreciation of porcelain, and pieces are to be found decorated in the 'Mughal' style.

Early eighteenth-century imports of hookah bases are recorded and it is not uncommon to come across pieces of *famille-rose* porcelain decorated with an elephant, produced later in the century. Generally, however, the trade in that period was controlled by the Portuguese and then by the English East India Companies, and imports tended to follow European rather than Indian tastes in form and decoration.

Farther to the west there was substantial trade with Persia and the Arab countries, and many pieces exist which bear fine calligraphic inscriptions and verses from the Koran. These inscriptions, many of which are dated, also appear on large bowls and other pieces decorated in Canton style during the nineteenth century.

The Topkapi Palace Museum in Istanbul houses a vast accumulation of Oriental ceramics, mostly Ming porcelain. The extent to which this accumulation was due to direct importations from China is unknown; considerable quantities were obviously acquired by conquest and as tribute from the occupied territories (at its height the Ottoman Empire extended over much of the Middle East and beyond, and reached northwards almost to the Caspian Sea, westwards to the gates of Vienna and, in North Africa, as far as Tangier).

subjects on a gilt, green-scrolled ground, referred to in America as Rose Medallion.

There had been a vast two-way trade between China and India from at least the thirteenth century. Porcelains (particularly celadons and blue-and-white pieces) and silks came from the one in exchange for peppers and other spices, pearls and gemstones, frankincense, rosewater and coral from the other. At first the import of porcelain into India was limited by the Hindu prejudice against eating or drinking

THE DECLINE OF
THE EXPORT TRADE

From the instructions given to the Supra-Cargoes each season by the Directors of the Company it is clear that the bulk market was declining by the 1770s as English porcelain manufacturers took more and more of the home market. At one sale only 500 out of 1800 lots were sold. Indeed, in the 1779–1780 season no

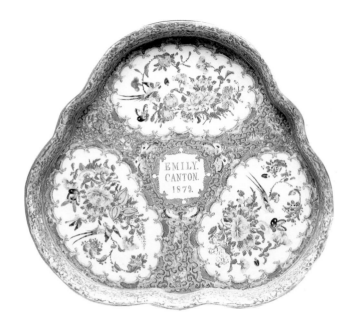

CANTON DISH, JIAQING PERIOD, 1796–1820 (40cm/15¾in)

The figure on this fine quality piece may possibly represent Earl Macartney, former Governor of Madras and Ambassador to China 1792–3, in audience with the Emperor Qianlong. (ABOVE)

CANTON DISH, dated 1879 (26cm/10¼in)

Inscribed and dated pieces of this late period are unusual and help to build up a chronology of the changing style of Canton, or rose medallion, decoration. Emily may have been the loved one of a member of the crew or the name of the ship. (ABOVE LEFT)

CANTON PERSIAN-MARKET BOWL AND STAND, dated AH 1297 (AD 1882) (33.5cm/13⅛in)

The blue ground is typical of Middle-Eastern market pieces. (LEFT)

new Chinese porcelain was ordered. One factor was the tax on imported Chinese porcelain, which was nearly 50 percent and later (1799) was to exceed 100 percent.

In 1791 the Directors of the English East India Company resolved to discontinue their bulk purchases of chinaware, which was running at two million pieces per annum. The decision of the Directors was kept secret for some considerable time because the Company had vast stocks that it hoped to sell as new importations. It was

not until 1795 that the China dealers petitioned the Company to resume the trade or to permit them to take over the importation at their own risk, but the Company declined. The cessation of bulk imports in the early 1790s served as a great fillip to the English pottery and porcelain manufacturers who increased production to fill the void. The English East India Company's monopoly in trading with China ceased in 1833 and the market opened to all traders and commercial enterprises.

PUNCH BOWL,
c.1775
(D28.6cm/11¼in)

The decoration is of a red-biased palette and the gilding is typical of the period, as are the complex panels of diapers and flowers.

DISTINGUISHING FEATURES OF EXPORT PORCELAIN

A Chinese teapot or plate is readily distinguishable from a near-contemporary English copy: the Chinese porcelains are of a true or hard paste which, being fired to between 1280 and 3500°C (2354 and 2462°F) is fully vitrified, with a thin, hard, close-fitting glaze. The English copies are soft-paste. The Chinese glaze, unlike English copies, does not run into tears or pools and should not have bubbles, at least not on the top surface. It is watertight and should not stain or discolour. It will be thinly potted and the foot-rim should be true – the plate should rest on the table without rocking. Yet, quite obviously, not every plate that is neatly potted and sits true must be a Chinese piece of porcelain.

The foot on a normal-sized plate will not be separately applied; instead, the underside will look as though it has been scooped or thinned away from the centre to form the surrounding foot. The central section will often show lathe-like thinning marks or rings. The glaze will have been cleaned away from the foot so that this is bare. The unglazed edge of the foot will probably be slightly tinted with green or light brown. If the undersides of two Chinese plates are rubbed together the resulting noise will be

both loud and grating. There will be no signs of the spur marks, stilts or other kiln furniture that can sometimes tellingly appear on English copies.

The edges of Chinese plates are thin and prone to chipping or glaze nibbles, but where these occur the underlying surface will, if clean, appear to be white and not clay-coloured. Hair-line cracks on Chinese porcelain can be very difficult to detect. The glaze should not have crazed or crackled, unless this was intended as a decorative feature.

If the object is decorated in underglaze blue, the blue should not have run into the glaze but be sharp and static. All decoration was hand-painted rather than printed. With overglaze enamels the pigments tend to sit on the surface rather than sink into the glaze. Some enamels are rather prone to flaking away from the glaze, not entirely but in small areas. When viewed at certain angles some Chinese enamels seem to have a slight halo around them, or the effect of oil dropped on a wet surface. If gilding is present it will be thin and rather watery-looking, not thick and tooled into a design as was some European gilding.

Some imported blue-and-white porcelain was 'clobbered'. Clobbering is a term usually used in a derogatory sense for overglaze enamelling and gilding which has been applied to existing decoration – normally underglaze blue – in an effort to enhance its value, by making the piece more decorative and colourful. Such later additions usually have the opposite effect

for modern collectors. The gilt border added in England on Chinese blue-and-white porcelain in the 1775–1800 period is not considered to be clobbering. It was then merely a fashionable way of taking the somewhat mundane Chinese blue-and-white tableware a little more upmarket, and to lend individuality to a dealer's stock when all were displaying much the same repetitive patterns. Although most gilding on Chinese blue-and-white was applied in England, some wares were imported with Chinese gilding.

Chinese teapots have the glaze trimmed away from the filling aperture; likewise, the inside flange of the covers is free of glaze. This enabled the covers to be fired on their pot without the risk of the glaze gluing the two pieces together. Many Chinese teapots do not have pierced strainer holes at the base of the spout – only a single large hole. This is especially so with early examples made before about 1740. When strainer holes do appear they are few in number, usually not more than three, and were punched through the glazed body from the outside. This addition usually results in the glaze having crudely flaked away around the holes.

However, the most reliable and simplest way to tell a Chinese teapot is to look under the handle where the top of the hand would be when tilting the pot. There, a small vent-hole is usually found, which allows air to escape from the hollow, moulded handle. This, on normal-sized teapots, jugs and creamers, is an almost 100 percent guarantee that the piece is Chinese.

Since tea was very expensive in the eighteenth century in relation to a weekly wage and was not a main meal as it was to become in the nineteenth century, the teapots were very small by today's standards. The tea bowls were also small with slightly flared rims, unlike the larger ones made in the 1770s. The body and glaze were very consistent over a long period and only the basic shape of the article and its style of decoration provide clues to dating. The early saucers tended to be very shallow, with a diameter of 14 cm (5½ in) or

BLUE-AND-WHITE TEAPOT, *c.*1790 (H12cm/4¾in)

Teapots such as this were usually gilded in England, the gilder often adding his number (in this case, 44) under the foot rim.

less. So shallow are they that it would be almost impossible to drink tea (certainly not hot tea) from such a vessel. Contrary to popular belief, a 'dish of tea' probably does not refer to the unlikely practice of drinking from a saucer.

Having given some guidelines for distinguishing Chinese-made wares from English examples in the same style, it must be pointed out that unless the decoration on the Chinese example is particularly rare or fine, then the English copy will be commercially more desirable, at least in the English market. There are far more eighteenth-century Chinese plates or teapots in existence than there are Bow or Worcester copies. Also, even though earlier examples tend to be rarer than later ones, they may not necessarily be more valuable. A rare late design or shape may well be more desirable than a standard piece made some 100 years earlier.

The quality of potting and decoration are sometimes cited as indications of age, the belief being that the older pieces or those of the 1720–1750 period are superior to later wares. This is broadly true, but one can have inexpensive, poorly finished, porcelain at any period, and some of the wares after 1800 are of superb quality. Likewise, the wonderfully trimmed, so-called 'eggshell' tea wares and other articles so typical of the 1720–1750 period can be very nearly matched on some later examples and can be surpassed, at least in thinness, by much later Japanese porcelain.

As a rough guide to dating porcelains,

BLUE-AND-WHITE VASE AND COVER, *c.*1880 (35.5cm/14in)

Vases such as these, along with ginger jars and beakers painted with prunus, often on a 'cracked ice' ground, were exported to the West in huge numbers during the second half of the nineteenth century. Many bear reign marks of the Emperors Chengua (1465–1487) or Kangxi (1662–1722).

blue-and-white Chinese porcelain with added gilt borders or other embellishments almost certainly dates after about 1780. Oval-shaped teapots, tureens or dishes date from about 1760 onwards, often *c.*1790–1810, and plates with a slightly concave condiment flange are also *c.*1790 or later. It must be remembered that large amounts of Chinese porcelain, mostly blue-and-white, were being imported into Europe in the second half of the nineteenth century, and even down to the present time when the flood-gates seem to have re-opened. Most of the post-1850 imports were based on Kangxi and Qianlong blue-and-white and frequently reproduced the reign marks on the base. Baluster vases, ginger jars and trumpet vases are most common. A 1910-period Liberty & Co. advertisement recommends Nankin blue-and-white porcelain as being 'Highly finished and important Decorative Art Objects, suitable for placing in Halls, Galleries, Rooms, Libraries, Smoking Rooms &c, on large Cabinets, Brackets or beneath Console Tables, &c, &c.'. Some post-1891 examples have the word 'CHINA' stencilled under the base and 'MADE IN CHINA' can occur after about 1920, but by no means all late pieces were so marked and, even when they were present, such markings could be removed at a later date.

In the middle of the eighteenth century some porcelain was imported in the white, almost certainly as private trade, and decorated in Europe. Attractive floral, landscape and figure painting was carried out in England, especially in the 1750s and 1760s, and a few examples are known with transfer prints; one such example has been dated 1757. The best-known independent decorating studio was that of James Giles in Soho, but there were probably more than a dozen other decorators at work who decorated English and Chinese white porcelain often to a very high standard. Similar decoration was done on the Continent, notably in Holland and in Germany (where the decorators were known as *Hausmaler*, or housepainters), although the Dutch work tends to be coarse.

JAPANESE
PORCELAIN

Ceramics have been made in Japan for some thirteen millennia. In the early period, up to about 7500BC, Japanese pottery resembled neolithic wares of other cultures. In the Jomon period, rouletted decoration gradually became elaborated until the upper areas of the pinched-up or coiled pots were decorated with fantastic semi-abstract modelling. Towards the end of the Jomon period continental influence is apparent and some doll-like figures, possibly fertility figures, were made. In the following Yayoi period (300BC–300AD) invaders from the continent brought the potters' wheel and decoration was on the surface only. For the tumuli of the Kofun period (300–600AD) large tube-like figures, haniwa, were used as external decoration on retaining walls.

Stoneware was introduced in the fifth century from Korea and glazing techniques on pottery from China by the eighth century. Stoneware and porcelain imports from China had a very strong influence on Japanese stoneware in the twelfth to fifteenth centuries and again in the seventeenth. Glaze-decorated stoneware was made in Japan from the twelfth century.

GROUPS OF JAPANESE EXPORT PORCELAIN VESSELS

This group includes early enamelled ware, Imari, Kakiemon and Kakiemon-related wares.
The dates span some 70 years; the vase on the left of the
front row was certainly made before 1695 when a similar example was
depicted in a ceiling-painting at the German palace of Oranienburg.

THE BEGINNINGS OF THE PORCELAIN INDUSTRY

Japan's long-standing tradition of the making of stoneware was reinforced, at the end of the sixteenth century, by an influx of potters from Korea. These men were brought to Japan by the returning forces from the invasions of Korea, either as immigrants or as captives. As little porcelain was made in Korea in the late sixteenth century, and almost no blue-and-white porcelain, these potters must have been stoneware potters, making the ware called *punch'ong*.

Many of these potters settled in the northwest of Kyushu, near the starting-off point of the invasions, near to the port of Karatsu. One of their major contributions was the introduction of the *noborigama*, the stepped, chambered, climbing kiln. This kiln, which allowed a close control of the atmosphere and temperature gradient around the pots during the course of firing, spread from the Karatsu area to Seto and Mino on Honshu. For 20 or more years the Karatsu industry flourished until, in about 1620, some Karatsu kilns in the southern area, an area that we could now call western Arita, began to make porcelain concurrently with stoneware. Sherds of porcelain and stoneware fused together in kiln accidents have been found at two kilns in this area, demonstrating the firing of the two together in the same firing of the same chamber of the same kiln.

The techniques for making and firing stoneware and porcelain are, after all, almost identical – it is the material that is different. Porcelain clay is a decayed granite, and a mountain of this material, Izumiyama, was found in the area of the town now called Arita. It seems possible that the Karatsu potters had used this porcelain clay as a component of their own particular transparent glaze.

The earliest porcelains made in these

SHOKI-IMARI BLUE-AND-WHITE DEEP DISH, c.1620–40

The mixture of patterned borders, formal at the outer edge, scrolling further inwards with a swiftly painted, somewhat perfunctory flower and bird motif in the well, is a typical feature of some of the early wares.

kilns, the earliest porcelains made in Japan, naturally enough closely resembled the Karatsu in shape and decoration. The shapes were those in demand at the same time, mostly bowls, bottles and small dishes, and the painting was pictorial or patterned, done with the brush in a metal oxide under a transparent glaze. In the case of the Karatsu this was underglaze iron-brown; in the case of the porcelain, it was an underglaze cobalt blue.

Legend in Japan ascribes the commencement of the industry to a Korean, Ri Sampei, but it seems more probable that this was a case of an industry being developed in order to supply a new demand. In this case there seems to have been a demand for relatively inexpensive porcelain decorated in blue and white or in celadon. At first rather simple, these Arita porcelains – *shoki-Imari* (early Imari) named from the port through which they were shipped – became increasingly sophisticated in shape and pattern, in spite of a tendency towards mass-production even in this inexperienced industry. Competition

from China in the form of the so-called Tainqi porcelain – *ko-sometsuke* (old blue and white) – specially made in Jingdezhen for the Japanese market, only increased the level of sophistication.

During the second quarter of the century the Arita porcelain industry expanded fast. New demand for porcelain, partly due to its acceptability into the ranks of 'tea taste' led to the opening of new kilns and ensured an increase in quality and in the range of product. For most of this time, the imported *ko-sometsuke* and the native *shoki-Imari* competed in the same market, each influencing the other. A wider range of kiln furniture enabled larger shapes, especially wide dishes, to be made in Arita; this was to have very far-reaching effects later. Meanwhile celadon dishes in imitation of Zhejiang celadons were made for a low-volume export trade to southeast Asia. This trade in turn stimulated the production of enamelled porcelain for the same market. These examples are apparently the first enamelled wares produced in Arita and are in the dark pigments that we call 'Kutani' enamels.

SHOKI-IMARI
BLUE-AND-WHITE
PLATE WITH
LANDSCAPE DESIGN,
*c.*1630–50 (22cm/8½in)

*With an unusual
rolled-over lip, this
plate otherwise bears a
fairly typical type of
landscape decoration
that owes more to
Japanese painting in
Chinese style (Kano
school) than it
does directly to
Chinese painting.*

The first recorded Dutch purchase was in 1650, some coarse porcelain; curiously, this was to be sent to Tonkin. Special shapes were ordered in 1653. Until 1656 the Dutch ordered Japanese porcelain for their various 'factories' throughout Asia, but these porcelains were for use, not for resale. In other words, the Dutch did not yet consider Japanese porcelain a worthy substitute for Chinese porcelain.

Then in 1657 a case of samples was sent to the Governors of the Dutch East India Company in Holland, the Chamber of Seventeen. This apparently included some enamelled wares. Presumably these samples were judged satisfactory, for in 1659 came the first large order for Japanese porcelain; whereas in 1656 the order had been for 4149 pieces, in 1659 the order was for 64,866 pieces. This is the beginning of the export trade in Japanese porcelain to Europe and to many Asian countries, in the hands of the Dutch and of the Chinese, that was to last almost until the middle of the eighteenth century.

EXPORT TRADE:

THE EARLY PERIOD

When the Portuguese had arrived in Japan in the mid-sixteenth century they had brought with them Jesuit priests as well as guns and trade. Their aims were always two-fold — conversion and profit. The Dutch, arriving in 1600, were Protestant or Calvinist. Tension between the Christians was exacerbated by some Spanish Franciscans. At first tolerant of or even welcoming to Christianity, the Japanese authorities began to believe in a possible European invasion of Japan and this led first to a massacre of both European and convert Catholics and then to complete expulsion. Successively stronger laws against foreign ships arriving in Japan and against Japanese ships or citizens leaving Japan culminated in the final Edict of Closure of the Country (*Sakoku*) in 1639.

Imports of *ko-sometsuke* were drastically curtailed in the late 1640s, as Jingdezhen was caught up in the civil wars that led to the downfall of the Ming dynasty in favour of the Qing (Manchu) dynasty. Arita took full advantage of this lack of competition and again expanded its production and the range of its products. The use of coloured glazes, celadon and *temmoku* had been widespread in the Arita kilns; now it became more adventurous. Underglaze copper-red was tried at several kilns, but it was never very successful and was soon discontinued. Shapes specifically for use in the tea ceremony and in the *kaiseki* meal that accompanies a formal tea ceremony were made at several kilns.

Not all the 30-odd Arita kilns were capable of producing high-quality wares and a sorting-out of kilns into different types of production had occurred over the years. Possibly this was due to local governmental pressure, more probably simply to the laws of supply and demand. A few kilns made only one or two types of product, while at the top end of the market the more sophisticated kilns made a very wide range of product, reflecting demands of differing sub-divisions of the market and of the price ranges.

Imports of Chinese porcelain ceased totally in the 1650s. Meanwhile the Dutch East India Company, the most powerful of the European East India Companies in the Far East and the only European Company allowed access to the direct trade with Japan, had begun to buy small amounts of Japanese porcelain. Hitherto the Dutch had been buying Chinese porcelain, specially made to their orders in Jingdezhen in shapes demanded by the European and Near Eastern markets. Now that Jingdezhen porcelain was no longer available, the Dutch could only buy southern Chinese porcelain, seemingly having difficulties in getting the shapes they wanted. Noting, apparently, the Japanese export trade to southeast Asia adapted both to the shapes demanded (the celadon dishes) and to the colours made available through the enamelling process, the Dutch turned to the Japanese market.

LARGE BLUE-
AND-WHITE DISH
IN *KRAAK* STYLE,
*c.*1660–70
(54cm/21¼in)

*This is a copy of a
Chinese Wanli period,
so called* kraak *dish.*
(RIGHT)

BLUE-AND-
WHITE MUG IN
TRANSITIONAL
STYLE, WITH
EUROPEAN LID,
*c.*1660–70
(16cm/6¼in)

*The painterly Chinese
Transitional style is
here travestied in Japan.*
(FAR RIGHT)

The Dutch thereafter shared with the Chinese the uneasy monopoly of the direct trade with Japan.

To the Dutch, the advantage of trading with Japan was threefold: firstly, no other European nation had direct access to the Japanese trade; secondly the Japanese could make to order the shapes, sizes and styles of porcelain desired by the Dutch; and thirdly, much of the porcelain could be coloured to Dutch specification.

Both the Dutch and the Chinese were allowed to carry on a strictly limited trade with a single 'factory' each. After the 1640s both factories were in the harbour at Nagasaki, the Dutch one on a fan-shaped reclaimed mudflat called Deshima. Conditions under which the Dutch worked were very severe and it was only the great profits to be made from the trade that induced them to undertake it. European nations who wished to buy Japanese goods could obtain them only from the Dutch or from the Chinese. As we shall see, the Chinese bought great quantities of Japanese porcelain for resale to European nations other than the Dutch.

Much of what the Dutch wanted was what they knew they could sell; in other words, imitations of Chinese porcelain. At this time, in the mid-seventeeth century, the Chinese styles favoured by the Dutch were the Wanli *kraak-porselein* style (*kraak* is a corruption of 'carrack', the vessel that is supposed to have brought the porcelain from China) and the so-called Transitional style, transitional between the Ming and Qing. The former, usually used in Japan for open shapes, bowls and dishes, took the form of a central pictorial element surrounded by a compartmented border. This style was called *fuyo-de* in Japan, as the border compartments suggested flower petals. In fact this had been a style of the end of the sixteenth and the beginning of the seventeenth centuries, but it can still be found represented in Japanese porcelain well into the nineteenth century. The Transitional style was based on more open designs of flowers or of landscapes, and is to be found on closed shapes, jars, bottles and vases.

Whereas the Chinese originals for the Transitional style had been carefully and

beautifully decorated in a distinctly painterly manner, the Japanese mimics are definitely crude. But we know from written sources that the Japanese potters were shown not the Chinese originals, but wooden models sent from Holland. Presumably these wooden jars had been painted by Delft potters, so it is hardly surprising that the curious bent figures and the bottle-brush trees bear scant resemblance to the Chinese; they were Japanese versions of European pastiches of Chinese originals that had already made concessions to European tastes. Over the years the number of different shapes ordered by the Dutch increased and the Japanese potters moved further and further away from the original designs.

Chinese porcelain for Europe had mostly been blue and white. Celadon was better known for the Near Eastern market, but in Europe the blue-and-white colour scheme signified porcelain, and the majolica potters of Holland, England and elsewhere in Europe imitated it by opacifying their lead glazes with tin oxide (delftware, or tin-glazed earthenware). Some enamelled

LIDDED JAR ENAMELLED WITH CHRYSANTHEMUMS, *c*.1660–80 (27.3cm/10¾in)

It is likely that this jar was enamelled by the Kakiemon when they were still enamellers only, before the commencement of the Kakiemon kiln at Nangawara. (LEFT)

JAR ENAMELLED WITH A LANDSCAPE, *c*.1660–75 (21.4cm/8⅜in)

During the early period of enamelled export porcelain different workshops apparently used different palettes of pigments. (FAR LEFT)

TEA-WHISK SHAPED BOTTLE ENAMELLED WITH A LANDSCAPE, *c*.1660–80 (27cm/10½in)

The use of the geometric patterning in matt red above a landscape enamelled in dark colours, shows that this bottle lies in the ancestry of the Imari wares. Such pieces used to be attributed to the Kutani kilns. (BELOW)

Chinese porcelain had come to Europe before the mid-seventeenth century (some *kinrande* pieces are inventoried in Schloss Ambras in 1596) but it was rare and the colours were dark. Early Japanese enamel had been similarly dark; by 1657 it must have been as bright as the earliest-known pieces for the Dutch market. These are the clear and brilliant colours which included an overglaze cobalt-blue unknown as yet in China. The earliest Japanese enamelled porcelain to reach Europe must therefore have been a revelation; it was porcelain as brilliantly coloured as majolica.

It has become the custom in England to call the blue-and-white wares Arita and the coloured wares either Imari or Kakiemon. This is a convenient description but it obscures the truth. The Arita and Imari wares were made at the same time in the same kilns (Imari is the name of the port through which the porcelain was shipped to Nagasaki), while the word Kakiemon denotes a style rather than the product of one kiln. In fact most Kakiemon seems to have been made at one kiln, but it was also made at rival kilns and it is not always clear which pots are from which particular kiln.

At first, the enamels used on the Imari wares were very varied. They evolved from the 'Kutani' style wares of the 1640s and 1650s, by gaining in brilliance and translucency. Only the red was matt and opaque. Different groups of workers appear to have used different pigments or palettes of enamels and it is possible, to some extent, to classify these. By and large, we can see that they fall into two lineages, those that lead to the Imari and those that lead to the Kakiemon. Even when this settling down period is over – perhaps in the late 1670s and early 1680s – there is wide variation within each group. Not only did each kiln make a wide range of wares for different levels of the market, but also, as fashions waxed and waned, innovations were quickly imitated, with consequent difficulties for the researcher.

Most of the shapes were those of European usage; thus the Dutch ordered the shapes they wanted: mugs, jugs, bottles, kendi, bowls, teapots, cups, some with saucers, figures of animals and people and so on. Presumably, the Chinese were able to order shapes for resale to European clients and it may be no coincidence that the Kakiemon porcelain, which is closer in taste to the Chinese than is the Imari, is most commonly found in the countries in Europe that had East India Companies that had no direct trade with Japan, whereas Imari is more common in Holland.

ARITA AND IMARI WARES

As we have seen, both these names are used for wares made in Arita, as it is English usage only to distinguish the enamelled wares as Imari. It might be possible to subdivide the Arita and Imari wares into groups according to which kiln was the producer, but this is difficult as there is so much overlap in the productions of the various kilns. We do not know whether this was due to the large orders being distributed by the local authorities, or to imitation and competition between rival kilns. It is easier to divide this very large and heterogeneous group by the palettes of enamels used upon them.

The earliest painters in enamels made use of a good range of enamel pigments, especially a strong aubergine as a dominant colour and with some use of underglaze blue. At this stage, the underglaze blue was used as circumferential lines or patterns to divide a dish or vessel into zones that could then be decorated in enamel colours. These enamelled areas tended to be around the middle of a bowl or vessel, as dividers between cartouches, or in the well of a dish, though dishes might have enamelled borders, too. Only later was the enameller forced to conform to the picture laid out by the painter in underglaze blue who left specific gaps for specific patterns (such as a flower of a particular shape and size) to be filled in by the enameller. This latter case implies a close connection between the potter (for underglaze blue is painted onto the unfired pot) and the enameller. This variation in the use of underglaze blue occurs in the Kakiemon porcelains, too.

Porcelain with underglaze blue only was

The pictorial scene is of a high-grade courtesan with her two kamuro *in a garden before the rolled blinds of a 'green house'. The rich decoration is typical of the Genroku period when some examples were even more over-decorated in even brighter colours.*

the commonest and the cheapest ware, as it underwent only one firing in a kiln, but the variation in quality and, no doubt, in price was very considerable. Variation in the range of enamel pigments used was perhaps even greater; the commonest and probably the cheapest of the Imari wares used underglaze blue, red and gold only, with black used for outlining, as it is on almost all types. At the other end of the scale, of those Imari wares that do include underglaze blue, the best use red, blue, yellow, two greens, aubergine and black.

Many of the best-quality Imari wares do not use underglaze blue at all. Possibly this was to compete with the best-quality Kakiemon porcelain, which also lacks underglaze blue on the finest-quality pieces. Some types of this group are richly polychrome; others use a restricted palette of, for example, red, gold and green.

Imari wares that use underglaze blue

make full use of it both for defining the areas of decoration and for the basis of pictorial design. The use of contrasting areas of decoration is marked; most obvious is the use of shaped reserves (fan shapes, poem-slip shapes etc.) against a powder-blue ground. Some of the earliest Imari wares made for Holland had only gold and silver painting on a blue ground. In other cases the underglaze blue is of patterning or of flower-work behind or beside brightly coloured major pictorial elements.

In the underglaze blue wares, landscape decoration is probably as common as the floral. In the coloured pieces, humans may appear as more important elements in any decorative scheme. Such decoration tends to be on a larger scale with time; in other words the later wares tend to be more lavishly and boldly decorated. There may be a tendency towards overdecoration that leads to fussiness. This is particularly evident in the characteristic large lidded jars, three of which, with two trumpet-shaped vases, made up the standard *garniture de cheminée*. In these the later examples are not only overdecorated, but the lids are

LARGE IMARI JAR AND COVER, *c.*1690–1700 (58.7cm/23⅛in)

Part of a garniture of three jars and two trumpet-shaped vases, this vase uses the standard Imari style of decoration with underglaze blue decoration that leaves spaces to be enamelled after the high temperature firing. (ABOVE)

IMARI FIGURE OF MAN, *c.*1700–20 (32.4cm/12¾in)

Such figures occur either free-standing or as knops to the lids of jars. Always exotic and therefore popular, figures of humans and of animals were a staple of the export trade.

This figure was present in Burghley House in 1688 and is therefore one of the earliest securely dated pieces of Japanese export porcelain. The Japanese modeller of this enchanting beast had never seen an elephant, but only somewhat fanciful Chinese illustrations. (BELOW)

KAKIEMON WARES

We have divided the production of the Arita kilns into two lineages; this second one, the Kakiemon lineage, is smaller in quantity and more restricted in range than the vast group we have called the Imari lineage.

The group is named after the potter Sakaida Kakiemon, a quasi-legendary figure to whom is attributed the origination of the enamelling process in Japan. Today the word covers both a more or less coherent style of decoration and the use of a particular palette of brilliant translucent enamels. Most, but by no means all, of these wares seem, in the mid-period and later, to have been made at the Kakiemon kiln.

In fact, as we have already seen, it is more probable that this group was, at first, one of many groups of enamelled porcelain

taller in proportion and the knobs of the lids larger. Often such knobs were modelled as human or animal figures. Freestanding models were common at all periods.

It was the cheaper blue-red-and-gold Imari wares that were most commonly imitated by the Chinese as Chinese Imari, though better-quality polychrome wares were also copied. The making of Chinese Imari may well have contributed to the decline of the Japanese export trade in the early to mid-eighteenth century.

KAKIEMON
SAUCER DISH
WITH THE
'THREE FRIENDS',
c.1690–1710
(21.2cm/8¼in)

This is a classic 'brown-edge' Kakiemon dish, made of the milky-white nigoshide *body and with an almost colourless transparent glaze. Enamels only are used, of the particularly translucent Kakiemon type, in an asymmetrical decoration of great delicacy.* (RIGHT)

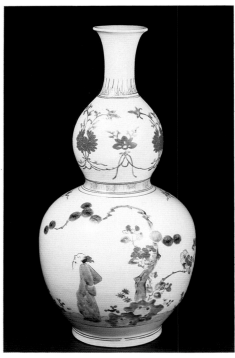

made by competing workshops of enamellers. The palette was securely established in the 1680s and in all probability the Kakiemon kiln was established at this time. The enamellers had either become potters or else were working almost exclusively with this new kiln.

It was this kiln that produced the famous milky-white (*nigoshide*) body, uniquely (for Arita) white and with an almost completely colourless glaze. Such pieces therefore lack the blue cast of all other Arita products. This body never bears underglaze blue decoration and seems to have been used almost exclusively for bowls and plates. Such pieces are lightly decorated, the asymmetrical patterns making full use of the beautiful white background.

Patterns of decoration at the kiln were usually landscape or floral – a famous exception is the 'Hob-in-the-well' pattern – though more formal patterning was frequently a feature. The painting was of a high quality both on these *nigoshide* wares and on the other products of the kiln; these products included both enamelled wares

KAKIEMON BLUE-AND-WHITE DISH, c.1690–1710 (31.5cm/12¼in)

Sherds of dishes painted in underglaze blue in this fine style have been found at the Kakiemon kiln-site in Nangawara in south-western Arita, along with sherds of the undecorated nigoshide *body.* (ABOVE)

DOUBLE-GOURD
BOTTLE
ENAMELLED IN
KAKIEMON
STYLE, c.1670–
1700 (43cm/17in)

As no closed shapes seem to have been made at the Kakiemon kiln, this piece must have been brought from some other kiln to be enamelled by the Kakiemon, a fairly common practice. The sages and the 'three friends' (pine, plum and bamboo), refer to the Chinese classics. (ABOVE)

that did make use of underglaze blue and wares in underglaze blue only.

Examination of the kiln site raises a serious problem: only open shapes (bowls, dishes, etc.) have been found in the spoil heaps. Closed shapes (bottles, jars, etc.) must have been bought in from other kilns for enamelling; those that bear enamels only were clearly chosen for their whiteness of body and clarity of glaze, in close resemblance to the true *nigoshide*. It is not known which kilns provided them.

The essentially lightly decorated Kakiemon porcelain makes a marked contrast to the more gorgeous Imari and to the bolder underglaze blue wares we call Arita. This, as we have suggested, may have been to conform to Chinese taste, whereas the Imari was more in Dutch taste.

Kakiemon porcelain was much imitated. Sherds of *nigoshide* dishes have been found, albeit uncommonly, at two other Arita kiln sites. The style of painting was, of course, imitated elsewhere and the palette of enamels could be imitated in other styles of decoration or with the addition of enamel colours not used by the Kakiemon (such as the brown enamels used on the 'Hampton Court' hexagonal jars). The Kakiemon style was rarely imitated in China, but was a major stimulus and inspiration to the porcelain industries of France, Germany and England.

THE END OF THE EXPORT TRADE

The third decade of the eighteenth century saw a decline in export from Arita. Partly this was the fruit of its own success. Japanese porcelain had been more expensive in Europe than the Chinese equivalents. As the novelty wore off, the cheaper Chinese porcelain, which was often of equally fine or finer quality, captured the market. It is strange, therefore, that the Kakiemon style was so influential in Europe during the first half of the eighteenth century and the Imari so influential in the second half.

Attempts to revive the flagging interest in Japanese porcelain were made by the Dutch, who commissioned Japanese porcelain to be made, bearing decoration designed by a Dutch artist, Cornelis Pronk, in 1734. Even this was a failure, as the Chinese produced better versions presumably at a lower price. It is worth remembering that at this date the Chinese were producing quantities of armorial porcelain decorated after European design and specification. Japanese armorial porcelain, usually dating nearer to 1700 or earlier, is, incidentally, rather rare.

In the 1740s, the export of Japanese porcelain virtually ceased, though there was a small volume of trade, usually to private order, throughout the century. The Arita kilns therefore suffered something of a slump until a small resurgence of the domestic market at the end of the century.

KUTANI

The term Old Kutani, *ko-Kutani* in Japanese, has been applied to several groups of porcelain, not all of which are related to each other either temporally or geographically. The porcelains thus described have in common a palette of enamel pigments in which dark and somewhat opaque colours are used in combinations which seem to depend upon aubergine (which varies as far as rich purple), dark green and yellow. The blue is usually rich and dark, and there is nearly always underglaze blue.

Underglaze blue is usually confined to the backs of dishes, where it may appear as circumferential rings, or as a definite decoration, usually floral.

Most of the so-called *ko-Kutani* wares are large dishes, though smaller dishes, jars, bottles and a few other shapes occur.

LARGE ENAMELLED DISH IN GEOMETRIC KUTANI STYLE, MID TO LATE 17TH CENTURY (34cm/13¼in)

*It is the dark colour of the enamels and the geometric pattern of this and other dishes that have caused them to be classified as Old Kutani (*ko-Kutani*), whereas most are almost certainly of Arita manufacture.*

Usually the surface area is more or less covered with decoration, often strongly asymmetrical or pictorial, on a large scale and of boldly drawn motifs. Sometimes the area is broken up into zones of geometrical patterns which may or may not leave spaces for pictorial decoration. Dishes of the latter type may have a shaped outline, usually nine-sided.

A variety is called green Kutani, *ao-Kutani*, from the predominant green enamel, though yellow is almost as common. In these wares the backs of dishes may be totally covered in yellow or green enamel, with black line decoration. These dishes are so thinly glazed as to appear to be biscuit and show signs of being underfired. The decoration on the face of such dishes leaves no space unenamelled, often with a crude design. All these types have at some time been called seventeenth century.

Excavations at the Kutani kiln site in Kaga, on Honshu, demonstrated that there was a kiln there in the middle of the seventeenth century. This was probably the only porcelain kiln of the time outside Kyushu. Sherds recovered from the site, however, resemble none of the porcelains traditionally ascribed to the kiln. Sherds of medium- to large-sized dishes do occur at the site, but these are poorly shaped and lack underglaze blue, thus differentiating themselves from almost all *ko-Kutani*.

Excavations at Arita sites, on the other hand, show that at least some of the *ko-Kutani* porcelain was made in Arita. Three kilns in Arita seem to have been involved in the production of the large dishes, during the second and third quarters of the seventeeth century (Maruo, Yamabeta and Cho-kichi-dani kilns), while others may also have made the smaller dishes, closely akin to *shoki-Imari*, that bore Kutani-palette enamels. It seems likely that all these types of pieces were made for the southeast Asian market, beginning perhaps as early as the 1640s.

Sherds of the body, with tell-tale patterns of underglaze blue and the typically smeared thin, greyish glaze of most *ko-Kutani*, have been found at Maruo and Yamabeta, while the more white-bodied type has been found at Yamabeta and Cho-kichi-dani. Sherds of enamelled *ko-Kutani* wares have been found (this is highly unusual, for enamelled sherds are rare at kiln sites) at the Yamabeta kiln site and also on the site of the enamellers' quarter, the *aka-e-machi*.

Both the *ao-Kutani* and the pictorial type (one sherd bears the picture of a tiger) have been found. The small dishes with the foot shaped in cross-section as a sharp V, which have similar enamels, but lack underglaze blue and have a whiter body than the norm, may be from the Arita kiln Otaru.

The controversy over the origin of the *ko-Kutani* porcelains is by no means settled. We can but suggest that most of the *ko-Kutani* porcelain that is seventeenth century was made in Arita. Much of it is later, often much later than the seventeenth century, and most of this later material seems to have been made in Kaga. There are, however, some porcelains of the so called *ko-Kutani* type that do seem to be seventeenth century, which were not made in Kutani and were not made in Arita.

DEEP DISH ENAMELLED IN KUTANI STYLE, MID TO LATE 17TH CENTURY (31.1cm/12⅛in)

The style of landscape painted on this dish in combination with the geometric border suggests an early date for this group, nearer to the middle than to the end of the century.

NABESHIMA

Towards the end of the seventeenth century, the Nabeshima lords of Hizen (now Saga-ken) seem to have decided that porcelain would make sufficiently grand gifts for the Shogun and for Court officials. Porcelain of export type would clearly be unsuitable as it would be of foreign shapes and would bear inappropriate decoration. Legend has it that the first kiln to make these presentation wares was in Iwayakawachi in southwestern Arita; workers were later transferred to Okawachi, some 8 km (5 miles) north of Arita.

Excavation does not substantiate the suggestion that any kiln in Iwayakawachi was the origin of the Nabeshima porcelain. In all probability the style used for the Nabeshima wares grew from an Arita style where dishes of shaped forms stood on a relatively high, attached, ribbon foot. Such wares have been called Matsugatani wares. Several kilns in Arita made such pieces; one of these, Sarugawa, is in the Iwayakawachi area, hence, perhaps, the story.

The Nabeshima porcelain made at Okawachi, beginning perhaps at the very end of the seventeenth century, is distinguished by perfection of shape and by careful and very beautiful decoration. The body and glaze were similar to that of Arita, for the whiteness of the Kakiemon *nigoshide* was never emulated.

Typically, the Nabeshima porcelains of the best period – thought to be the first half of the eighteenth century – are dishes in three sizes: of diameters approximately 30cm (12in), 20cm (8in), and 15cm (6in). Usually these have a curved profile, the best having a perfect catenary curve, though sometimes there is a narrow out-turned flattened lip. They stand on a tall vertical foot, though occasionally the larger dishes stand on three moulded feet. Cups are also not uncommon, either of bucket shape or of a narrow and more elaborate cross-section. Shaped dishes are relatively rare, and there is some argument over the origin of some of the small moulded dishes, which are sometimes classified, on no evidence, as Matsugatani. At the Okawachi kiln site, sherds have been found of large celadon figures,

but these seem rarely to have survived. There was, of course, an evolution towards the 'standard' shapes, and the earlier dishes seem to have been more flattened in profile.

Decoration on the Nabeshima porcelain depends on extremely skilful use of glaze and of the *wu-tsai* technique, which uses underglaze blue to outline an area that will later be enamelled, a technique that is almost unknown in Arita wares. The Nabeshima celadon glaze was particularly fine and though often thickly applied was perfectly controlled, especially in the area adjacent to the foot-rim. Frequently celadon was used in conjunction with blue and white, in reserves, or with iron-brown and with enamels. Sometimes the cobalt blue was used in the celadon and sometimes enamels appear on the celadon.

More typically, Nabeshima dishes use blue and white, with or without the addition of overglaze enamel. On such pieces the back is invariably in underglaze blue only. On the earlier pieces, the back may be boldly decorated with a floral scroll and the tall foot bear some regular pattern. On the typical pieces the decoration on the

NABESHIMA DISH WITH CAMELLIAS AND A BANDED HEDGE, EARLY 18TH CENTURY (20cm/7¾in)

Flowers occur on Nabeshima porcelain more commonly than do inanimate objects or abstract patterns. (ABOVE)

NABESHIMA DISH WITH 'AUSPICIOUS TREASURES', EARLY 18TH CENTURY (31cm/12in)

Chinese 'auspicious treasures' are painted in underglaze blue and in the typically Nabeshima method of underglaze blue outlining an area of colour. (ABOVE LEFT)

back is usually in three areas and may be a linked cash pattern or a rather perfunctory flower pattern. The foot almost always bears the famous comb pattern. There is never a mark.

The painted decoration on Nabeshima porcelain is careful and extremely sophisticated; the painting, whether in underglaze blue or in enamel is very skilfully applied. Underglaze blue may be used as a background either as a wash, or in a careful stencilled pattern.

The subjects for decoration vary widely, but are usually based on formal and sometimes geometric abstract patterning, on inanimate objects such as jars, or on trees or plants. Patterns may be arranged around the perimeter only, or asymmetrically over the whole surface, or even cover the whole surface. There is rarely a central motif within a border. Areas of two different backgrounds may cover approximate halves of a dish, or be divided by an overlaid pattern. There is always a distinct tendency towards patternmaking.

It is generally thought that the weaker designs date from the later periods; by the nineteenth century imitations were being made at Hirado and elsewhere.

Excavation at the Okawachi kiln site shows that not only the Nabeshima official wares were made there, but also a large quantity of ordinary domestic wares. In all probability the Nabeshima pieces were fired in two of the chambers towards the centre of a large *noborigama*. The ruins of the kiln now on the site are too large to be those of the eighteenth-century kiln.

NABESHIMA *MUKOZUKE* CUP WITH ABSTRACT PATTERN, EARLY 18TH CENTURY (H6.5cm/2½in)

The shape of this small food bowl is bilaterally but not radially symmetrical.

OTHER KILNS

SUISAKA

Certain *temmoku* and underglaze blue dishes, sometimes with enamel, usually of non-round shape, have in the past been attributed to the Suisaka kiln in Kaga. This site is known only from literary sources and its location is unknown. Some, at least, of such wares are from Arita; the early and crude types were made in at least three kilns, the later and more sophisticated type has been found at one kiln site in Arita. It is, of course, possible that such wares were also made at Suisaka, or indeed elsewhere, too, but there is no evidence for this.

MATSUGATANI

As with the Suisaka, the Matsugatani wares are a heterogeneous group of small porcelain dishes, usually not round in shape, that is attributed to a site on no evidence. No sherds of anything resembling these pieces have been found at the Matsugatani kiln site, which lies between Arita and Saga. On the other hand, so-called Matsugatani sherds are not uncommon at several kiln sites in Arita and it is inescapable that most of them, if not indeed all of them, are of Arita manufacture.

A connection is often drawn between the Matsugatani wares and the Nabeshima wares of Okawachi. While they may indeed be the inspiration of the early Nabeshima style, perhaps towards the end of the seventeenth century, there is no certain connection. In style they are usually beautifully though strongly painted in a pictorial scheme that may ignore a moulded pattern on the body.

SHIBUEMON

A very beautiful style of carefully painted enamelled porcelain has been singled out as the Shibuemon style. In decoration these pieces fall into no known category but are sometimes seen as intermediate between the Kakiemon, whose enamels they utilize, and the Nabeshima, to which they owe a stylistic debt. They are even sometimes called *Kaki-nabe*.

Usually they are attributed to the late seventeenth century, for some of them bear inscriptions that suggest, somewhat tenuously, that they are Genroku (1688–1703) in date. Shibuemon is thought to be the name of a relative of the Sakaida (Kakiemon) family. It is possibly more plausible to suggest that they are from the late eighteenth century and represent the finest achievements of Arita at a low ebb in the town's fortunes. They were not made for the export trade, but for a luxury domestic market.

LATER JAPANESE PORCELAIN

The problems of nomenclature and chronology that beset our knowledge of Arita, Imari and Kutani wares around the mid-eighteenth century continue well into the nineteenth century. The stimulus of Japan's export trade on the development of her home market gradually weakened towards the middle of the eighteenth century, as the cheaper products from China displaced Japan as supplier to the various European East India companies. This situation was compounded by a policy of political, cultural and economic isolationism that was not broken until the 1850s, when the Americans finally succeeded in imposing a trade treaty. Japan was a convenient fuelling station on the trade route between Shanghai and the newly acquired western seaboard state of California. The British, Dutch, French and Russians followed up the advantage with their own enforced treaties.

Eventually, internal pressure for political reform within Japan brought about her participation in the newly instituted International Exhibitions. The effect on European artistic communities and taste following the 1867 Paris Exhibition in which the

HIZEN WARE,
FROM *KERAMIC
ART OF JAPAN* BY
G. A. AUDSLEY
AND JAMES LORD
BOWES, 1875
(LEFT)

*Hizen ware of this
type would now be
attributed to Arita.*

ENGRAVING OF
THE JAPANESE
COURT AT THE
1862 LONDON
EXHIBITION

*Major international
exhibitions helped
spread the vogue for
'Japonisme'.*
(BELOW)

Japanese arts were represented was
dramatic. It led to a craze for all things
Oriental. 'Japonisme', as it was dubbed,
combined with 'Chinamania' and Aestheti-
cism, from which, around the year 1900,
Art Nouveau would emerge. The opened
door allowed artistic and technological
influences to pass in both directions once
more and permitted Japan to lay the
foundations of an industrial state. The
export of Japanese ceramics to Europe
resumed after a gap of more than 100 years.

IMARI

By far the most common of these export
wares is the group known as Imari: porcelain painted first in underglaze blue, then
glazed and fired, then enamelled in colours
(including at least an opaque iron-red),
fired, then gilded and fired again. This
group continues an Arita type evolved at
the end of the seventeenth century, a style

HIRADO BLUE-AND-WHITE BOTTLE,
1835 (22cm/8⅛in)

This piece is decorated in underglaze blue with the crest of the Wakigawa family. (BELOW)

GROUP OF IMARI DISHES AND JARS,
LATE 19TH CENTURY

Imari decoration was popular in Europe. (BELOW)

produced for the domestic Japanese market throughout the country's period of isolation in the eighteenth and nineteenth centuries. Its quality varies enormously, from the downright bad – stencil-printed blue outlines perfunctorily filled with poor-quality pigments – to the technically and artistically superb productions exemplified by the Fukagawa factory in Hizen.

Some time after 1879 Eizaiemon Fukagawa, eighth in a line of succeeding generations of potters, established a factory in Arita. Under the picturesque trade-name of 'Fragrant Orchid Company', the factory perfected a wide range of overglaze enamels and mastered underglaze blue and grey. By successfully exploiting the three levels of on-glaze, glaze and underglaze the painting often achieves an optical depth usually appropriate to a strongly three-dimensional design. The visual effect may be further heightened by the addition of moulded or even relief ornament.

OTHER FACTORIES

The underglaze palette was expanded by other factories, notably by the 'Makuzu Kozan' group whose work brings into the twentieth century the eighteenth-century Nabeshima style, through the use of immaculately graduated blues and soft reds. (It is interesting to note that a similar expansion of the underglaze palette was being achieved almost simultaneously in Europe at the Royal Copenhagen factory, itself stimulated by 'Japonisme'.)

Another group of factories, which specialized in the use of underglaze blue and is believed to have been started around the middle of the eighteenth century, is that of Hirado. Hirado is an island which lies off the northwestern extremity of Kyushu, a short sea-crossing from the kilns of Arita, Imari and Nabeshima. Porcelain attributed to this area is usually of a much finer 'grain' than other factories, and where the biscuit

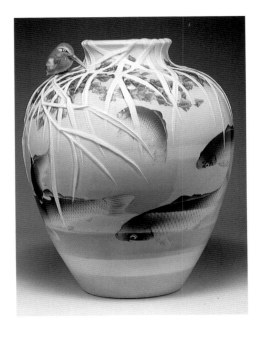

FUKAGAWA VASE, LATE MEIJI/TAISHO
PERIOD, *c.*1900–20 (44.5cm/17½in)

TRIPOD CENSER, MAKUZU KOZAN, MEIJI PERIOD, 1868–1912 (D28.5cm/11¼in)

This piece is signed Makuzu yo Kozan sei, and is decorated in underglaze blue with enamels depicting dragons over lotus flowers. (BELOW)

KUTANI TEAPOT AND COVER, MEIJI PERIOD, 1868–1912 (H18.5cm/7¼in)

This teapot or ewer has a bird head and ho-o *spout.* (BELOW RIGHT)

porcelain emerges from underneath the glaze (usually around the foot-rim) it may leave a characteristic orange stain caused by oxidation. Also, the porcelain is very white. These qualities recall the Chinese porcelains of Fujian (the so-called *blanc-de-Chine* wares), and like them lend themselves to finely detailed modelling and reticulation. Although Hirado certainly produced flatwares, the forms associated with these kilns are often more complex, such as zoomorphic censers, *sake* pots and teapots perhaps in the form of boys clutching puppies or of a *minogame* (an auspicious sea turtle). On such pieces the complexity of form is sufficiently ornamental in itself. The use of cobalt-blue is often very understated to prevent upstaging a ceramic modeller's *tour-de-force*. For similar reasons and to the same effect, minor details such as eyes, mouth and hands may be unglazed, thereby exploiting the effect of orange oxidation already mentioned.

Where Hirado forms are simpler or more formal, panels may be reserved with landscapes painted in the late-seventeenth and early-eighteenth century Chinese style.

By the 1880s the already complex issue of Kutani wares (see page 77) was further confused by the Kutani mark that appeared not only on a translucent porcelain body but also on opaque earthenware of an oat-coloured body. In both cases the decoration is predominantly iron-red enhanced by gilding and often with black or *grisaille* detail. Additional clear enamels may often be used within panels and on border motifs but in no case is underglaze blue used. The quality, as of nineteenth-century Imari, is variable: some pieces are clearly mass produced (including European tea wares), whereas others, in which the painting is meticulous, are clearly not. The genesis of these nineteenth-century Kutani wares is unclear but the variety of clays that bear a similar palette and manner of painting points to a number of separate potters and enamellers working in a 'style' rather than a single tradition.

This intermarrying of once separate ceramic 'families' is further exemplified by the mutation of the Satsuma earthenware style onto a porcelain body. Such hybridization is no doubt symptomatic of a country rapidly accelerated through an industrial revolution. It also reflects a growing demand for porcelain from Europe.

China had once furnished Europe with enormous quantities of exportware throughout the eighteenth century; so too Japan moved into the twentieth century with massive production of tea wares for the Western market. 'Eggshell' porcelain potted to almost paper thinness satisfied this demand at all levels. By far the majority is of poor quality, often coloured within transfer-printed outlines thus allowing for mass-production (just as had English bone china teaware of the mid-nineteenth century). On average, for every 50 services of this type seen today one may demonstrate a very high quality of both potting and decoration. The subject-matter is usually various figures shown out-of-doors, luscious garden flowers or exotic birds by a shore.

Just as the Chinese had eventually subsumed their exportwares to European forms and decoration towards the end of the eighteenth century, so Japanese factories were quick to follow European originals: thus Noritake, perhaps the most famous of these factories, manufactured pieces clearly inspired by the Royal Wor-

cester Works both in painting and form.

Intent as Japan certainly was upon re-entering the international community of the 1860s after its years of isolation, the basic strands of an essentially traditionalist nation remained unbroken. It resurfaced in the twentieth century in a return to pre-industrial simplicity of line, form and decoration. Though it is as yet unclear how some strands of the eighteenth-century ceramic tradition tie into the late nineteenth-century export wares, it is apparent that throughout her isolation from the rest of the world Japan's potters had sustained and developed their numerous domestic porcelains, earthenwares and stonewares. The home market continued to be furnished with traditional tea wares, maintaining a tradition which, in the second half of the twentieth century, would provide the platform for a return to and reinterpretation of the Chinese Song Dynasty – where porcelain originally began.

EARLY

CONTINENTAL

PORCELAIN

---

*A*fter the short-lived Medici porcelain factory in Florence, there was a long gap before anyone else in Europe succeeded in making either artificial or true porcelain. During this period, the quantity of imports from China increased greatly because the Dutch East India Company had taken over from the Portuguese and Spanish as the major importers from the Far East during the whole of the seventeenth century. Large quantities of porcelain, particularly of blue-and-white, reached Europe, though there were also coloured wares and, more rarely, monochromes. It became the fashion for northern European rulers, particularly in Germany and Holland, to install a porcelain room where every part was covered in porcelain vessels of various shapes and sizes.

MEISSEN CHINOISERIE COFFEE POT AND
CHOCOLATE CUP, *c.*1730 (coffee pot: 20.3cm/8in)

———

The pieces are painted with lambrequin borders of Böttger lustre.

MEDICI PLATE,
*c.*1575–87
(24cm/9½in)

The underglaze blue painting suggests at first sight a direct link with Chinese porcelain. The painter, however, has almost certainly based his work on a Turkish version. (LEFT)

MEDICI JUG,
*c.*1575–87
(14.6cm/5⅝in)

The dangers of high-temperature firing are evident in this piece. The body has started to 'sit down' in the kiln. (FAR LEFT)

MEDICI PORCELAIN

That a number of Italian Renaissance principalities should have attempted to discover the secrets of producing a rare, exotic and expensive material so prized that only princes and potentates might afford it, is not surprising. Thus, Florence, Padua, Ferrara and Venice are all known to have conducted experiments in manufacturing porcelain.

Of these, only Florence succeeded in achieving a recognized production, from which only about 64 examples have been identified. These pieces represent a period of output of approximately 12 years, from 1575 to 1587. Modest as this corpus may be it nevertheless confirms the Medici experiments as the first successful 'manufacture' of porcelain in Europe.

In China, hard-paste porcelain production had evolved over many years and out of locally available and congruent materials. Such a genesis was unlikely to be repeated elsewhere without detailed knowledge (or inspired guesswork) of the actual materials to be prospected and used. Where the experimental procedure was one of imitation based largely upon trial and error, an altogether different product could be expected. This was so of Medici porcelain; it was composed of a very different material from that of the Chinese ware in that it was an 'artificial' or soft-paste porcelain. It was totally unlike the porcelain seen by the Venetian adventurer Marco Polo during his 17 years at the Yuan court of Kubilai Khan (*c.*1280s), 300 years before.

Three men are recorded as being central to the making of the first European porcelain. The most important was undoubtedly Grand Duke Francesco I de Medici, himself an experimental chemist with an interest in many of the applied arts. According to Andrea Gussoni, Venetian ambassador to Florence at the time, research into producing a translucent ceramic material had already been under way for 10 years prior to the first successes around 1574. In other words, work may have started around 1564 when Francesco was created Regent, owing to the bereavement of his father, Cosimo I, upon the death of his wife. In view of his scientific interests Francesco may be regarded not merely as the princely sponsor-patron but as an active collaborator in the porcelain-producing enterprise.

Cosimo's distinguished servant, Giorgio Vasari, also chronicles the achievement of producing porcelain in his *Lives of the Artists*, ascribing this success to Bernardo Buontalenti. Buontalenti is principally known for his drawings and designs for fashionable operas and mechanical garden amusements, in addition to which Vasari credits him with the production of 'Indian Porcelain'. Gussoni, however, indicates that 'a Levantine' provided the key to the discovery (or rather invention) of the new material.

It is in fact unlikely that any one man fused the divergent strands that converge in the physical and decorative properties of Florentine porcelain. Until documentation to the contrary appears it would be reasonable to assume that Francesco, Buontalenti and the 'Levantine' played some crucial part in the production of porcelain.

TECHNOLOGY

Florentine porcelain is made from a recipe entirely different from any indigenous Italian or Chinese formula: it is composed of 15–25 percent white clay suspended in a glass-like quartz silica. Such a material is close to Persian frit porcelain and may represent knowledge brought by 'the Levantine' to Florence. However, the silica component of the body is in fact derived from the glaze covering it and laboratory analysis has shown this to correspond closely to Piccolpasso's 1557 formula for an Italian maiolica tin-glaze. The Medici body and glaze, therefore, fused together a Persian-type porcelain body with a modified Italian earthenware glaze. They were united by being fired to 1100°C, well beyond 959°C–1000°C, the maximum temperatures previously attained or required in the manufacture of the indigenous maiolica ware. Indeed, at this level traditional uninsulated maiolica kilns would undoubtedly have begun to buckle.

Quite apart from the likelihood of kiln failure was the danger of the objects themselves collapsing in the firing. The fact that only 64 pieces have been recorded is a further indication of the experimental nature of the production. But, though imperfect, they represent a real, if expensive and temporary, innovation in the European tradition. That a faulty piece, at least to twentieth-century eyes, should have been presented to a person of the highest rank (a flask dated 1581 was destined for Philip II of Spain and bore his coat-of-arms) is a further indication of the esteem in which the makers held their own invention. The enterprise seems to have lapsed following the death of Francesco, which confirms how extravagant it must have seemed to his successors.

FORM AND DECORATION

The potters were adventurous in their construction, and shapes included dishes and plates with everted flat rims; double cruet bottles; pilgrim flasks; Renaissance ewers; and wine-jars with handles and spouts. Body moulding with gadroons (copied from metal shapes), embossed ornamental borders, applied overhead handles, fluted spouts and grotesque masks modelled in full relief all testify to a confidence of handling, whatever surprises the kiln might then hold. Rarely, if ever, do firing cracks appear around luted joints or applied ('sprigged') ornament, faults which were common enough on many eighteenth-century porcelains.

Pieces were painted with underglaze cobalt-blue, often outlined in manganese. The use of this pigment, well known in Chinese porcelain manufacture, is not surprising since it was also employed in the maiolica industry. The colour of the blue varies from piece to piece. Mostly it has a greyish, out-of-focus look due to the refraction of light by millions of tiny bubbles trapped in the soft-looking glaze. Sometimes the blue has a blackish tone, reminiscent of the *kraak-porselein* being produced in China and imported by the Portuguese at the same time.

The painting on these wares is executed in an altogether new and self-conscious style that brings together elements of Near Eastern flower meanders with fashionable 'grotesques' and anthropomorphic scrolls with spiky chrysanthemum blooms. Sometimes, by outline and shading, the blue merely emphasizes the moulded form of the object. There are no obviously transferred Chinese motifs – such influences merely whisper from the wings.

Medici, the first of all European porcelain, which preceded its French successors by 100 years, encapsulates a Renaissance determination to manipulate matter. In its uncompromising pursuit of difficult forms it demonstrates a successful and attractive fusion of Science and Art.

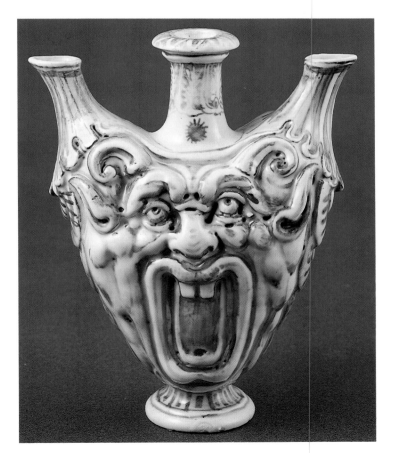

MEDICI VASE OR BOTTLE, *c.*1575–87 (H19.7cm/7¾in)

The complex form of a grotesque Pan mask is remarkable for a factory working in a totally experimental material, and reflects the influence of maiolica design.

MEISSEN

As early as 1675, Count Ehrenfried Walter von Tschirnhausen (1651–1708) was experimenting with radiant heat and a reflective mirror to find out the melting point of refractory substances such as kaolin. This is a vital ingredient of true porcelain which must reach 1450°C (2640°F) in the kiln. While he may have made some form of soft-paste or artificial porcelain, von Tschirnhausen was not successful in finding the secret of true porcelain until he was joined by Johann Frederich Böttger (1682–1719) who had started his adult life as an alchemist working for Frederick I of Prussia. Unsuccessful in solving this impossible task, Böttger fled from Berlin in the year 1700 but was seized by Augustus of Saxony and taken to his castle, the Albrechtsburg, where he was told to assist von Tschirnhausen in looking for the secret of porcelain. In 1708 he produced his first experimental wares, and by 1710 had achieved his first proper production. By that time, they were already making faience and were experimenting in red stoneware.

Many pieces of red stoneware, teapots in particular, had been imported from Yixing in China, and these had been copied in the late seventeenth century by the Delft potter Arij de Milde. Böttger's pottery was harder than either the Chinese or the Dutch copies, which enabled it to be polished until the surface was as shiny as jasper, after which he named it, and also allowed the surface to be engraved and cut in a variety of designs. The workshop also produced a softer stoneware which was glazed and decorated by Martin Schnell, a Dresden lacquerer, and was based on Chinese and Delft models.

The porcelain clay originally came from Kolditz, but a more satisfactory kaolin clay was found at Aue, and this was used until the nineteenth century. The early Böttger porcelain is creamy and thinly potted, with a slight green tinge to the foot-rim. To begin with, stoneware models were used, in particular those with moulded acanthus leaves round the lower parts of the vessels, and the porcelain was painted both in colours and gold. One of the first colours was an unusual pink lustre, known as mother-of-pearl pink or Böttger lustre. In the mid-1720s, the formula was changed to a much whiter glaze and less creamy colour, and stayed basically the same until the Seven Years War in 1756. The glaze has a slightly oily surface and, where it meets an unglazed foot-rim or unglazed base, there is a thickening that one does not find in later Meissen pieces or even the best imitations.

MEISSEN'S PAINTERS

When Böttger died in 1719 aged 37, he left the factory in a desperate financial situation. In 1720 Johann Gregor Herold was brought from du Paquier's factory at Vienna by Stölzel who had defected to Meissen in 1719, and in 1723 he was appointed court painter. One of the more gifted painters employed by Herold was David Köhler, who perfected the use of underglaze blue and, before his untimely death in 1723, painted a few fine large vases. After that date the underglaze blue painting at the workshop was confined mainly to table wares.

Herold brought an enriched palette of colours to Meissen and was particularly adept at painting chinoiserie scenes. In fact, he made his own drawings based on earlier prints by various artists and, from these, the painters in his employ decorated the wares with delightful small figures on terraces, quite often painted within lace-work cartouches known as *Laub und Bandelwerk*, the earliest being just iron-red and gold, but later with the addition of puce. Tea and coffee services were very popular and the earliest ones were usually unmarked. In 1724 the KPM (Königlich Porzellan Manufactur) mark was introduced and in 1725 the factory started using the crossed-swords mark in underglaze blue (which is still in use today), as well as gilt numerals added by the decorator.

The very early chinoiserie landscapes had clouds painted in the background, but after 1725 these no longer appeared. Early on, there were rarer European landscapes and harbour scenes also with clouds.

In the late 1720s and throughout the 1730s, copies of Japanese Kakiemon wares became popular. These were taken from the Japanese originals in the collection of Augustus the Strong. The Meissen painters also developed a mixture of Kakiemon and Chinese *famille verte* which evolved into flower painting known as *Indianische Blumen*.

The Kakiemon-style pieces often have the caduceus or overglaze blue enamel crossed-swords marks, and many are wheel-cut with the Johanneum inventory marks. Up to 1733, certain large vases have the underglaze blue AR monogram (of Augustus Rex), though this is very rare on smaller pieces. Some vases were left in the white and decorated in the 1740s, whereas a few have fine late nineteenth-century decoration very close to the original. Dresden copies are described in chapter 10.

Japanese Imari patterns are much less common and then almost entirely on useful wares, but were also popular for export to the Near East towards the end of the eighteenth century. Chinese *famille verte* was also copied, but again, this is fairly rare. In the 1730s, coloured grounds appear, the most common of which are yellow, a sea green known as *seladon fond*, and a lilac; other colours include orange, blue, brown, gold and lime-green.

One of the best-known painters at Meissen, who started work at the age of 12 in 1726, was A.F. von Löwenfinck who painted animals and chinoiseries after Schenk. He left for Bayreuth in 1736.

Among other painters who worked under Herold was J. Stadler, who specialized in chinoiseries, but rather more loosely painted than Löwenfinck's. Another was C.F. Herold, kinsman of the chief painter, who also specialized in chinoiserie painting, though he painted

BÖTTGER RED STONEWARE FACETED TEAPOT, *c.*1715 (ABOVE)

MEISSEN BOTTLE, *c.*1730 (19.5cm/7$\frac{11}{16}$in)

While the shape and panel decoration are based on a Japanese Kakiemon original, the turquoise ground was a Meissen invention. It bears the mark of Augustus the Strong's Japanese palace. (LEFT)

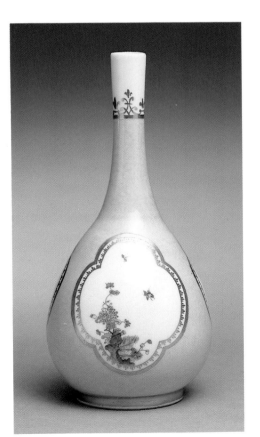

landscapes as well. J.G. Heintze, who was slightly younger than both the Herolds, painted landscapes particularly in the late 1730s and early 1740s, while B.G. Häuer was mainly known for mining scenes. At this time, battle scenes after Rugendas appeared, as did garden landscapes painted after Watteau, and hunting subjects.

In the 1730s European flowers had started to appear as decoration. The best-known exponent of these was J.G. Klinger, who probably started painting them in 1731. His early flowers were particularly beautifully painted in a botanical style known as *Ombrierte Deutsche Blumen*, with shading and the addition of insects.

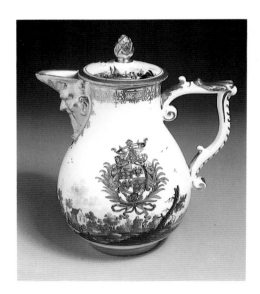

HOT MILK JUG, *c.1740* (15.2cm/6in)

After chinoiserie, this form of decoration was the most popular for tea and coffee services between 1725 and 1745. In this case, the jug is decorated with the arms of a Venetian family painted with figures in landscapes. (ABOVE)

MEISSEN HARLEQUIN FIGURE, *c.1733* (16.1cm/6⅜in)

Of all J. J. Kändler's figures from the Commedia dell'Arte this is perhaps the most beautiful. On some examples, the jug bears a date and the crossed swords. (ABOVE)

MEISSEN *SCHNEEBALLEN* PART TEA SERVICE, *c.1745*

This type of decoration with encrusted flowerheads first appeared in 1740; J. J. Kändler's Arbeitsberichte *of that year describes a* Schnee Ballen *(snowball) service. The painting of galants and ladies is after Watteau.* (TOP)

In the 1740s and particularly in the 1750s, this flower painting, which was the most common decoration on Meissen, changed from the German flowers to what was known as *Manier Blumen*, painted in a rather looser and more naturalistic style. Birds were almost as frequently used as flowers in the decoration of Meissen dinner services.

In the early 1730s there were a number of armorial dinner services made for Augustus of Saxony, the earlier ones in Kakiemon style. Later in the decade, armorial tea services were created for German, Venetian and other European families, with either chinoiserie or landscape views on the reverse. The most famous of these armorial services was the Swan service ordered for Count Brühl in 1738. (Count Brühl had been put in charge of the porcelain manufactory in 1733.)

After the Seven Years War ended in 1763, Meissen lost many of its workmen to Berlin, and it was no longer the dominant factory in Germany. Herold was pensioned off and C.W. Dietrich became the art adviser in 1765. The period from 1763 to about 1780 was known as the Academic or 'dot' period, after the small dot that appears between the hilts of the crossed-swords mark. From 1780 until the early nineteenth century, known as the Marcolini period after the director of the factory, the dot was changed to a star. As well as the blue marks, there are various marks impressed into the glaze. In the 1730s the formers' or repairers' marks were impressed near the rims on the underside of the pieces. From about 1740 these marks were replaced by a two-figure number.

MEISSEN FIGURES

Meissen is as famous for its figures and groups as for its wares. The earliest, which were also made in red stoneware, either copied Chinese *blanc de chine* models or Bernini saints. There were also Italian Comedy figures, dwarves, and small seated all time, succeeded Kirchner, and most of the large white animals from this period are in fact Kändler's work.

Kändler soon found the large figures too difficult to make and of those that survive many are fire-cracked. Small figures were then popular for table decoration, and Kändler was the chief modeller of these until his death in 1775, only four months after Herold. In 1735 he was joined by J.F. Eberlein, who died in 1749. In 1743 P. Reinicke came to the factory where he worked until 1768. F.E. Meyer arrived in 1748 and stayed until 1761, moving soon afterwards to Berlin in 1762.

In the late 1730s there were many finely from peasants of different nationalities at their respective trades. A large series of miners was modelled in 1750 together with the famous Meissen shepherds and shepherdesses, artisans and street traders. The first series of street traders modelled in the late 1740s have plain bases or are slightly encrusted with flower sprays. They were modelled after drawings by E. Bouchardon, while a second series was taken from either the 'Paris Cries' from designs by C. Huet, or from the 'London Cries' by P. Tempest after M. Laroon. These have Rococo scroll bases. Less common is a small series of chinoiserie figures and of Middle Eastern figures taken after a book by de Ferriol, the

Chinese known as pagods. The first sculptor employed was G. Fritzsche, shortly followed by J.G. Kirchner. Kirchner began modelling in 1727, and was entrusted to make the very large white figures of birds and animals for Augustus's Japanese palace at Dresden, which was started in 1721 and enlarged in 1728. However, in 1733, the year that Augustus died, J.J. Kändler, perhaps the greatest porcelain modeller of dressed figures and groups of ladies and gentlemen of the Court often attended by servants. Italian Comedy figures were also popular subjects, especially a wonderful series of harlequins modelled by Kändler between 1738 and 1744.

As time went on, these figures were re-issued in various ways, either singly or in groups. The 1740s and 1750s showed a multitude of different figures, some taken French Ambassador to the Turkish court. Figures of famous mythological subjects were also popular in the 1750s, and there was a fine series of religious figures, first modelled in the 1730s, but these were usually made only to special order.

In 1753 came the series known as the Monkey Band, modelled by Kändler and Reinicke after the drawings by C. Huet, which was copied at Chelsea and by

MEISSEN PORTRAIT SNUFFBOX, 1748

The portrait of Lady Caroline Fox was commissioned by her husband, Henry Fox, on the birth of an heir and is attributed to the miniaturist Johann Martin Heinrici who started work at Meissen in 1741. The gold cage mounts were also made in Dresden. (RIGHT)

PAIR OF MEISSEN INDIAN RING-NECKED PARAKEETS, *c.*1745
(taller: 35.3cm/13⅞in)

The Louis XV gilt-bronze bases of these figures modelled by J. J. Kändler have the crowned 'C' marks to show that they were made between 1745 and 1749. It was the fashion in Paris and elsewhere in the middle of the eighteenth century to mount porcelain in elaborate gilt-bronze. (BELOW)

numerous nineteenth- and twentieth-century factories. The three court jesters – Fröhlich, Schmiedel and Schindler – were also the subjects of a series of figures in the late 1730s and early 1740s. But one of the most popular models was Count Brühl's tailor, dressed in court finery riding a goat, and forming a pair with his wife.

The scope of these figures was rich and varied. As well as human beings, animals and birds modelled after original prints and drawings were popular, particularly the brightly coloured parrots. Dogs, cats and many other animals were produced, the most popular being the pug dog, an emblem of one of the forms of Freemasonry invented by Augustus of Saxony for the ladies of the Court. Ladies with pug dogs represent members of this Masonic order.

In the 1730s the rockwork bases were either plain or encrusted with flowers generally with turquoise leaves. About 1740 these leaves were no longer painted turquoise but a more naturalistic green. Also the earliest models of some of the figures had legs which stuck out or had minimal bases. In the 1740s the popular figures of this type were remodelled without the legs being so vulnerable. About 1750 the flower-encrusted rockwork bases or the plain oblong bases were replaced by Rococo scroll bases, sometimes fairly high.

In the mid-1730s the undersides of the figures were often glazed and marked, but by 1740, an unglazed base with a blowhole was usual. The mark on these was often ground away when the base was flattened and by 1750 it was painted very small at the back or side. In the 1760s a hollow glazed base was reintroduced.

After the resumption of production at the factory in the 1760s, it turned more and more to a Neoclassical style, and Kändler found himself unable to go along with this new fashion. The factory then employed two new master modellers, one a Frenchman called M.V. Acier who came to Dresden in 1764 and stayed until his death in 1795. The other was J.C. Schönheit who came to the factory at the age of 15 years in 1745 and stayed until his death in 1805.

MEISSEN
TUREEN, c.1760

This model was first made by J. J. Kändler in 1750, and is here delicately painted with farmyard birds, butterflies and other insects. (RIGHT)

MEISSEN BUTTER TUBS OR PIE DISHES
AND A TEA BOWL AND SAUCER, c.1730

The gilt decoration on these pieces was added in Augsburg either in the Seuter or the Aufenwerth workshops c.1730 (BELOW)

MEISSEN FIGURE, 1772 (27.7cm/10⅞in)

This figure of a female fruit seller was based on an earlier design, remodelled by J. J. Kändler in 1772. (ABOVE)

Since Meissen was no longer the leading porcelain manufacturer, these Neoclassical designs and models followed the lead of Sèvres or were based on sentimental French paintings by Greuze or Moreau le Jeune.

HAUSMALERS AND IMITATORS

From the first decade of its manufacture, Meissen porcelain was sent to Augsburg to be mounted in silver or silver-gilt; in addition, a number of pieces of Böttger porcelain, still undecorated when the formula of the paste was changed in the early 1720s, were sent there to be painted by independent painters known as Hausmalers. The most famous of these was the Seuter family, who specialized in gilt chinoiseries as well as figures in hunting scenes in a rather crude hand. The other major Augsburg painter was J. Auffenwerth who, with his daughters, also painted Meissen porcelain with figures in a rather feathery style. The most important of the Hausmalers was Böttengruber of Breslau, but his work is now extremely rare. Ignaz Preissler also worked at Breslau and is particularly famous for painting beautiful

MEISSEN PLATE, MID-18TH CENTURY

This piece was painted by the Hausmaler Franz Ferdinand Mayer of Pressnitz and possibly depicts the famous bear-pit at Berne. The painting is c.1750, although the plate is probably earlier.

and exact small scenes in black monochrome. His style was very similar to that of J. Helchis, who did particularly attractive harbour scenes. Among Böttengruber's pupils was H.G. Bressler, who painted putti among strapwork.

In Bayreuth, too, there were a number of outside decorators working mainly on Meissen blanks. The most famous of these was J.F. Metsch, (*fl.*1735 and 1751). His painting was characterized by rather neat and stiff Baroque scroll cartouches enclosing chinoiseries or harbour scenes and other landscapes. He also often painted in black (*Schwarzlot*). Perhaps the most famous of the painters who worked with Metsch was J.P. Dannhofer who painted chinoiseries and hunting scenes. There was also F.F. Mayer, who worked in Pressnitz from the late 1740s up to the 1770s. His style is particularly idiosyncratic. His borders are characterized by very distinctive bouquets of flowers or by elaborate gilt scrollwork. His distinctive landscapes, often painted around bowls or in the centre of plates and dishes, had a rather individual light-green colour to them.

Somewhat similar to Mayer was another outside decorator called F.J. Ferner whose place of work is still a mystery, though he may have assisted Mayer. Ferner is particularly well known for buying Meissen blue-and-white porcelain and over-decorating it with gilding and flowers in bright colours. His more elaborate pieces have figures of sportsmen as well.

A completely different technique was used by the amateur Auguste von dem Busch (1704–1779). He was a Canon of the Catholic Church who worked at Hildesheim and specialized in engraving his designs with a diamond infilled with black.

From the mid-1760s, any piece sold in the white from the Meissen factory should have an incised line through the blue crossed-swords mark. The outside decorators from this time on are usually not of comparable quality to those of the mid-eighteenth century, but their work was produced right through the nineteenth century and up to the present.

As well as genuine factory pieces that were decorated by outside painters, the Meissen mark was copied in different parts of Europe. The Thuringia mark of Volkstedt can be mistaken for that of the Meissen factory, though in fact it is a crossed pitchfork. The French mark of de la Courtille has crossed arrows, and in the nineteenth century a number of factories, including Sitzendorf and Carl Thieme of Potschappel, used a form of crossed sticks or crossed lines.

Meissen copies by Edmé Samson of Paris can be very deceptive, particularly if the bases are hidden. There are a few easily identifiable signs of forgeries. In most cases when the nineteenth-century modellers used eighteenth-century moulds, the colours they applied were quite different: the decoration of the late 1730s and early 1740s is strong, whereas that of the late 1740s and early 1750s is in pastel shades.

THE VIENNA FACTORY

The Vienna factory was founded by an Austrian court official of Flemish origin called Claudius I du Paquier (*d.*1751). The Meissen workman C.K. Hunger was persuaded to come to Vienna after he had made preliminary experiments in firing china clay, but, as at several other factories he went to later, was not successful. However, in 1719, Samuel Stölzel, who was Böttger's kilnmaster, arrived in Vienna and immediately porcelain began to be made. Unfortunately for the factory, Stölzel was dissatisfied with his pay and returned to Meissen in 1720, taking with him J.G. Herold. Though the porcelain made in Vienna is extremely attractive, financially it was never very successful, and in 1744 the factory was taken over by the Empress Maria Theresa.

Some of the porcelain is difficult to distinguish from the early Meissen porcelain made by Böttger, but it is often slightly bluer and smokier in colour. The decoration on du Paquier porcelain is usually different from that on Meissen, and

the shapes of the wares are often more unusual and imaginative. The style is generally Baroque, and much more of the painting is in black and gold.

European flowers were first used as decoration in about 1730, which is earlier than at Meissen, and were painted in a very beautiful and precise style. Chinoiseries and landscapes painted by A. Anreiter and Z. Schulz are also typical of this period, but their Oriental decoration is copied from Japanese Imari rather than Kakiemon. As well as *Schwarzlot*, they used puce and iron-red monochrome and a more restricted colour range than at Meissen. Battle scenes after Rugendas and hunting scenes after J.E. Riedinger were popular. A fine chinoiserie dinner service made for the imperial family, as well as a Jagd service painted in

black by J. Helchis and others with hunting scenes, were among the best-known wares produced at Vienna. J.J. Ringler, the arcanist, started as a painter at Vienna, but through his friendship with the director's daughter, discovered the secret of making porcelain which he took to many other nascent porcelain factories. Figures at this early period were unusual, but there is a famous porcelain room now in the Österreichisches Museum in Vienna in which moulded figures appear.

Vienna became a state factory in 1744. Artists included C.D. Busch, and J.G. Klinger who arrived from Meissen in 1746 and stayed until his death in 1781. The most famous of the modellers was J.J. Niedermayer, who was at the factory from 1747 until he died in 1784. He was also

PAINTING (DETAIL) DEPICTING A BANQUET AT SCHONBRUNN FOR THE MARRIAGE OF THE EMPEROR JOSEPH II AND ISABELLA OF PARMA IN 1760, MARTIN VAN MEYTENS

The mirrored surtout de table *is set with Rococo porcelain groups and shows how these were used in the eighteenth century.*

joined by L. Dannhauser, who died in 1786; in 1778 Anton Grassi succeeded Niedermayer as Modellmeister. By this time the factory's style had become Neoclassical and Niedermayer's figures were much stiffer and more formal than earlier.

Because of its proximity to the Ottoman Empire, Vienna exported wares to Turkey, particularly during the third quarter of the eighteenth century; these were usually brightly painted, but less finely than those for the domestic market. At one stage, the trade with the East reached 120,000 pieces annually. The mark of the State and later periods is a beehive-shaped shield either impressed or painted in blue.

The potting dates were impressed underneath each piece, starting with 83 for 1783, and continuing into the nineteenth century with 801, and so on.

In 1784 there was a financial crisis and Konrad von Sorgenthal (d.1805) became the director of the factory, immediately reorganizing it. Sorgenthal introduced a very brilliantly coloured Neoclassical decoration with minutely painted classical figures and arabesques in panels on brightly coloured grounds, somewhat based on Sèvres. This fashion continued through the nineteenth century into the twentieth and was made by minor factories in Bohemia after the closure of the Vienna factory in 1864. These later productions, however, were of much coarser quality.

HÖCHST

The 1740s saw a number of factories starting production all over Europe and the same names crop up in different factories as workmen went from place to place, particularly at the beginning of this period when those who had secrets to sell tried to capitalize on their knowledge. On 18 February, 1746, a privilege was granted to start a porcelain factory at Höchst by the Elector of Mayence. A.F. von Löwenfinck arrived in 1743 from the Fulda faience factory, and stayed until

VIENNA TUREEN AND COVER, c.1740; EN SUITE STAND c.1730 (D45cm/17¹¹⁄₁₆in)

These pieces are from a Jagdservice *(hunting service) manufactured by du Paquier's factory, probably for the Imperial court.*

PAIR OF HÖCHST MINIATURE HARLEQUIN AND COLUMBINE FIGURES, c.1750–55 (8.1cm/3¼in)

1749. J.J. Ringler, the arcanist from Vienna, was also at the factory between 1750 and 1752, and it was not until his arrival that there was any serious production of porcelain. The business side was organized by J.G. Goltz, who died in 1757; his step-son J.F. Clarus subsequently took over his position.

The early Höchst painters included C.W. von Löwenfinck who left in 1748, and J.P. Dannhofer, who arrived from Bayreuth and worked between 1747 and 1751. In 1749 Louis de Farty was made the director, and he was succeeded by J.K. Benckgraff in 1751. The well-known painter J. Zeschinger also worked there, though he went to Fürstenberg in 1753 with Benckgraff when he left the factory. Simon Feilner started his career at Höchst and it was probably he who, among other things, modelled the very fine Höchst series of Italian Comedy figures on pedestal bases. He left in 1753. L. Russinger was modelling at Höchst between 1759 and 1767 (and became master modeller in 1762), but in 1767 was succeeded by J.P. Melchior. The work of both Russinger and Melchior is typified by coloured grassy bases and rather sweet figures of children at various pastimes, as well as pastoral and mythological figures lying asleep under trees watched by their companions, after such famous French artists as Boucher.

The early Höchst porcelain has a soft milky-white glaze over a coarse grey-white body. The mark was originally a wheel painted in red or puce which later changed to underglaze blue. It is sometimes impressed. The moulds were sold and the faience factory at Damm copied a number of Melchior models in the late nineteenth century. A factory at Passau used them to make quite deceptive porcelain copies at the beginning of the twentieth century.

NYMPHENBURG

When Maria-Anna Sophia, the granddaughter of Augustus the Strong of Saxony, married Prince Max II Joseph of Bavaria in 1747, her interest in porcelain caused him to open a porcelain factory in an old hunting lodge at Neudeck. He employed F.I. Niedermayer as a potter, and also the painter J. Helchis, who arrived from Vienna in the autumn of 1747 and stayed until 1750. Although Niedermayer was the guiding spirit, he was ousted for a short period, but returned in 1749 when he was joined by Count S. von Haimhausen in 1753. J.J. Ringler was there between 1754 and 1757 when he was discharged, and was succeeded by the chemist P.R. Härtl who was sacked in 1761.

Perhaps the greatest modeller of European porcelain figures after Kändler was F.A. Bustelli, who arrived in 1754. He was influenced in his modelling by the wood sculptor, F.I. Günther, and many of his figures and groups appear to be based on carved wood originals. Bustelli is particularly famous for his beautifully modelled set of 16 Italian Comedy figures with exaggerated Rococo poses. He also executed delightful groups of figures among ruins, chinoiseries, and more mundane subjects.

In 1761 the factory moved to Nymphenburg, the palace of the Elector. Unfortunately, Bustelli, who had so much promise, died young in 1763; D. Aulikzek succeeded him as Modellmeister in January 1765. The Palatinate took over the factory in 1770, and in 1797 J.P. Melchior and D. Aulikzek the younger were the chief modellers. When Frankenthal closed in 1799 it transferred many of its moulds to Nymphenburg, and since that date Nymphenburg has reproduced both old Frankenthal and

HÖCHST AMYNTHAS AND SYLVIA GROUP, c.1770 (H26.1cm/10¼in)

Modelled by Johann Peter Melchior, this piece was taken from an engraving by René Gaillard after the picture by François Boucher of the play 'The Aminta' written by Torquato Tasso in 1573. This piece has a blue wheel mark on its base.

NYMPHENBURG FIGURE, c.1755 (14.5cm/5⅝in)

Franz Anton Bustelli produced some charming figures of vendors, such as this eggseller, as well as his more famous Italian comedy series.

Nymphenburg models. Many of Bustelli's figures are still in production.

Early Nymphenburg paste was a slightly creamy white, becoming greyer during the last quarter of the eighteenth century. The nineteenth- and twentieth-century copies are a white smooth porcelain.

There is a certain amount of controversy as to how many of the Nymphenburg figures were originally left in the white and decorated at a later date. This, combined with the fact that they were still being made in the late 1760s and 1770s, means that there is often doubt about the exact period of manufacture and/or decoration of the earlier groups and figures. The later ones, however, can be distinguished by a difference in paste and the shape of the impressed Bavarian shield mark. The wares include two royal services, one finely painted with European flowers within Rococo blue-and-gilt borders dating to 1760, the other in Neoclassical style by Aulikzek, with monochrome landscape vignettes within pearl borders. Well-known designs on wares were the 'Chintz' pattern and *trompe l'oeils* of prints on wood-grained grounds.

STRASBOURG AND FRANKENTHAL

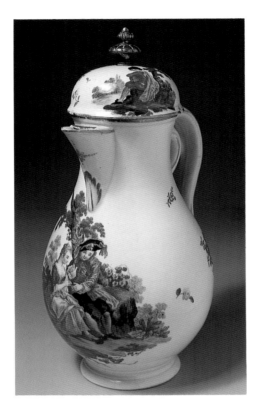

Charles-Francois Hannong started a faience factory at Strasbourg about 1709. But, though porcelain is mentioned in records, it is unlikely to have been made before 1752, when the ubiquitous J.J. Ringler joined Hannong to give him the secret of true porcelain. For two

FRANKENTHAL COFFEE POT AND COVER, c.1770 (25.5cm/10in)

This piece was possibly painted by Osterspey with lovers in a landscape after Antoine Watteau.

FRANKENTHAL *DEJEUNER*, DATED 1777

These wares are painted with Allegories of the Arts from the engraving by Etienne Fessard. (BELOW)

years he produced some interesting figures and groups, but in 1754 Louis XV forbade any porcelain competition against his factory at Vincennes. As a result Hannong, while retaining the faience factory in Strasbourg, moved the porcelain works north to Frankenthal, just outside the city of Mannheim. J.W. Lanz, who had been at Strasbourg, became the chief modeller at Frankenthal. He made all the usual German subjects of the period but preferred those taken from everyday life. His Strasbourg figures were usually based on modelled grassy mounds, whereas after he moved to Frankenthal he substituted slightly Rococo style bases with little puce scrolls.

In 1757 J.F. Lück may have joined the factory and made figures and groups in the style of Lanz, but was probably under the direction of G.F. Riedel (*fl*.1757–1759) who also worked at Höchst. Riedel was originally responsible for modelling designs on table wares. In the same year Carl Hannong, who had been managing the

factory at Frankenthal for his father, died, and Hannong sent his second son, Joseph-Adam, to take his place.

Like so many porcelain factories in Europe, Frankenthal was not quite able to meet expenses, and in 1762 the factory was sold to the Elector, who employed Adam Bergdoll, who had formerly been at Höchst, as technical director. He was succeeded by Simon Feilner in the early 1770s, who, however, was only appointed director in 1775.

In 1762 the court sculptor, Konrad Linck (1732–1793), was made chief modeller and introduced a somewhat more Neoclassical style. His figures were distinguished by the sculptural quality of their draperies and the mound bases with gilt scroll borders had strong yellow and green grass work with shredded clay added here and there. K.G. Lück, a relation of J.F. Lück, was one of the most prolific modellers at the factory at the time that Linck was there, and he worked from about

He did some very amusing chinoiserie figures and groups as well as hunting subjects, all with finely modelled heads with pointed chins. These figures often had striped and spotted clothes decorated with floral sprigs.

From 1777 to 1779 Adam Bauer created mythological scenes and children acting as peasants and shepherds. In 1779 J.P. Melchior arrived and began making biscuit figures and reliefs.

A few very fine painters, including J. Osterspei (1730–1782) who arrived in 1759, specialized in mythological scenes. These scenes were particularly popular on Frankenthal porcelain and were also painted by J.B. Magnus between 1762 and 1782, and Winterstein who worked between 1758 and 1781.

The Frankenthal porcelain was a fine creamy white with a well-fused glaze. This quality declined after a cheaper clay was introduced in 1774. By 1790 the output of the factory had dropped considerably, and

BERLIN

The Berlin porcelain factory was started by W.K. Wegely in 1751, but his productions are comparatively rare. During the Seven Years War (1756–1763) he hoped to get the workmen and the secrets from the Meissen factory, but when Frederick of Prussia seemed unlikely to allow this, he gave up in 1757. The Berlin porcelain of this period was white with a thin glaze and the enamel colours were inclined to flake. The models were similar to the contemporary Meissen. The mark that was used at the factory was a 'W' in blue.

Having beaten Saxony in this war, Frederick and the Prussians were able to obtain porcelain from the Meissen factory, but in 1761 Frederick allowed J.G. Gotzkowsky to start his own factory in Berlin. However, in 1763 Gotzkowsky went bankrupt and the king purchased the factory

BERLIN
*DEJEUNER, c.*1767

The very fine, white nature of Berlin porcelain lends itself to the landscape painting in grisaille.

1756 until 1775, becoming Modellmeister when Linck gave up his job in 1766. Lück carried on the techniques and style introduced by Linck, but was still much more Rococo in his feeling for figures and groups. Like so many other porcelain modellers he took his subjects from prints after pictures, as well as European subjects after Greuze.

after the French occupation in 1794 the models and moulds were removed to Nymphenburg. The early mark is an impressed 'P H' followed by a lion rampant and the Palatinate arms in blue. After 1762 a crown above the monogram 'C T' was used; the last two numerals of the date were sometimes added between 1770 and 1788.

from him. The chief modeller was F.E. Meyer (*fl.*1761–1785) who had come from Meissen, and was helped by his brother W.C. Meyer between 1766 and 1783. When Meyer died in 1785, J.G. Müller became Modellmeister at the factory for a short time, and was then succeeded by J.C.F. Riese (1789–1834).

The Berlin porcelain in the eighteenth century was extremely fine, almost white though with a faint yellowish, slightly grey tinge. The painting was particularly delicate. At first it was set off by crisp moulded borders, which like everywhere else evolved from the osier pattern of the 1760s. Later in the century Neoclassical designs were also very finely executed. The factory is chiefly noted for its magnificent dinner services. The mark was a sceptre in blue.

FÜRSTENBERG

The Duke of Brunswick had been experimenting between 1744 and 1747 with making porcelain, but it was only in 1747, when the works were transferred to Fürstenberg, that a proper factory was founded, where the experiments continued. In 1753 J. Benckgraff arrived from Höchst together with J. Zeschinger and Simon Feilner. Benckgraff died that year, but by the following year the factory was making true porcelain. Feilner became the chief modeller, and is particularly famous for his series of figures of the Italian Comedy on plain mound bases, modelled in 1754, and also of miners, modelled in 1757. The porcelain, however, was not particularly good and often had black spots and impurities in it. Two other modellers joined Feilner – J.C. Rombrich, who stayed for over 30 years until 1794, and A.K. Luplau, who joined in 1765 and in 1776 left for Copenhagen.

Some of the Fürstenberg models were direct copies of Meissen but after the mid-1760s the factory concentrated more and more on wares. The figures were revived in the 1770s, with smaller versions of the comedy and miner figures among others. The wares frequently had moulded borders and Rococo scrollwork to disguise the imperfections of the paste.

In 1774 the painting workshop was moved to the ducal palace and, at the same time, the colours improved. The bronzes and ivories in the palace provided the

PAIR OF FÜRSTENBERG HARLEQUIN AND COLUMBINE FIGURES, c.1755 (19.6cm/7¾in)

Though Simon Feilner had neither the Baroque mastery of Kändler nor the Rococo genius of Bustelli, he produced a forceful series of Italian comedy figures.

inspiration for biscuit figures and reliefs, and after 1790 there was a strong emphasis on designs after the antique. The main mark used by the factory was a distinctive cursive capital 'F' in blue.

LUDWIGSBURG

Like many of the other Electors and Princes in Germany, the Duke of Württenburg wanted his own porcelain factory. His first attempts in 1737 were unsuccessful, and it was not until 1759, when J.J. Ringler was made director, that the factory was able to make proper porcelain. This was Ringler's final workplace, and he remained there for the next 40 years. He brought with him G.F. Riedel from Frankenthal, the influence of whom is clearly visible in the models produced in the early period.

The factory's best period was between 1764 and 1775 after which it declined when the Court returned to Stuttgart, and it finally closed in 1824.

The paste of Ludwigsburg is very much greyer and smokier in tone than most of the other factories already mentioned. Models were quite prolific and naïvely charming. The first of the well-known Modellmeisters was J.J. Louis, who held the post from 1762 to his death in 1772. It is more probable that it was he rather than his predecessor J. Göz (fl.1759–1762) who modelled a series of rather stiff but attractive dancers taken from the court ballet, as well as miniature figures and groups after designs by Riedel, from the annual Venetian fair traditionally associated with the Duke and his Court. A series of figures of peasant types and another of musicians was probably made under the influence of or by J.C.W. Beyer who was active at the factory between 1761 and 1767.

All the figures were sensitively modelled and carefully decorated in pastel colours influenced by the smoky tone of the glaze. Much of the tableware produced at the factory was beautifully modelled with Rococo scrolls and simply painted with flowers, though more elaborate scenes are also known. The main mark of the factory was the interlaced 'C' monogram surmounted by a crown in blue.

PAIR OF
LUDWIGSBURG
FIGURES, c.1760
(15cm/5⅞in)

*The delicate painting
and great charm of
these dancers,
probably performing a
minuet, are
characteristic of the
romantic style
prevalent around the
middle of the
eighteenth century.*

THE SMALLER
GERMAN FACTORIES

There had been a faience factory at Ansbach since the early years of the eighteenth century, but it was in the late 1750s that the Markgraf of Brandenburg started a porcelain factory there with a very young workman, J.F. Kändler, a relation of the famous Meissen modeller. The porcelain from this factory is very rare and it is of fine quality, resembling that of Berlin rather more than Meissen, from which the majority of its workmen were derived. Kändler died in 1791 and the factory did not last much longer. The main mark used by the factory was a capital 'A' in blue.

Kelsterbach was another rare factory, owned by the Landgrave of Hesse-Darmstadt, which was run in combination with a faience factory under the direction of C.D. Busch from Meissen. Its figures were modelled by K. Vogelmann and were somewhat baroque and craggy-looking. The factory functioned from 1761 to 1768

FULDA GROUP, 'THE APPLE PICKERS',
c.1778 (26.4cm/10⅜in)

*This piece, modelled by Neu, is probably based on
a picture by Boucher or Lancret.*

and from 1789 to 1802. The later period produced some undistinguished pieces.

The Prince Bishop of Fulda's small factory, which existed from 1764 to 1789, is particularly famous for its figures of the Fulda court orchestra and 'Cris de Paris' modelled by G.L. Bartolème from Ansbach, who arrived in 1770 and whose work resembles that of K.G. Lück of Frankenthal. Sporting and peasant figures were made as well as comedy groups by Wenzel Neu. The earlier figures were reminiscent of Höchst with hollow mound bases, slender elongated heads and a sweet sentimentality. Flower painting, landscapes and birds also appear. There were also pieces with biscuit busts of the Prince Bishop and other notables. The early mark is a cross in blue followed by that of the monogram 'F F' surmounted by a crown.

Porcelain was also made at Cassel, from 1766 to 1788, with models by J.B. Xaveri. It consisted mostly of blue-and-white wares and Kakiemon designs. The porcelain is very smoky and imperfect and the mark is similar to that of Frankenthal, a lion rampant in blue, save that the Cassel lion has a double tail. Pfalz-Zweibrücken (1767–1775) had a factory run by L. Russinger of Höchst and nearby Ottweiler (1764–1794) made somewhat similar wares. Porcelain was made in the early years only followed by creamware, and it had a much more French feeling than most German factories. The factory at Würzburg (1775–1788) made a few table wares as well as very rare religious and other figures. Porcelain was also made at Ellwangen by J.J. Ringler in about 1758 but has not yet been satisfactorily identified.

THURINGIA

In Thuringia a number of porcelain factories were started up in the eighteenth century, and had a certain success. The first of these was Gotha, which flourished from about 1756 to 1834. Its chief products were table services and tea

SET OF LIMBACH FIGURES, c.1775 (20cm/7¾in)

These provincial figures, emblematic of the Continents, are stiffly modelled with doll-like features, but they possess an appealing, naïve quality. (ABOVE)

and coffee sets, influenced by Fürstenberg with a fine but creamy paste. Wallendorf, which was founded in 1764, was where G. Greiner went into partnership with J.W. Hammann. The mark was a 'W' in blue, at first badly written to look like crossed swords. Like most Thuringian porcelain it had a grey paste. In 1772, Greiner left for Limbach, which used a crossed 'L' mark with a star below, deliberately meant to resemble the crossed swords of Meissen, as well as an 'LB' monogram. Later, the mark was a trefoil and the porcelain is much greyer. Limbach specialized in stiff doll-like figures with a naïve charm. The Greiner family also had factories at Grosz-beitzenbach (existing from 1777 to the present) whose eighteenth-century wares were virtually indistinguishable from those produced at Limbach.

Perhaps the most famous of the Thuringian factories was that of Kloster-Veilsdorf which flourished from 1760 to the present. A charming series of Italian Comedy figures are attributed to Wenzel Neu before he went to Fulda, and classical figures on square or polygonal bases are of note. The paste is whiter and finer than the other Thuringian factories. The mark was a 'CV' monogram until 1797 when the factory was bought by the Greiner family.

Volkstedt (*c.*1760 to the nineteenth century) at first produced soft paste but soon learned the secret of hard paste. It was also bought by the Greiners and is famous for making fakes and forgeries in the nineteenth century. The eighteenth-century paste is grey and the figures are naïve. Wares are usually crude copies of Marcolini-period Meissen, and the mark of a pitchfork can be mistaken for that of the Meissen factory.

THE VENICE FACTORIES

The city of Venice was the setting of the third European factory to produce true hard-paste porcelain. This factory was founded by Francesco

COZZI VASE, VENICE, 1769 (40.6cm/16in)

This piece is painted with an allegorical figure of Venice with the lion of St Mark's and inscribed: Primo Esperimento in Grande fatto li 15 Maggio 1769 nella Privil (egiata) Fabbrica di Geminiano Cozzi in Canalregio. *The reverse has a view of St Mark's, the companion vase Neptune and a country view, possibly of Bassano.*

Vezzi (1651–1740), a goldsmith. He was joined by C.C. Hunger of Meissen and Vienna in 1720 and manufactured porcelain there between 1720 and 1727. The porcelain resembled that of Vienna and Meissen somewhat but was not quite as finely finished. It can be white or creamy, but is more often grey in colour, very translucent and thinly potted. It is painted in gold, a strong brown-red, bright leaf-green and other colours with both chinoiserie and Imari designs, and the majority of the production comprises cups and saucers, with occasional teapots, and more rarely plates. Pieces of unusual form can be found but the entire known remaining products of the factory are possibly not much more than 100 pieces. It closed in about 1735. The usual mark is a shortening of Venezia, Vena.

After a gap of 30 years, another small factory was set up in Venice between 1758 and 1763, by N.F. Hewelke. This porcelain is even rarer than that of the early Vezzi factory, and was composed of a hard, slightly yellow paste, marked with a 'V'.

In 1764 G. Cozzi started a third factory in Venice which was much more successful, and lasted until 1812. Its wares were made of a thin hard grey paste with a shiny wet-looking surface. The colours were bright but rough, and of note are an iron-red, a violet and an emerald-green. The pieces were painted both with classical and contemporary subjects. The factory also made characters from the Italian Comedy, though they are particularly rare. Cozzi used an anchor mark, often in red, but much larger than that used at Chelsea.

About 1752 P. Antonibon, who already had a faience factory, started up at Le Nove near Bassano with the help of J.S. Fischer who had come from Dresden and Vienna. His production was very similar to that of Cozzi, and the colour of the paste can often be mistaken for that of the other factory. The Le Nove mark was a star. The porcelain factory appears to have gone into abeyance in 1773, until Antonibon leased it to F. Parolin in 1781, and in this latter period they had a painter, G. Marcon, who painted contemporary scenes and chinoiseries.

DOCCIA

The most important Italian factory is that of Doccia, near Florence. It was founded by the Marchese Carlo Ginori in 1735 and remained in the Ginori family until 1896. Ginori employed J.C.W. Anreiter, a Hausmaler from Vienna together with his teenage son Anton who remained in the factory until about 1746 when he returned to Vienna. His chief modeller was G. Bruschi who stayed until 1778. The first pieces that were actually sold do not appear to have been made before 1746. In 1757 Carlo Ginori died, and was succeeded by his son, Lorenzo, who carried on from 1757 until 1791.

The early paste of the factory is known as *masso bastardo*, which is a hybrid hard paste with a very grey, rather rough, sticky and smeared surface extremely prone to fire cracks. Between 1770 and 1790 the paste was greatly improved, and an opaque tin glaze was applied to it. Some of the earlier pieces have double walls in imitation of the Dehua *blanc de Chine* porcelain. Also at this time an unusual technique of decorating in blue and white with a stencil known as *stampino* was used. The polychrome painting often utilized stippling, and although this was also done in the Venetian factories of Cozzi and Le Nove, the Doccia stippling is more pronounced. It was used to produce flesh tints, both on figures in the round and for figure painting on the wares.

Two of the best-known Doccia patterns are known as *'a Tulipano'*, a rather formal

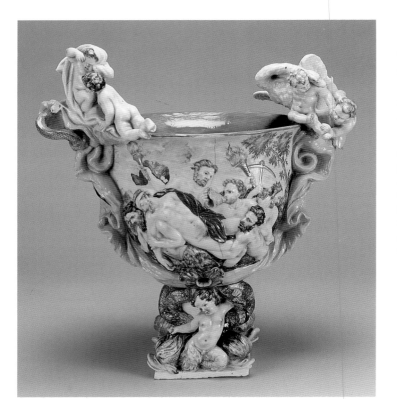

DOCCIA CENTRE-PIECE FROM A SIXTEEN-PIECE *SURTOUT DE TABLE*, c.1755–58 (H42cm/16½in)

The type of relief decoration used on this piece made for the Earl of Bristol served as a model for pieces made at Doccia and elsewhere in the second half of the nineteenth century.

THE *CABINETE DE PORCELANA* IN THE PALACIO REAL, MADRID, *c.*1770

There are two chinoiserie rooms modelled by Giuseppe Gricci for the Capo de Monte palace between 1757 and 1759 and Aranjuez between 1763 and 1765, the latter costing 571,555 Spanish reales. The room shown here, smaller and in the Neoclassical style, is by Carlos Schepers and dates from the 1770s. This cost 256,958 reales.

Oriental red peony spray, and *'a Galletto'* with Chinese style cocks in red and gold.

Doccia is also well known for its bas-relief decoration of classical subjects. This was originally done for Ginori when copies of Renaissance bas-reliefs were made in the white *masso bastardo* porcelain. One of the outstanding productions in this style formed a table centre decorated with figures in relief and with shells. A complete example still exists at Ickworth, Suffolk, made for George William, 2nd Earl of Bristol and Envoy Extraordinary at Turin between 1755 and 1758.

The Doccia figures also somewhat resemble those made in the Veneto, and these include Italian Comedy, classical, peasant and contemporary subjects.

CAPO DI MONTE, BUEN RETIRO AND NAPLES

The most famous of all Italian porcelain is that of Capo di Monte (1743–1759). Charles III of Bourbon, who had become King of Naples and Sicily, and married Maria Amalia Christina of Saxony in 1738, was very interested in making a porcelain of his own. Though he tried to imitate the hard paste of Germany, he never succeeded. However, the soft-paste Capo di Monte porcelain is more beautiful, though much more difficult to fire than any of the hard-paste porcelains. This superb paste was invented by G. Schepers.

The chief modeller at the factory was Giuseppe Gricci, while the chief painter was Giovanni Caselli, who died in 1752. He was succeeded by J.S. Fischer who came from Le Nove in 1754 until his death (from eating poisoned mushrooms) in 1758. Gricci's modelling equals that of Kändler at Meissen and Bustelli at Nymphenburg, and is admirably set off by the wonderful translucent soft paste of Capo di Monte. He modelled a series of delightfully observed figures of contemporary subjects, mostly with small heads, as well as bold Italian comedy figures and groups. He was less successful in his classical figures, but is well known for the fabulous Chinoiserie room made entirely out of porcelain in the Capo di Monte Palace in Naples.

Caselli and his niece Maria painted the most beautiful natural flowers and fruit as well as contemporary figures in the landscapes, while G. della Torre specialized in battle scenes, landscapes and figures. These scenes are particularly easy to recognize from the clouds, which are painted in violet and pale orange-red. The Capo di Monte mark was a fleur-de-lys either in blue or impressed in the base in relief in a roundel.

In 1759 the King succeeded his father as Charles III of Spain, and left his young son Ferdinand IV as King of Naples and Sicily. He took the workmen and the factory with him to Madrid to the Palace of Buen Retiro (1759–1808) and continued to make porcelain there, concentrating on figures. His

greatest accomplishment was a porcelain room modelled by Gricci in his Palace at Aranjuez similar to the one in Naples.

The quality of the porcelain deteriorated later in the century, and in 1803 a hard paste was introduced. The factory was destroyed by the British in 1812. Some of the porcelain made between 1770 and 1783 was in fact a form of creamware, similar to Wedgwood's Queen's ware.

Ferdinand IV revived a Royal porcelain factory at Naples (from 1771 to 1806). The secret of the paste was solved by G. Tucci, who had worked at the Capo di Monte factory, while F. Celebrano was the chief modeller until 1781. It was not until the first director Peres died in 1779 that his successor Venuti brought success to the factory. The porcelain, like that of the earlier factory, was a very translucent and glossy soft paste, but now it was in the fashionable Neoclassical style. Biscuit and glazed figures were made with classical subjects based on the finds from Pompeii and Herculaneum as well as other antiquities in Naples. Figures in peasant dress, birds and animals were made. Wares included tea, coffee and dinner services as well as vases. They were similarly painted with local scenes, classical ruins and peasants in national dress. The usual mark is a crown over 'N' in blue.

VINOVO

Vinovo (1776–1820), which is about 10km (6¼ miles) outside Turin, was started by G.V. Brodel. Brodel employed Paul-Anton Hannong, the black sheep of his family who had betrayed his brother at Strasbourg and Frankenthal and had to flee. Vinovo ware has a rather creamy body resembling soft paste, and is painted in the French style.

There were several other small factories in the north of Italy, one being Este, which was started up in 1781 by G.B. Brunello who had come from Le Nove. Este also made faience, but few actual pieces can be definitely attributed to this factory.

PORTUGAL

Attempts were made to produce porcelain at the faience factory at Alcora in the second half of the eighteenth century. Although the records list pieces, the only known true porcelain appears to date from about 1784 to 1786, and even of this very few pieces are known.

FRENCH

PORCELAIN

All the early French porcelain factories made soft paste rather than hard paste, unlike those in Germany and most of the rest of Europe, with the exception of England. The secret of true porcelain, as mentioned earlier, was only discovered at Meissen in 1708. The early experimenters imagined that true

CAPO DI MONTE GROUP OF RABBIT CATCHERS, c.1750 (H16.5cm/6½in)

This piece was modelled by Giuseppe Gricci. In the composition of his groups, he rivals the German modellers Kändler and Bustelli. The painting is by an unidentified hand and appears on certain other fine Capo di Monte groups.

ST. CLOUD BLUE-AND-WHITE VASE, PROBABLY BEFORE 1700 (15cm/5⅞in)

The Bérainesque style of this vase is similar to the few pieces still attributed to Rouen, but the paste makes a St. Cloud attribution far more likely.

porcelain was a form of glass and therefore used common glass mixed with white clay and other ingredients. The resulting porcelain was of exceptional beauty but entailed serious disadvantages in that many more pieces collapsed in the kiln, or became so misshapen in the firing as to make them virtually unusable.

In 1673 a patent was granted to open a factory at Rouen, to Louis Poterat, son of Edmé who was already known as a maker of faience. A few pieces very similar to St. Cloud decorated in blue were attributed to Rouen, but most of those are now thought to be St. Cloud. A silver-mounted mustard pot in the Sèvres Museum with a coat of arms is almost certainly of Rouen manufacture. The glaze is somewhat more blue or green-toned than that of St Cloud, and the blue is a dark inky colour. The borders with arabesques are painted with fine dots.

ST. CLOUD HOT MILK JUG, c.1725
(15.2cm/6in)

St. Cloud used the blanc-de-Chine *invention of applied prunus branches on European shapes.*

ST. CLOUD

Though it is claimed that porcelain was made at St. Cloud as early as 1678, it was only in 1702 that the widow of P. Chicaneau, who had married H.-C. Trou in 1679, was granted letters patent to make porcelain, Trou having obtained the patronage of the Duke of Orléans for the factory. In the next generation the Trou family and the Chicaneau family probably separated, the latter setting up a branch establishment in Paris.

The St. Cloud paste has a rather creamy or ivory tone with a soft and shiny surface. It is difficult to date but the earliest designs are likely to have been those painted in underglaze blue. Lambrequins based on textile originals are common in the decoration as are other Bérainesque designs. A number of the shapes and patterns appear in Rouen faience.

In the second quarter of the eighteenth century much of the porcelain was left in the white and moulded in relief with prunus and other designs, originally based on those of Dehua, but latterly of a purely European format and feeling. These pieces were often mounted in silver.

When it came to painting, unlike the other French factories, adaptations of Imari and *famille verte* patterns were made as well as the more usual Kakiemon, and indeed the Kakiemon is much more derivative than directly copied from the Japanese porcelain originals.

Figures of mainly chinoiserie origin were made during the second quarter of the century, and in about the middle of the century elaborate pot-pourri vases encrusted with flowers on rockwork bases became a speciality of the factory. Like the other French factories, St. Cloud also made numerous snuff boxes, knife, fork and cane handles and other small pieces. Some of the small pieces have raised-and-tooled gilding impressed with designs and with translucent enamel panels in the style of Hunger. The usual mark of the factory is an incised 'St. C.' over a 'T'.

CHANTILLY

The Duc de Condé (1692–1740) founded a factory at Chantilly in 1725, but did not obtain a patent until 1735. His director was C. Cirou until 1751. The factory is most famous for its pieces painted in the Kakiemon style. The Duc de Condé had a large collection of Japanese Kakiemon porcelain and this was used by the factory partly as inspiration and partly for direct copies. They also copied similar designs via the Meissen factory. J.-A. Fraisse published a series of Chinese drawings in 1735 which were used by the factory as source material, which explains how certain pieces are inspired not only by Kakiemon but also Chinese *famille verte*. The figures too are a mixture of Chinese and Japanese styles often with Japanese decoration on a truly Chinese-type figure. Some of the figures, though, must be based on unknown Japanese originals.

Chantilly can be distinguished from its contemporary French porcelain by the fact that it had an opaque tin glaze until about 1750. From that date a normal lead glaze,

CHANTILLY CACHEPOT, c.1735–40
(13.9cm/5½in)

This piece is painted in a Kakiemon-inspired palette with a design based on an engraving in the Livre de Desseins Chinois Tirés d'après des Originaux de Perse, de la Chine et du Japon *by J.-A. Fraisse, painter to the Duc de Condé.*

slightly yellow or creamy, was substituted, though occasionally later pieces used the tin glaze. Because of the edict forbidding competition with the Royal Factory at Vincennes, elaborate and fine pieces were rarely made after 1755. However a great deal of tableware with underglaze blue decoration of sprigs of flowers or with pinks was produced, and the same patterns appear in enamel pink or blue. The finest service is the one painted with flowers on a blue-and-gilt trellis pattern ground. Chantilly also made snuff boxes and other small items. The usual mark is a hunting horn in red.

MENNECY

The factory at Mennecy was started by François Barbin (1689–1765). Barbin started a small faience factory in the grounds of the Duc de Villeroy's chateau. In 1734 he bought a house in the Rue de Charonne in Paris, probably using it only as a decorating establishment, while the porcelain was made at Villeroy, which is close to Mennecy.

GROUP OF CHILDREN, MENNECY STYLE, c.1760 (ABOVE)

In 1748, because of pressure from Vincennes, the decorating shop in the Rue de Charonne was closed and Barbin had to remove his kilns to Mennecy itself. He was joined by his son, Jean-Baptiste, but both died in 1765, and the factory was then bought by J. Jullien and S. Jacques who also made porcelain at Sceaux. In 1773 they left Mennecy and set up at Bourg-la-Reine.

The early Mennecy porcelain can easily be mistaken for St. Cloud. It has the same sort of creamy tone with a greenish surface, particularly when it is painted in the Kakiemon style. The factory also produced some beautifully modelled chinoiserie figures. After the removal to Mennecy the style changed and became more like that at Vincennes-Sèvres with European flower sprays. Gilding was not used and the rims were usually painted in pink but occasionally in bright blue. Covered custard cups as well as miniature campana vases were produced in large numbers and the former were often modelled with spiral reeding. Flowers, birds and peasant figures in landscapes were common subjects in the painting. The popular later figures were more often children grouped on rockwork bases. The chief modeller of these was Nicolas Gauron. Arriving at Mennecy in 1753, he later moved to Tournay and Derby. Many small snuff boxes, knife handles and cane handles were made. The usual mark is an incised or painted 'DV'.

VINCENNES

The Vincennes factory opened in 1740, as an experimental workshop producing soft-paste ware, in converted premises at the royal château of Vincennes. Five years later, the company was granted a royal warrant which gave it the exclusive right to manufacture 'porcelain in the style of Saxony, painted and gilded and depicting human figures . . .'. In other words, it was to emulate the products of the factory that had been established in Meissen in 1710, the first in Europe to

produce genuine hard-paste porcelain decorated with a range of opaque colours which made it possible to produce pictorial images. The factory at Vincennes was financed by two joint stock companies incorporated by Charles Adam (1745–1752) and Eloy Brichard (1752–1759) and assisted by grants from the Royal Treasury. In 1756, the porcelain factory was moved to a purpose-built building in Sèvres, a village ideally situated between Paris and Versailles. In 1759, it was taken directly under royal administration.

As an experimental workshop, Vincennes had to devise everything from scratch. Whereas the discovery in Saxony of deposits of kaolin (the essential component of true hard-paste porcelain) made possible the foundation of the Meissen factory in 1710, in France, kaolin was not discovered until 1768. Up to this time a substitute was produced, a sort of opacified glass with the same qualities of translucency and hardness as glass. This product was called soft-paste porcelain purely because its glaze was very easily scratched.

Neither at Saint-Cloud nor at Chantilly, the only porcelain factories in France until

VINCENNES SOFT-PASTE WATERING CAN, 1753 (20cm/7$\frac{7}{8}$in)

Bardet's delightful painting epitomizes the romantic flavour of many pieces produced by the Vincennes factory in the middle of the eighteenth century.

1740, could a satisfactory soft paste be produced. The workshop at Vincennes was the first to manufacture a clay of perfect whiteness, with a fine, transparent glaze. Claude-Humbert Gérin, responsible for this significant achievement, had first to perfect a kiln to fire the pottery and the glaze. It took him up to 1746 to master the firing of biscuit and glaze. Then in 1748 he invented a kiln which could fire decoration at a low temperature, the first continuous kiln in the history of ceramics.

In addition, while Saint-Cloud and Chantilly were decorating solely with transparent, unmixed flat colours on the surface, Vincennes commissioned enamellers who had mastered vitrifiable colours between 1744 and 1748 to perfect a range of colours which could be mixed and shaded with appropriate fondants. In 1748, after many abortive attempts, the secret of ground gold and its mordants was discovered. Manufacturing could commence.

The first phase at Vincennes included the production of numerous porcelain flowers, faithful copies of a wide variety of natural species. *Marchands merciers* would mount these flowers on varnished brass stems with natural foliage. These were then used to decorate a variety of objects, such as lamps, chandeliers and wall sconces among others. The factory also produced small, freely modelled or moulded figures – the figures were enamelled and often coloured. They included birds and animals, nymphs, hunters or children, singly or in groups. In 1749, Marie-Josèphe of Saxony presented her father with a magnificent piece consisting of a porcelain vase containing mounted flowers, flanked by two groups of figures symbolizing the Arts, the whole mounted on a gilt-bronze plinth.

Production was gradually diversified under the influence of the goldsmith Duplessis, who was hired in 1748 to create shapes to contemporary taste. The first such pieces consisted of tableware and items suitable for the dressing-table or for serving hot drinks in. The designs were inspired by Chinese (reliefs of prunus blossom) or Saxon (latticework) motifs, or borrowed

from the goldsmith (fluting and ribbonwork) with a predilection for objects taken from nature (shells and reeds). The decoration of this early period was also influenced by Meissen. There were lively landscapes and stiff flowers with dark outlines taken from engravings and painted in muted colours or monochrome.

The year 1751 was marked by major changes for Vincennes. J.J. Bachelier, a flower painter, was engaged to supervise the painters. After the death of J.L. Orry de Fulvy, the first patron of the establishment, Louis XV charged J. Hellot, Director of the Academy of Sciences, to record and improve all the formulae. At the same time, advice was sought from connoisseurs to adapt the factory's products more to the tastes of its clientele. The result was that shapes became infinitely more diversified and decoration was inspired by topical subject-matter and painted in pure, clear colours. Vincennes introduced porcelain depicting children in the style of François Boucher and fanciful birds.

In 1751, J. Hellot perfected a brilliant blue (*bleu beau*) and produced a perfect ground in cobalt blue on biscuit. The mordant and the composition required considerable reworking until a satisfactory hue and application were achieved. Since this blue ground had a tendency to run at the edges, the decorators masked the defect by tracing designs in gold, with consistent virtuosity and richness. The ground colours – violet and turquoise blue (*bleu céleste*) in 1753, green (*verd*) in 1756 – associated with this gilding and lively decoration in polychrome or cameo, were applied in cartouches of symmetrical shapes and were characteristic of the second phase of production at Vincennes (1752–1756).

It was in the course of the same transitional year of 1751 to 1752 that another important change occurred, this time in sculpture production. The first generation of sculptors had worked directly with the clay, which had resulted in products of very uneven quality. It was decided that experienced modellers would be commissioned to produce sculpture in

VINCENNES SOFT-PASTE TANKARD, *c.*1752 (15.3cm/6in)

The birds and vegetation that adorn this covered cup are typical motifs of the mid-eighteenth century.

the round from designs by François Boucher. In order not to lose anything of the quality of the originals, these sculptures were produced from exact moulds, which enabled accurate copies to be made. To show the work off to the best advantage, these moulded figurines were not glazed before firing and the unglazed biscuit was lightly polished, an invention which was soon copied throughout Europe.

SÈVRES

The first years of porcelain production at Sèvres were a continuation of the work of Vincennes. A bright pink ground, now known as *rose Pompadour* after Madame de Pompadour, mistress of Louis XV and patroness of the factory, was created in 1757. More variety was introduced into the shapes of vases, for use or purely for decoration, in the same measured, baroque style, despite such extravagant creations as the *Vase à têtes d'éléphants* or the *Pot-pourri Vaisseau*. Gradually, the Neoclassical style predominated in the continually changing shapes of the vases. Decoration also evolved. The rich, gold ornamentation moved onto the coloured grounds, leaving simple guilloched bands framing the paintings. Decoration on the vases was inspired by fashionable paintings by Teniers, Berchem or Boucher, unless the subject-matter was purely ornamental (such as birds, bouquets or trophies). Tableware was decorated predominantly with floral or geometric designs.

The decorators were almost invariably specialists in particular genres. Among them were Ch.N. Dodin and Ch.E. Asselin, who painted figures in pastoral, mythological or military scenes; J.L. Morin, who painted naval scenes; A.V. Vielliard who painted children or small lively landscapes; F.J. Alconcle and E. Evans who concentrated on birds; J.J. Dieu and L.F. Lecot who produced chinoiseries. There were many others, including the virtuoso gilders E.H. Le Guay and H.F. Vincent.

The most important event of this period was the discovery in 1768 of deposits of kaolin in Limousin, which meant that true hard-paste porcelain could be produced at last. Because of this new paste, the range of coloured grounds could be extended considerably and the vocabulary of decoration varied, for instance with unusual enamel decoration on gold foil, which was in vogue in the 1780s. The two types of paste were both produced until 1804, when soft paste was abandoned. After the 1770s, the production of vases slowed, but that of tableware, which had been lagging somewhat since the Vincennes days, increased. A service in an antique style was created for the Empress Catherine II of Russia and there were 'Etruscan-style' *déjeuner* services designed by J.J. Lagrenée le Jeune, who was artistic director from 1785.

Towards the end of the century, new decorative designs began to appear. These included imitations of fabric and representations of flowers and birds which were often very faithful to natural history books, as well as innumerable variations on poly-

SÈVRES SOFT-PASTE EWER AND BOWL, PAINTED BY A.T. CORNAILLES, *c.* 1757
(ewer: 17.1cm/6¾in)
(LEFT)

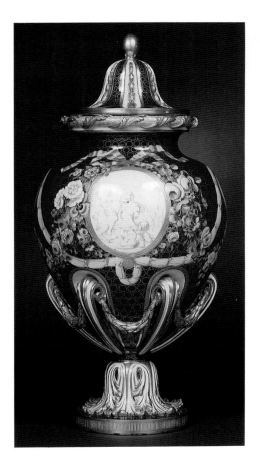

SÈVRES SOFT-PASTE URN, 1769
(49.4cm/17½in)

The fine painting on this piece is by J.B.E. Genest and Mérault the Younger. (ABOVE)

SÈVRES BISCUIT GROUP OF 'L'EDUCATION DE L'AMOUR', 1763
(32cm/12½in)

This group of figures demonstrates E.M. Falconet's compositional abilities. (ABOVE)

SÈVRES DESIGN
FOR CUP, JEAN-
JACQUES
LAGRENÉE THE
YOUNGER, 1788

*The cup shown in this
design was destined for
Marie Antoinette's
dairy at Rambouillet.*
(RIGHT)

SÈVRES HARD-PASTE CUP AND SAUCER,
*c.*1778

*Motifs used on this cup and saucer are typical of
European chinoiserie decoration.* (ABOVE)

THE DINING ROOM, PAVLOVSK,
RUSSIA

*The table is set with the eighteenth-century Sèvres
'Rose' service.* (ABOVE LEFT)

chrome patterns based on archaeological excavations in Italy and 'Etruscan' figures.

The plaques used to decorate furniture or decorative objects (clocks, barometers, *escritoires*, etc.) made a hesitant appearance at Vincennes, but were very successful at Sèvres and were bought in quantity by *marchands merciers* who had them mounted by the best cabinet-makers.

Sculpture developed in approximately the same way. E.M. Falconet was in charge of the workshop between 1757 and 1766. He continued the production of figures and groups of children in the Boucher style, but introduced more ambitious sculptures in biscuit, such as his celebrated *Baigneuse*. When he left for Russia, the workshop was placed under the direction of Bachelier who designed several items himself but made frequent use of sculptors such as Lemoyne, Saly or Pigalle. In 1773, the running of the workshop was entrusted to L.S. Boizot who imposed his rather stiff, classical style upon it.

Louis XV and Louis XVI clearly registered their interest in the establishment by generously presenting to foreign sovereigns and diplomats sumptuous services and ensembles so that the perfection of French arts could be displayed around the world. Among the dignitaries given services were the kings of Denmark, in 1756 and 1768; Empress Marie-Thérèse of Austria, in

1758, and Emperor Joseph II of Austria, in 1777; and the Duke of Bedford, then English ambassador, in 1763. A toilette set was ordered for the future Empress of Russia in 1782. Pipes and spitoons were given to the ambassadors of the Tipu, Sultan of Mysore, in 1788.

Apart from orders for their own residences – the most sumptuous of which was the ceremonial service commissioned for Versailles in 1783 – the kings of France organized exhibitions of Sèvres ware every New Year at Versailles. Thus, they regularly gave the factory an opportunity to display and sell its most recent creations.

THE REVOLUTION

The revolutionary period is generally considered to have been extremely difficult for a factory primarily dedicated to the production of luxury items. The only clientele possible at that time was found among Dutch or English dealers, which explains why so few decorative designs (trophies or symbols) or sculpture subjects (medallions, busts, allegorical figures) were inspired by republican ideals. Almost all such items are confined to the period of the Terror (autumn 1793); most of them were classically inspired forms or purely decorative subjects. It is therefore surprising that richly decorated chinoiserie started to be produced, using designs in coloured gold and platinum on a black ground.

SMALLER FRENCH FACTORIES

In 1762 J.-A. Hannong returned to France from Frankenthal and with a certain amount of difficulty produced hard-paste porcelain around 1768. Most of the output from his factory comprised figures of children in the style of the faience but he also made Neoclassical tableware. Flowers were the usual form of decoration.

The wares of the Niderviller factory resemble those of Strasbourg. It was founded as a faience factory by Baron de Beyerlé and was bought in the early 1770s by the Comte de Custine, who was guillotined in 1793. The production was carried on by his partner C.-F. Lamfrey. The factory is best known for its fine biscuit figures. These were made by P.-L. Cyfflé of Lunéville, whose moulds were removed to Niderviller in 1780. The sculptor Lemire was also employed by the factory. The usual mark is the double 'C' monogram under a crown similar to that of Ludwigsburg.

In the factory at Lunéville, which existed briefly from 1766 to 1777, porcelain, *terre de Lorraine* and *terre cuite* were made, but the stock was sold to Niderviller in 1780. Porcelain was also made at the faience factory of J.G. Robert in the south of France at Marseilles from 1733 to 1793.

TOURNAY

Though made in Flanders, Tournay ware is very similar to French porcelain, particularly Sèvres, and forms a link with early Chelsea as well. The factory was started in 1751 by F.J. Peterinck. R. du Bois became director in 1753, and it is possible he brought the secret of soft-paste porcelain with him. Peterinck died in 1799 and his son, who owned the factory

from 1797 to 1799, decided to concentrate on making earthenware elsewhere.

The chief painter H.-J. Duvivier (1763–1771) was well known for exotic birds, very like those on Chelsea and Worcester porcelain. He is also reputed to have painted the pink monochrome landscape vignettes that were popular at the factory.

Tournay porcelain is somewhat greyer than that of the French factories but later on becomes whiter with a slight yellow tinge. The finest Tournay can have a mottled dark-blue ground similar to that of the Chelsea gold anchor, and a fine royal-blue ground, which was used for the Buffon service made for the Duke of Orleans in 1787. After Duvivier, birds were chiefly painted by J.-G.-J. Mayer who became the head painter in 1774. The chief modellers were N. Lecreux, J. Willems, who also worked

TOURNAY PART SERVICE, 1787

Made for Louis-Philippe, duc d'Orléans, this service is painted with birds after Buffon's 'Natural History' chiefly by Jean-Ghislain-Joseph Mayer. It was the most ambitious enterprise of the Tournay factory; much of it is in the Royal Collection today.

at Chelsea during the red anchor period, A. Gillis, and N. Gauron (1758–1764). A number of the earlier figures resemble those of Mennecy, and later figures, particularly when they are left in the white, the biscuit figures of Derby. Tournay stopped manufacturing in the mid-nineteenth century. The mark was crossed-swords with stars or a tower, both in gold, but also in blue on the simple wares.

There were two minor factories in this region, Arras (from 1770 to 1790), and St.-Amand (from 1771 to 1778). At this period these two factories were inclined to make simple blue-and-white wares similar to those of Tournay and Chantilly, but later on de Bettignies, who had worked at Tournay, made a number of forgeries of Sèvres, Tournay and other soft pastes.

HOLLAND

The factory at the Hague started in 1776 by decorating white Tournay porcelain and is famous for its farmyard birds and its blue borders. It subsequently manufactured a hard-paste porcelain, somewhat similar in style to that of Tournay. It was run by A. Lyncker, who was of German origin. After his death in 1781 his son, Johann, carried on until the factory's closure in 1790. The mark was a blue enamel stork.

WEESP, OUDE
LOOSDRECHT
AND AMSTEL

The Weesp concern was started in 1757 by D. McCarthy who had come from Copenhagen. But he sold the factory in 1759 to Count Gronsveldt-Diepenbroek, who made hard-paste porcelain with the help of N. Paul, who later went to Fulda. In 1771 the factory was

ZURICH
MINIATURE
FIGURES, *c.*1773
(pattern seller:
9.5cm/3¾in)

Figures such as this trinket seller and a pattern seller were widely collected all over Europe at this time.

once more sold to J. de Mol, who had the help of L.V. Gerverot. Then it was moved to Oude Loosdrecht. After de Mol's death in 1782 it was put under the direction of F. Däuber and moved to Amstel; it closed in 1820. This factory mainly produced tableware, though a few figures were modelled in the earlier days by N. Gauron, who had come from Tournay. The porcelain was a fine white hard paste, and its decoration included landscapes with peasants in a palette dominated by brown. The mark was 'M:O.L.' in the 1770s and 1780s, followed by 'Amstel' in script.

SWITZERLAND

A factory was founded close to Zurich at Schoren in 1763. The poet and painter S. Gessner (1739–1778) was among its founders. The director was A. Spengler, whose son J.J. Spengler was one of the modellers and subsequently worked at Derby. After A. Spengler's death

in 1790 the factory was run by his son-in-law M. Nehracher from 1793–1800.

The original porcelain was soft paste, but this is extremely rare. A hard paste made from kaolin from Lorraine was introduced in about 1765. The porcelain is somewhat like that of Ludwigsburg but rather more brilliant, with a smoky tone, either faintly brownish or a sort of green-grey.

As well as Gessner, Heinrich Fuseli, a relation of the famous Anglo-Swiss painter, painted landscapes between 1771 and 1781. These paintings were usually stippled with soft greens and browns with touches of blue and red. European and Oriental flowers were also painted. They also made blue-and-white wares, particularly copying the Meissen onion pattern.

Zurich figures are particularly attractive, and the best modeller was J.V. Sonnenschein who worked at Ludwigsburg but came to Zurich between 1775 and 1779. These figures often resemble the Ludwigsburg originals and represent peasants and fishermen as well as soldiers, shepherds and shepherdesses, musicians and other contemporary figures. Classical subjects are less common. The factory stopped producing porcelain towards the end of the nineteenth century. Its mark was a 'Z' in underglaze blue.

A factory was founded at Nyon in about 1780 by F. Müller, who was reputed to have come from Frankenthal, and whose partner J. Dortu had been at various other factories. The porcelain is hard paste, white, and resembles that of the contemporary Paris factories. The style of painting is also based on that of Paris of the same period. The mark was a fish in blue.

DENMARK

The first Copenhagen factory was run by L. Fournier who had originally been at Vincennes and Chantilly. Many other famous names were also at Copenhagen for a short time, including C.C. Hunger in the 1730s, J.C.L. Lück in the 1750s and D. McCarthy at the same period. Fournier made soft-paste porcelain, usually fairly simple and painted with flowers very much in the French style. The Royal Factory was founded in the early 1770s under F.H. Müller, who formed a company in 1774, with the Queen as the principal shareholder, which was taken over in 1779 by the King. The factory declined in the early nineteenth century, but was revived after 1885.

Unlike the creamy soft paste produced by Fournier, the earliest hard-paste porcelain from the Royal Factory was blue-grey in tone. Like so many other European factories the osier border was often used as well as flowers. One of the better-known Copenhagen designs was of silhouetted portrait heads, while vases with historical figures painted in panels were also very popular in the 1780s.

The most famous of the eighteenth-century Copenhagen wares is the Flora Danica service, started for Catherine II of Russia in 1789, and finished in only 1802. The designs are taken from a book by Oeder, begun in 1761. The painting was done by J.C. Bayer from Nuremberg. This service is still being produced today. Neoclassical models, Norwegian peasants and other folk types, miners (similar to those at Fürstenberg) and busts of royalty were all produced. The best-known modellers were J.J. Holm and A. Luplau, formerly of Fürstenberg. The biscuit figures after the sculptor Thorwaldsen were late nineteenth-century productions. The mark is three wavy lines in blue.

SWEDEN

The factory at Marieberg was founded by a German, J.L.E. Ehrenreich in 1759 and originally produced a soft-paste porcelain. It made very little true porcelain and concentrated on faience. In 1776 P. Berthevin, a Mennecy modeller, came to the factory and much of the Marieberg wares of this period resemble Mennecy with its creamy soft paste, in particular spirally fluted custard cups painted with flowers. Berthevin left in 1769 and H. Sten from Rörstrand, the rival faience factory, arrived and made a semi-hard paste porcelain. In 1777 J. Dortu came to Marieberg, and, for a short time until the factory was closed in 1782, produced a true hard paste. A few figures representing Swedish peasants are also known.

RUSSIA

Various experiments in true porcelain were carried out in St. Petersburg by Hunger, who had left Stockholm in 1744. He was followed by D. Vinogradoff who succeeded in making some small objects, including snuff bottles. But it was only when he died, in 1758, that the Saxon J.G. Muller (apparently no relation of the Copenhagen worker) managed to produce any serious wares. The factory was under the directorship of A.

Tschepotieff until his death in 1773, and under Prince Viazemski until 1792, assisted by an alchemist from Vienna, J. Regensburg. The factory is most famous for its dinner services made for Catherine II as well as a remarkable service made for Count Orlov. Figures of Russian peasants taken from a contemporary book were modelled by D. Racette, who was first employed in 1779. The eighteenth-century mark was 'EII' in blue.

Francis Gardner, an Englishman, formed a porcelain factory in Moscow about 1765, and the quality is almost as good as that of the imperial factory. His most famous products were the four services made for the imperial orders of St. George, St. Andrew, St. Alexander Nevskii and St. Vladimir between 1777 and 1785, with badges in the centres of the plates and ribbons round the borders. The mark was a 'G' in underglaze blue. A lesser-known rival factory was that of A. Popoff, though this mainly produced wares in the nineteenth century. There was also a factory making porcelain at Korzec in Poland.

EARLY ENGLISH PORCELAIN

*M*any of the characteristics of early English porcelain, which distinguish it so sharply *from that made on the Continent, were dictated by economic factors. The English factories were private enterprises with none of the financial advantages of royal or aristocratic patronage that underpinned the prosperity of their French, German and Italian counterparts. Consequently, their survival depended entirely on commercial success in an extremely competitive market. Of the fifteen or so factories established in England prior to 1780, only two sustained production into the nineteenth century, a vivid commentary on the technical and economic hazards of mid-eighteenth century porcelain manufacture. Indeed, in the early pioneering days of the 1740s and 1750s, when trial and error was a necessary expedient and there was constant experimentation with porcelain bodies and glazes, some factories survived for only a year or two, while the history, output and exact location of others is still shrouded in uncertainty.*

Few of the English factories could rival the sophistication of the figure modelling and the domestic forms produced by the major factories on the Continent. Yet the English potting shapes had a pleasingly forthright quality which was often rooted in their earthenware origins. Similarly, if much of the decoration has a naïve and derivative appearance, in both its conception and execution, it reflected the tastes and priorities of a far wider cross-section of society than was allowed on the Continent. On the one hand, such factories as Chelsea, Derby and Worcester produced superb porcelain which echoed the Meissen and Sèvres taste, while on the other, factories such as Bow, Lowestoft and those in Liverpool concentrated on far less ambitious forms and decorative styles.

GROUP OF ENGLISH TEAWARES, *c.*1760–70

Left to right: a Liverpool teapot; a Worcester cup and saucer with the Plumber's Arms; a Bow teapot; and a Worcester cup and saucer.

EARLY PORCELAIN

Despite a long tradition of pottery manufacture which stretches back to the seventeenth century and beyond, England was slow to emulate other European countries in the field of porcelain. Whereas in France and Germany, the manufacture of porcelain had flourished since the early years of the eighteenth century, it was not until 1744 that the first two English factories were established, both of them in London.

In the mid-1740s, there was a tremendous demand for porcelain in England, stimulated by the popularity of tea drinking. Prior to this time the only porcelain available to slake this demand was the Chinese wares imported by the East India Company. To meet the competition of these imports the first English factories sought to imitate them. At Bow in particular, Oriental patterns were copied on a very substantial scale, almost to the exclusion of all other decorative idioms. In addition, much of the imported Oriental porcelain was blue and white, and underglaze blue quickly became the staple decoration for most of the early factories. It was relatively inexpensive to produce, requiring a simpler process of manufacture than polychrome wares and less skill in its decoration. The English factories thus sought to undersell the imported Chinese porcelain that had held sway since the seventeenth century. In this cheaper end of the market, there were also opportunities to compete with, and eventually replace, the waning delftware factories whose output of tin-glazed earthenware was far less durable and technically less accomplished than true porcelain.

TECHNOLOGY

Whereas Oriental, German and most Italian porcelain was 'true' or hard-paste porcelain, the majority of the English factories prior to 1780 utilized a soft-paste or 'artificial' body. This consisted, in essence, of a mixture of white clay and ground glass, the exact composition varying from factory to factory. Hard-paste porcelain was fired at a temperature of 1400°C, whereas a soft-paste body required the far lower temperature of 1100°C.

From the 1740s onwards, experiments were made continually as potters sought to invent and master new porcelain bodies, glazes and firing techniques. Some factories, notably Bow and Lowestoft, included bone ash, a highly versatile ingredient which reduced the likelihood of collapse in the kiln, a recurring hazard in the manufacture of soft-paste porcelain. An even more effective innovation, introduced first at Bristol in 1750, and at Worcester a year later, was the use of soapstone (steatite) in the composition of the body, which made it impervious to sudden changes of temperature. This was a crucial improvement in the manufacture of tea wares in particular.

The first relatively successful attempt at hard-paste, or 'true' porcelain, was made at Plymouth in 1768, after extensive experiments in preceding years. Although the history of 'true' porcelain in England was brief and commercially unsuccessful, its ingredients, together with that of the bone-ash body, were eventually to become

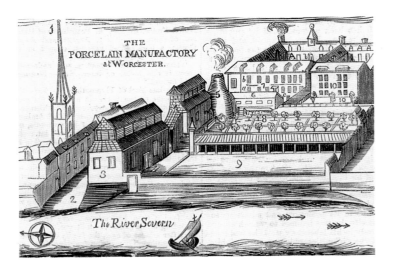

ENGRAVING OF 'THE PORCELAIN MANUFACTORY AT WORCESTER'

BOW SAUCEBOAT, c.1752–54 (H14.3cm/5¾in)

The shape and moulded decoration show the influence of George II silver form.

the basis of English 'bone china', the standard body to this day.

Two principal potting methods were used in the manufacture of domestic wares: 'throwing and turning', a process used mainly on hollow objects, and 'press moulding' in a plaster mould. An alternative to 'press moulding' was 'slip casting' which involved pouring liquid clay into a porous plaster mould. Figures were modelled and then dissected by the master modeller so that moulds could be made for each of the separate component parts of the figure. The resulting components were then joined together, an operation carried out by a skilled craftsman known as a 'repairer'. Some further hand-modelling was sometimes necessary before the figure was ready for firing and decoration.

DECORATION

Hand-painted decoration, whether on figures or domestic wares, was always applied over the glaze, when executed in more than one colour. Despite some early experiments with manganese, the only underglaze colour used in the eighteenth century was blue, obtained from cobalt oxide. In some instances, the underglaze blue was used in conjunction with overglaze colours, as for example on the celebrated blue-ground decoration at Worcester in the 1760s and 1770s.

The technique of transfer printing was developed at Worcester and Bow in the mid-1750s, at first in overglaze, and later in underglaze blue. In essence, the process involved inking a copper plate with a ceramic pigment and then transferring the design to paper. While the colour was still wet, the design was placed on the porcelain surface. Naturally, this process cut costs dramatically, and gradually rendered all but the most skilful painters more or less redundant. The development of transfer printing was one of the very few real innovations in the English ceramics industry in its early years. It is a baleful irony that this important technique led directly to both a lessening of artistic standards and to

much hardship among china painters, many of whom were forced out of the industry.

In almost every aspect of decoration and potting shapes, the English porcelain factories were fundamentally derivative. Chinese and Japanese patterns were readily imitated and adapted, both directly and absorbed through the influence of Meissen. Factories such as Chelsea, Worcester, and Derby closely followed many Meissen shapes and styles of decoration, in both their domestic wares and their figure models. By the late 1760s, the Meissen influence gave way to that of Sèvres, which was to hold sway for the following two decades. Yet a more pervasive and less pretentious influence on the ambitious domestic wares was that of English delftware. It was from this long-established industry, by then in decline, that the early porcelain factories derived much of their necessary expertise and all their painters and workmen. The movement of labour, from the delftware potteries to the porcelain factories, often located nearby, is evident in the underglaze blue decoration that constituted so important an element in the output of most of the early factories.

FIGURES

Yet, if the long tradition of English earthenware and stoneware exerted its often slightly rustic influence on much utilitarian porcelain, the figure modellers looked almost entirely to Continental sources to provide the element of sophistication that they sought. Nearly all the figure subjects from about 1750 to 1780 derived either from Meissen or from Sèvres. Only a few English figures were original creations.

English porcelain figures were invariably conceived in pairs, sets (as in the Four Seasons, the Four Continents, etc.) or as components of a series. Classical subjects were much in vogue, as were figures from the Italian Comedy and allegorical subjects. The earlier figures, from the 1750s, tended to be restrained in their modelling, though at their best were full of movement and vitality. Colouring was generally subdued

CHELSEA FIGURE, c.1754–55
(19.8cm/7¾in)

This figure of a carpenter was modelled by Joseph Willems. Unlike the majority of models from the red anchor period, which were derived from Meissen, this figure seems to have been an original creation and is amongst the finest of all Chelsea models. It bears a red anchor mark.

and indeed many subjects of the 1750s were issued 'in the white'. Bases were usually flat or of a simple scrolled form, in great contrast to the later elaborately scrolled versions. From the 1760s onwards there was a movement towards the extravagance of the late Rococo, as figures became increasingly ornate in both their colouring and their bocage. Gilding, which was used sparingly on the earlier figures, began to appear in profusion. The onset of the restraining influence of Neoclassicism in the mid-1770s finally swept away the excesses of the Rococo embodied in the Bow and Chelsea figures of the late 1760s.

WARES

The domestic forms of the 1750s and 1760s also mirrored Continental shapes to some extent, but an even more important influence was that of silver. Silversmithing, with its Rococo overtones, was most apparent in the early years of the Chelsea Factory. Apart from Chelsea, silver forms were associated with particular shapes rather than with factories. Almost all the sauceboats, tureens, coffee pots and mugs of the period from 1745 to 1765 derived to some degree from earlier silver prototypes, and in certain cases the porcelain shape can be traced back to its exact silver counterpart. One of the most engaging features of early English porcelain is this sympathetic fusion of Oriental or Continental decorative idioms with silver-inspired shapes.

The names of only a handful of the early modellers and painters are known to us today, because few records of the mid-eighteenth century factories have survived. Yet it is possible in some cases to identify the work of a particular modeller or painter, either from its high quality or through various idiosyncrasies peculiar to one hand.

CHELSEA

Chelsea holds a unique place in the history of eighteenth-century English porcelain, as being the single factory to concentrate its entire output on the luxury porcelain market.

Nicholas Sprimont, the proprietor of the factory and its guiding artistic spirit, was a Huguenot silversmith born in Liège in 1716. With his background in an essentially luxury trade, it was not surprising that Sprimont devoted his entire creative energies to making porcelain for the affluent and discerning echelons of London society. He made this intention clear in many contemporary newspaper advertisements for the factory, with their frequent references to 'The Quality and Gentry' and the 'Nobi-

WORCESTER COFFEE POT AND COVER, c.1754–55 (H17.5cm/6⅞in)

This shape is strongly influenced by contemporary English silver whereas the decoration is in the Chinese idiom.

lity'. In this endeavour he was assisted by the location of the Chelsea factory, near the fashionable Ranelagh pleasure gardens which had been opened to the public in 1742. Although Sprimont had no patron to subsidize his enterprise, he did have influential contacts, among them Sir Everard Faulkener, secretary to the Duke of Cumberland.

The history of the Chelsea factory falls into four distinct periods, each associated with a different mark. From time to time the chemical ingredients of the porcelain body and glaze were altered, probably to a greater extent than at any other factory.

INCISED TRIANGLE PERIOD

Sprimont's earliest porcelain forms, with their fluid lines, shell and marine motifs and asymmetrical curves, echo the sauceboats, dishes and salt cellars that he himself had created in silver. The Oriental influence evident throughout the first decade of the

factory found its earliest expression in the tea-plant and strawberry-leaf moulding on coffee pots, beakers and tea wares. Restrained painted decoration in European, Chinese and Japanese taste was used to accentuate and complement the powerful rhythm of the moulded designs, and a high proportion of the earliest Chelsea was left 'in the white'. This first period, during which an incised triangle was utilized, ended in March 1749, when Sprimont suspended sales of porcelain while the factory was moved to an adjoining site at the corner of Lawrence Street.

RAISED ANCHOR PERIOD

The relaunching of the factory was announced in the *Daily Advertiser* on 9 January 1750, summarizing the new stock as 'a great Variety of Pieces for Ornament in a Taste entirely new'. A recipe had been devised for a new porcelain body, suitable for a range of shapes and more utilitarian in both design and purpose than the Rococo forms of the 1740s. Perhaps symbolizing the dawn of a new era for the factory, a fresh mark was introduced: a raised anchor on an oval medallion.

The years between 1750 and 1756 were the most successful for the factory in both artistic and commercial terms. Every aspect of its production, relating to shapes, patterns and figure modelling, was permeated by the influence of Meissen. Yet at the same time the beautiful soft white body with its waxy glaze, whitened by the addition of tin oxide, bestowed upon these Chelsea wares a tactile dimension unmatched by hard-paste porcelain. Three principal decorative themes were preeminent: the Kakiemon style, floral designs, and figure and landscape scenes.

Kakiemon patterns, inspired by late seventeenth-century Japanese porcelain, had been popular at Meissen since the 1720s. The designs were composed of such motifs as flowers, banded hedges, Oriental birds, trees and bamboo, all painted in the distinctive Kakiemon palette which included iron-red, dark-green, yellow,

CHELSEA COFFEE POT AND COVER, c.1744–49 (H22cm/8¾in)

This classic Chelsea form is probably derived from repoussé silver and may have been intended for holding chocolate. The 'teaplant' moulding, sometimes picked out in enamel colours, was confined to the first few years of the factory's lifetime, when an incised triangle mark was utilized as with this piece.

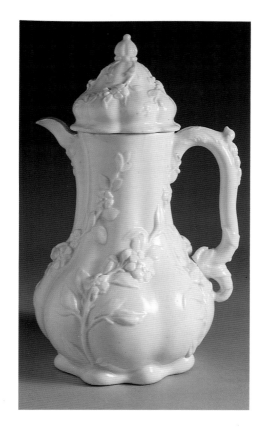

CHELSEA PLATE, c.1752 (20cm/7¾in)

Decoration in the Kakiemon taste, inspired by late seventeenth-century Japanese porcelain, but derived directly from Meissen, was very popular at Chelsea during the early 1750s. Shapes were characteristically octagonal or hexagonal and the palette was dominated by a beautiful iron-red, subtly enhanced by gilding.

turquoise and blue, often embellished with a subtle use of gilding. Floral designs tended to be either in the Meissen taste, or echoed the vibrant palette and almost botanical detail of Vincennes. Landscape and harbour scenes were loosely based on those executed by C.F. Herold at Meissen, either in enamel colours or puce monochrome. A speciality of the factory was the depiction of fable subjects, principally drawn from engraved illustrations by Francis Barlow, of *Aesop's Fables*, published in 1687. Much of this painting was the work of Jefferyes Hamett O'Neale, an accomplished miniature painter who endowed his fable subjects with a whimsical humour, often evident in the facial expression of his animals.

Some potting shapes were of Japanese derivation, translated through the medium of Meissen, while others were inspired by silver originals. In the 1750s, the expanded production of figures, birds and animals was almost entirely adapted from Meissen. The majority were the work of the principal Chelsea modeller, Joseph Willems. His creations had none of the biting sense of caricature of their German prototypes, but instead a more gentle satire was conveyed by less angular modelling and softer outlines. The colours were restrained in tone and for the most part, sparingly used. Chelsea models of the mid-1750s are widely considered to be among the finest of all English figures.

RED ANCHOR PERIOD

In about 1753 a new mark was introduced, this time an anchor painted in red. A year or so later, a new formula further modified the porcelain body, adapting it to the manufacture of the more elaborate forms that were coming into vogue. The glaze lost much of its tactile allure and became more transparent and prone to crazing, possibly due to underfiring in the kiln. This new body, however, had the advantage of permitting much thinner potting, and wares became correspondingly lighter in weight.

By this time, the output of the factory had greatly expanded both in quantity and variety. The celebrated fruit and vegetable forms belong to this period, as does the range of animal and bird tureens. The sense of grandeur of the Chelsea production is conveyed by the surviving catalogue of the second of a series of auctions held by Sprimont, in St. James' Hay Market in March 1755. Alongside the domestic wares, vases and figures from the previous year's production are listed Partridge tureens, sunflower leaves, cabbage lettuces and 'artichoaks'. Still more exotic were tureens formed as fighting cocks, carp, eels, boars' heads and even 'a beautiful tureen in the form of a Swan large as life in a fine dish'. This shift in emphasis towards naturalistic themes reflected the continuing influence of Meissen. Yet by contrast, the botanical decoration, mainly on plates and dishes, seems to have been original and must be counted among the foremost achievements of the factory. The production of botanical motifs was stimulated by the proximity of the Chelsea Physick Garden, on land leased from Sir Hans Sloane. Despite an impression of scientific accuracy these botanical designs were laid out for decorative effect. Several designs, however, match illustrations from the first volume of *Figures of Plants* (London, 1755) by Philip Miller, the curator of the Garden, whilst others have been identified as being copied from botanical illustrations after Georg Dilnysius. An advertisement for the Chelsea factory in *Faulkner's Dublin Journal* for July 1st, 1758, describes 'Table Plates, Soup Plates, and Desart Plates enamelled from the Hans Sloane's Plants'.

A speciality at Chelsea from the early 1750s onwards were the so-called 'toys', miniature scent bottles, seals, étuis and bonbonnières. These delightful little pieces were also made at the 'Girl-in-a-Swing' factory, so-named after its most celebrated figure subject. This mysterious class of porcelain, with its elusive connection with the Chelsea factory, was produced from about 1752 until 1754. Apart from the 'toys', its idiosyncratic output was limited to a relatively small range of figures and an even smaller production of domestic wares.

CHELSEA PLATE, c.1755 (24cm/9⅜in)

CHELSEA PLATE, c.1755 (24cm/9⅜in)

Botanical subjects were a speciality of the Chelsea factory during the mid and late 1750s. They depicted specimens of plants, fruit, vegetables, flowers, leaves and insects, some taken from contemporary book illustrations. Others were more imaginatively devised for the exotic nature of their visual impact. This piece is marked with a red anchor.

GIRL-IN-A-SWING SUGAR BOX AND COVER, c.1752–54 (H13.4cm/5¼in)

This mysterious class of porcelain is mainly confined to miniature pieces, or 'toys', and figure subjects.

GOLD ANCHOR PERIOD

The prosperity of the Chelsea factory was interrupted early in 1757 by Sprimont's ill health. By the time of his recovery, a year or so later, the influence of Sèvres had replaced that of Meissen. This final 'gold anchor' period was characterized by the addition of bone ash to the porcelain body, a greatly increased use of gilding, the introduction of ground colours, including the celebrated mazarine blue, and a far greater elaboration of both shape and colouring on tableware and vases. Bird and fruit decoration remained popular and was painted with the greatest élan, as were the fanciful chinoiserie figures in the manner of Watteau. Garnitures of three, five or even seven vases were often of the utmost opulence, with the last excesses of the Rococo gradually yielding to the Neoclassical symmetry of Sèvres. Figures, derived both from Meissen and Sèvres, were more fully and richly painted, often with sumptuous gilding and elaborate bocages. This last period at Chelsea drew to an end in August 1769, when Sprimont sold the factory.

BOW BASKET,
c.1754–56
(D23cm/9in)

*The 'Partridge' or
'Quail' pattern was
derived from Meissen,
though it originated
on Japanese porcelain.
It was used at Bow on
a wide range of wares,
from the early 1750s
until the mid 1760s.
Openwork baskets of
this type were made in
three sizes.*

CHELSEA GROUP,
c.1765
(H32.5cm/11⅞in)

*One of a pair of
marked gold anchor
groups emblematic of
'Winter' and 'Summer'
from the Seasons. The
relatively small heads
are typical features of
Chelsea figures.*
(ABOVE)

CHELSEA VASE,
c.1765

*The influence of Sèvres
is strongly evident in
this elaborate form,
decorated with a
Mazarine blue ground,
richly gilded with
exotic birds. The vase
is marked with a gold
anchor.* (RIGHT)

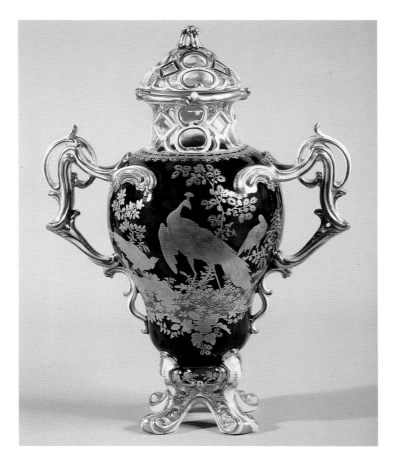

BOW

Founded in 1744 by Thomas Frye and Edward Heylyn, the Bow factory shares with its metropolitan neighbour, Chelsea, the distinction of being one of the first two English porcelain manufactories. Of them, Bow sought a far wider market, its production ranging from fine figure models and vases, to a very large output of relatively inexpensive 'sprigged' and blue-and-white porcelain. Indeed, judging from the size of the factory and the number of hands employed, it seems likely that Bow was the largest of all the eighteenth-century English factories. The contrasting nature of their output, in terms of quality, quantity and marketing, suggests that far from being commercial rivals, Bow and Chelsea were, initially to some degree, complementary. The primary objective at Bow was to manufacture porcelain in imitation of the Japanese, and in particular the Chinese, for a thriving export market. The exterior of the factory was copied directly from the East India Warehouse in

*A comparatively late
example of the raised
prunus blossom or
'sprigged' decoration,
derived from Chinese
Fukien porcelain and
popular at Bow
throughout the 1750s
and early 1760s. The
moulded flowers
around the base,
picked out in
underglaze blue, are a
very rare feature.*

of cutlery. Blue-and-white remained a significant proportion of the Bow output through the 1760s. Perhaps the most outstanding decoration in this style were the powder-blue designs derived from early eighteenth-century Chinese porcelain. Yet by the late 1760s there was an overall deterioration in the standards of both the decoration and of the porcelain itself. Worcester patterns were imitated with more enthusiasm than subtlety and the Bow palette often degenerated into garishness.

FIGURE AND ANIMAL SUBJECTS

Throughout the 1750s and 1760s, a large range of figure and animal subjects was produced, outstripping every other factory

Canton and indeed the factory itself was styled 'New Canton'. Almost throughout the factory's history the bulk of its production was decorated in the Oriental taste and it was only in the last decade that European themes predominated. Bow used a bone-ash body rather than the glassy, lighter body of the Chelsea factory, which proved to be an important factor in its successful production of figures.

Prior to 1750, Bow's output was restricted to a small class of wares, mainly decorated either in the *famille-rose* taste or in underglaze blue. In 1749, John Weatherby and John Crowther joined the factory and from that time onwards, production increased rapidly. Apart from *famille rose* the prevailing styles of decoration were white wares 'sprigged' with raised prunus blossom, derived from Fujian porcelain, Imari patterns in underglaze blue and overglaze iron-red and gilt, and Kakiemon designs. The last were applied to a variety of wares from superb-quality vases and tankards painted with great panache and verve, to the vast quantity of domestic wares painted in the enduringly popular 'Partridge' or 'Quail' patterns. Overglaze transfer printing was done from about 1754 onwards, though not on the scale of the production at Worcester.

By far the greatest portion of the Bow output of the 1750s was its blue-and-white, particularly in the form of plates and dishes, for which its bone-ash body was especially suited. In the early 1750s, the underglaze blue was a bright vivid colour, but within a few years it became progressively darker. Patterns were almost invariably of Chinese derivation, although the influence of English delftware is often evident. Potting shapes generally followed Oriental forms, but the influence of silverware can often be discerned in the shape of sauceboats and tankards. Shell salts and centrepieces encrusted with applied shells and seaweed were a popular theme, left 'in the white', coloured, or in underglaze blue.

Designs of European flowers, though in the Meissen taste, were probably absorbed from Chelsea, and became popular at Bow in the late 1750s. Other non-Oriental idioms which date from this period include leaf-moulded forms, bird decoration and botanical painting, all themes derived from Chelsea, without ever attaining the excellence of that factory. Oriental figure decoration, scarce in the 1750s, became more common in the following decade, yet its quality was uneven by comparison with Worcester. Dinner services continued to be a speciality, together with a vast quantity

BOW COFFEE POT AND COVER, *c.*1752
(23cm/9⅛in)

This is a rare coffee or chocolate pot and cover displaying many features of early Georgian silver. The underglaze blue decoration, derived by way of Chinese porcelain, originated on Dutch delftware of the so-called 'Van Frytom' style, dating from the 1680s.

in quantity, if not always in the quality of the modelling. Classical subjects were something of a speciality and other popular models included pairs of 'sporters', cooks, musicians, monks and nuns, and allegorical subjects. The Seasons, The Continents, and The Elements were among the figures issued in sets of four.

Unlike the 'slip-casting' process used at Chelsea and Derby, Bow figures were press-moulded and consequently relatively heavy in weight. A few of the earliest Bow figures have a sculptural quality which places them among the finest English models, but most are notable less for their sophistication than for their rustic charm. A series of models which include the Muses have an engagingly primitive appearance, with their spirited

modelling, heavy-lidded eyes and somewhat simian facial features. These figures, heavy in weight, thickly glazed and often left 'in the white' were done by an unidentified workman, known only as 'the Muses modeller'.

It was not until about 1753–1754 that the Meissen influence on Bow models was fully manifested. The direct imitations of models by Kändler and Eberlein had an appealingly homespun naïveté, with their fresh colouring, innocent expressions and low mound bases. The typical Bow palette of the middle 1750s included an opaque light blue, yellow, crimson and a transparent emerald green, colours which sparkled on human figures and especially on the vivid range of bird models. The sheer

VAUXHALL

The Vauxhall China Works was the third main London porcelain factory, and spanned a period from about 1751–1764. Following a trial dig on the factory site in 1988, a class of porcelain previously attributed to William Ball of Liverpool was re-allocated to Nicholas Crisp of Vauxhall. The porcelain body was a soapstone recipe which would have contributed to more successful manufacture of tea wares than was attained at Bow.

The output of the Vauxhall factory consisted primarily of blue-and-white wares decorated in the Chinese taste, but also shared strong similarities with delft-

BOW FIGURE, c.1754–56 (20.5cm/8in)

The Thames Waterman can be identified by his distinctive Doggett's coat with its special badge worn upon the arm. The tone of the green on the coat and the floral decoration on the waistcoat and base, are especially typical of Bow during this period.

VAUXHALL CHAMBER CANDLESTICK, c.1755–60 (H5cm/2in)

The bright, vivid tone of underglaze blue, together with the fluid, delft-like style of decoration and the neat potting, are typical characteristics of Vauxhall porcelain.

exuberance of many of these Bow figures compensated for their often indifferent modelling, but by the 1760s the palette had lost its freshness and the modelling had degenerated further. Figures were perched upon high, Rococo-scrolled bases and often surrounded by elaborate bocages, with no surface left unpainted.

No factory mark was used at Bow, although a range of incised and painted marks occur, most notably the anchor and dagger mark of the 1760s. The existence of some 40 or so pieces of dated Bow is helpful in the chronology of shapes and styles of decoration. The factory, which had been experiencing a slow decline since the early 1760s, was finally sold in 1775.

ware, an inevitable influence in view of the immediate proximity of the Lambeth delft potteries. The tone of the underglaze blue is variable, but most typically it is a bright vivid colour which conveys the impression of being freshly painted. Potting shapes display a broad range of influences, embracing delftware, saltglaze stoneware, silver, Chinese porcelain and Bow. For a relatively small factory, there was a surprisingly varied production, including chamber and upright candlesticks, flowerpots, mortars, 'goat and bee' cream jugs and even snuff boxes. Alongside their tea wares, perhaps the most successful forms were sauceboats – over 20 different types are known.

The coloured wares fall into three

VAUXHALL MUG,
*c.*1755–60
(7.2cm/2¾in)

A delightful mug, its shape clearly influenced by contemporary English silver. The floral decoration is printed in outline colours and over-painted in enamels, a technique almost entirely confined, at this period, to the Vauxhall factory.

categories, one of which is of underglaze blue, embellished with overglaze iron-red and gilt, an Imari palette much used during the same period at Bow. The more conventional hand-painted polychrome decoration was usually either in the Chinese taste or of European floral designs, and was sometimes of superb quality. Many of the motifs have an elusive quality, drawing parallels with early Derby, 'Girl-in-a-Swing' porcelain and Chinese wares decorated in London. Significantly, in the light of Crisp's subsequent West Country connections, several Vauxhall shapes and decorative idioms foreshadow those at Plymouth. An innovation at Vauxhall was the use of polychrome transfer prints: this process involved printing in two or three outline colours which were then over-painted with enamels.

It is clear from contemporary newspaper advertisements that figures were made at Vauxhall, though none have so far been positively identified. It is likely that, in due course, some late Longton Hall models will be re-allocated to Vauxhall. Following the closure of the factory in 1764, Nicholas Crisp seems to have attempted to set up another at Bovey Tracey, near Exeter, and it was there that he died in 1774.

LIMEHOUSE

Almost our entire knowledge of the Limehouse factory, which was situated by the side of the Thames in the East End of London, is drawn from advertisements in the *Daily Advertiser*, between September 1746 and June 1748. It was probably in production from about 1745 to 1748, and the experiments conducted there pointed the way ahead for the more successful factories of the following decade. Contemporary advertisements imply that the Limehouse factory concentrated on blue-and-white china including a 'great Variety of Sauce-Boats, Tea-Pots etc.' Until the excavations on the site of the Limehouse factory, during the spring of 1990, no examples had been positively identified. Fragments and sherds have now been found of the class of porcelain previously attributed to William Reid's Liverpool factory. These wares, primarily teapots, sauceboats shell-shaped dishes and pickle leaves, nearly all decorated in underglaze blue, could therefore be firmly re-assigned to the Limehouse factory. Contemporary with the triangle period at

Chelsea, Limehouse was the first English factory to produce blue-and-white porcelain and, almost certainly, the first to use a soapstone formula. Many of the Limehouse shapes can be linked to contemporary salt-glaze stoneware and to George II's silver forms, whilst others foreshadow early Bow and Lund's Bristol.

LUND'S BRISTOL

Throughout the second half of the 1740s, attempts were made in London, Staffordshire and Bristol to produce porcelain. In 1970, excavations on the site of 'The Pomona Potworks' at Newcastle-under-Lyme in Staffordshire, unearthed a series of porcelain and pottery wasters, including a porcellaneous bowl dated '25th, July 1746' in underglaze blue, the earliest such piece ever recorded. However these discoveries were of a misfiring, involving kiln failure and as yet, no proof exists that porcelain was made successfully in that location in the 1740s.

Nevertheless, these extended and interconnected experiments finally bore fruit in 1750, when Benjamin Lund opened his factory in Redcliffe Backs on the River Severn at Bristol. Using a soapstone formula, and with the aid of workmen who had previously been at Limehouse, Lund concentrated chiefly on blue-and-white wares. A restricted range of shapes included teapots, mugs, coffee cans, patty pans, pickle leaves and shells, but perhaps significantly, virtually no teabowls, coffee cups or saucers. Some creamboats, sauceboats and white figures of Lu Tung-Pin, the Chinese immortal, bear on their bases the embossed mark 'Bristol' and the date 1750. Lund's porcelain was generally well potted, with a slightly heavy glaze and a tendency for the underglaze blue to blur, losing some definition and creating the illusion of the decoration being out of focus. It has never been satisfactorily resolved whether or not polychrome decoration was carried out at the factory.

c.1754–56 (D13.5cm/5¼in)

This rare shape was inspired by a silver original, but the pattern, sometimes used on English delftware, can be traced back to early eighteenth-century Chinese porcelain. No factory mark was used on Worcester porcelain until about 1760, but this piece bears the painter's mark.

WORCESTER

Early in 1752, Benjamin Lund's factory was 'united' with the Worcester factory, founded in the previous year by Dr. John Wall and 14 other partners, and situated in the grounds of Warmstry House, on the banks of the River Severn. The brief years of experimentation at Bristol account for the astonishing degree of sophistication evident in the Worcester production, almost from the start. Decorative idioms were mainly inspired by Chinese *famille verte*, and to a lesser extent, Japanese porcelain. Fanciful chinoiserie scenes were created, evoking a fairy-tale atmosphere of figures in loose-fitting robes, crane-like birds, meandering blossom and miniature islands. These delicate and elusive compositions adorned an array of delightful potting shapes, some derived from Oriental forms, but others, especially sauceboats, tankards and cider jugs, harking back to silver originals. Many of the earliest teaware shapes, including cream jugs, coffee cups and creamboats, with their lobed forms, cursive rims and elaborate Rococo handles, were more successful

from an aesthetic than from a practical standpoint, and by about 1755 shapes had generally become simpler in outline and much more functional.

These changes coincided with a period of rapid expansion, fuelled by the introduction of overglaze transfer printing, a greatly increased output of blue-and-white wares and, most particularly, an ability to produce tea wares which could withstand the impact of boiling water. In this endeavour, the soapstone body devised at Bristol, together with a tough and durable glaze, gave the Worcester factory an enormous advantage over its commercial rivals. Both patterns and shapes were strongly influenced by Meissen, yet the Rococo forms adopted by Chelsea, Longton Hall and Derby never found favour with the Worcester designers, probably because they were unsuited to the soapstone recipe. Floral and bird patterns echoed those of Chelsea, while the Oriental designs were generally derived from Meissen, rather than directly from the Chinese.

Transfer printing over the glaze was developed at Worcester from 1753–1754, and within two years or so, the factory was unequalled in its mastery of the technique

(5.7cm/2¼in)

A 'sparrow beak' cream jug painted in a brilliant, though subtle, famille-rose palette. This style of decoration, often appearing in association with elaborate shapes, was confined to the first few years of the factory's production.

WORCESTER 'KING OF PRUSSIA' MUG,
c.1757–58 (11.8cm/4⅝in)

WORCESTER OPENWORK BASKET,
c.1770–72 (25cm/10in)

The 'pine cone' pattern was the most popular of all the underglaze blue transfer prints at Worcester. It was used principally on plates, dishes and baskets of the 1770s, and was copied at other contemporary factories including Lowestoft and Caughley. This piece bears a crescent mark. (ABOVE)

WORCESTER BLUE-SCALE DECORATION,
c.1768–72

This is the most celebrated of the three underglaze blue grounds at Worcester, the others being gros bleu and powder blue. All occur in conjunction with European flowers, exotic birds, Oriental flowers and, more rarely, figure painting. These pieces are marked with a crescent, fretted square and 'W' marks. (LEFT)

in terms of output, quality, clarity and aesthetic effect. This was largely the work of Robert Hancock who was later to become a full partner at the factory. From the mid-1750s until the early 1770s, a standard of transfer printing was set which was unmatched by any other factory. Underglaze blue patterns, usually painted in the Chinese taste, echoed styles found on English delftware, and from the early 1760s onwards an increasing proportion was printed rather than hand-painted.

By the late 1760s, a more opulent style of decoration prevailed at Worcester. Alongside the more mundane floral and Chinese figure patterns, the 'Japan' patterns and those derived from Sèvres were coming into fashion. So too were the celebrated ground colours, including blue scale, powder-blue and *gros bleu*. These rich underglaze blue grounds were embellished with overglaze designs within circular, oval and mirror-shaped panels, which ranged from floral motifs and exotic birds, to landscapes and Oriental patterns, invaria-

bly enriched with gilding. Still more sumptuous were the overglaze grounds, among which were claret, yellow scale, green and turquoise, derived from several sources including Meissen, Sèvres and Chelsea. Increasingly, in all but the most simple patterns, the porcelain body had become primarily a canvas for painted decoration, and the balance between form and decoration had undergone a radical transformation. The gradual introduction of these coloured grounds, together with the increasing elaboration of the decorative idioms, coincided with the decline and eventual closure of the Chelsea factory.

It was perhaps the progressive decline of Chelsea which inspired the Worcester partners to establish a commercial outlet in London. In 1767, the factory entered into an arrangement with James Giles, an independent decorator, to supply white porcelain for him to enamel in his workshop in Berwick Street, Soho. For the next four years, until the termination of this agreement in 1771, the Giles atelier under-

took much of the most prestigious decoration on Worcester porcelain. Not only did Giles decorate the plain underglaze blue grounds sent from the factory, but he was also responsible for many of the overglaze coloured grounds and border designs. His fruit, flower and bird designs were characterized by a looser, freer composition than was typical of the factory decoration, utilizing such distinctive motifs as cut fruit, agitated birds and sumptuous ciselé gilding. For the most part, Giles' patterns reflect a Meissen influence rather than that of Sèvres, and at their best they outshine all the Worcester designs of the same period.

In the years from 1751 until the death of Dr. Wall in 1776, Worcester excelled in almost every facet of porcelain production. The factory was deficient only in the manufacture of figures, the soapstone body being unsuitable for that medium. The few models made were wooden in posture and have a lifeless quality, though their consequent scarcity causes them to be much prized by collectors.

The Worcester factory has the distinction of being the only eighteenth-century English porcelain manufactory to remain in continuous production until the present day. Unlike most of its early competitors, factory marks were used from the middle 1760s onwards, the most common of which were a crescent, a script 'W' and a fretted square, all in underglaze blue.

DERBY

The Derby factory, which began production in 1750, was unique among the early English factories because during the first six years of its existence its output was almost entirely limited to figures, vases and ornamental items. It was not until 1756, when William Duesbury took control, that production assumed a more conventional course. For the next 12 or so years, the influence of Meissen so permeated the potting shapes, decorative styles and figure models that

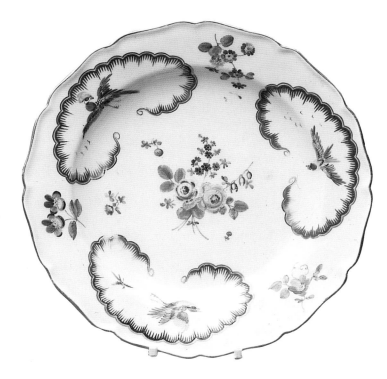

WORCESTER PLATE, *c.*1770–72
(22.4cm/8¾in)

Inspired by a Sèvres original, this plate was decorated outside the Worcester factory, in the London atelier of James Giles. His work can be identified by the loosely bunched central bouquet, the distinctive floral sprigs on the rim and the characteristic style of bird painting.

DERBY SUNFLOWER DISH, c.1756
(D16.5cm/6½in)

Naturalistic forms of this kind, echoing those at Meissen in the 1740s, were popular at Derby, Longton Hall and Chelsea during the mid-1750s. The opaque yellow is characteristic of early Derby wares.

'CHELSEA-DERBY'

In February 1770, Duesbury and his partner Heath acquired the recently closed Chelsea factory. For the next 14 years, both factories were in production, a phase widely termed as the 'Chelsea-Derby' period. A factory mark was employed for the first time, a capital 'D' conjoined with an anchor. With the purchase of the Chelsea factory came an improvement in the china body, through the addition of bone ash, first used at Chelsea in 1758. The Sèvres influence had by now superseded that of Meissen, and was evident in both the Neoclassical forms of the 1770s and the formalized patterns of classical urns, festoons of flowers, putti and cherubs. At the same time, the first of the Derby 'Japan' patterns made their appearance, a style which was to remain strongly associated with the factory for the succeeding 100 years. On a grander scale were the claret and turquoise ground colours, though these seldom reached the quality of their Chelsea and Worcester counterparts.

FIGURE AND ANIMAL SUBJECTS

From the very earliest period, figure models were a crucial component of the Derby production and for the next 20 years only the Bow factory could rival their output. The earliest models were the work of Andrew Planché, and his figures and animals, most often left 'in the white' but sometimes coloured, are perhaps the most outstanding examples of English figure modelling. They embody the vitality and spontaneity of the best Continental figures and have a dynamic energy and spirit most appropriate to such sculptural subjects as 'Pluto and Cerberus', the 'Florentine Boars', the 'Charging Bulls' and the 'Pair of Goats'. Chinoiserie groups representing the Senses, as well as more derivative models such as shepherds, seasons and classical subjects have a vigour and rhythm which is entirely free of the static, posturing sentimentality of many English figures. Planché's figures are usually termed 'dry

contemporary newspaper advertisements describing the factory as '. . . the Derby or second Dresden . . .' were no more than candid. Shapes of the 1756–1765 period included circular and oval openwork baskets, asymmetrical Rococo vases, leaf-moulded plates and dishes, sauceboats, mugs and conical coffee pots. Tea wares were uncommon until after 1760, because the porcelain tended to crack on the impact of boiling water, a problem which remained with Derby for the next 20 years.

DECORATION

The decoration on Derby wares was most often of freely drawn floral designs, in a predominately iron-red tone, by a hand known as the 'cotton-stem' painter. Moths, butterflies and even fruit were scattered on the borders which surrounded bird and landscape patterns. Most remarkably, on English porcelain, the decoration on tableware was strongly linked to that on figures. Leaf-moulded dessert dishes, vine-leaf dishes and fruit forms often echoed

those of the red anchor period of Chelsea.

A more distinctive Derby idiom was tiny figures in landscapes, which occurred on characteristic Derby shapes such as ink sets, pot-pourri vases and covered salts with mask handles. Foot-rims during this period were customarily ground, and flatware, when held up to transmitted light, showed 'moons' or captured air bubbles in the paste, a phenomenon also found on Chelsea porcelain. The Derby palette up until the late 1760s had a fresh, delicate and slightly pastel feeling, entirely appropriate to the ornamental forms that they adorned.

Underglaze blue painting, first used in about 1758, never attained the commercial significance it had at Worcester, Bow and elsewhere. Initially, it was used on the same baskets, dessert dishes, butter tubs and shell centrepieces more frequently decorated in colour. The blue was a bright rich colour, most impressive when seen in the border designs of the period. Somewhat less common was the underglaze blue printing, introduced in about 1764, but with limited technical or artistic success.

CHELSEA-DERBY
PLATE, *c*.1775
(23.6cm/9¼in)

*This plate bears a
gold anchor mark.*

edge', a description which originates from the characteristically unglazed area around the bases of most models.

Like all Derby figures, the models of the middle 1750s were slipcast, and many were decorated in attractively pale colours. They tended to be light in weight and often had a blue tinge to their glaze. Models invariably imitated Meissen originals and both human figures and birds were openly advertised as 'after the finest Dresden models'. From about 1760 the palette became stronger and the modelling lost some of its delicacy and vitality. Many subjects were issued in several sizes and they became progessively more fully decorated. By the middle 1760s, bases had become higher and more scrolled and bocages were more prominent. Classical subjects remained popular, as did themes from contemporary life, albeit in a somewhat idealized guise. In contrast to the preceding decade, where it had been used with the greatest restraint, gilding was

PAIR OF DERBY FLORENTINE BOARS,
c.1750–54 (L12.7cm/5in)

*These magnificent boars convey something of the
strength and vitality of the modelling on the
earliest Derby figures.* (ABOVE)

DERBY 'EUROPA AND THE BULL',
c.1765–68 (H28cm/11in) (RIGHT)

applied lavishly, emphasizing the impression that the lower standards of modelling were being masked by a fecundity of painted decoration. Patch marks on the bases of figures, a distinguishing characteristic of Derby, resulted from the practice of standing them on pads of clay during the process of glaze firing.

Figures of the so-called 'Chelsea-Derby' period continued many of the themes of the previous decade, though the influence of Sèvres had become increasingly apparent. Unglazed models, left 'in the biscuit' were often of superb quality, because they were spared the inevitable blurring of detail caused by the liquid glaze. Other innovations of the 1770s included a vogue for national heroes such as John Wilkes and General Conway, theatrical subjects, and, especially, allegorical groups such as Leda and the Swan, some of which had been first issued in the previous decade. Indeed, many models, such as Apollo, and Venus and Cupid, which originally dated back to the Planché period of manufacture, were re-issued in the 1770s, though by this time their sculptural vigour and rhythmic vitality had been diluted beyond recognition.

LONGTON HALL

The motivating creative force behind the Longton Hall factory, founded in Staffordshire in 1750, was William Littler. His earliest products were a class of white figures of birds, animals and human models, which from their thick glaze, glassy paste and poorly defined features have come to be known as the 'snow-man family'. This was the initial, experimental stage in the development of what was almost certainly the first Staffordshire factory to succeed in manufacturing porcelain, and it set an illustrious precedent for a long and distinguished tradition.

From 1753 onwards, the figures and tableware lost much of their primitive appearance, though both the decoration and the shapes retained a distinctive visual impact which was firmly rooted in Littler's earlier experience as a maker of saltglaze stoneware. The domestic output was distinguished by a fine series of leaf-moulded plates, dishes, pierced baskets, sauceboats, fruit and vegetable forms and strawberry-moulded flatware. Although derived from Meissen, the freshness of the yellowish lime-green on the leaf-moulding, and the charming flower and bird painting, lend these pieces an unmistakably English appearance. Idyllic rural scenes of castles and ruined arches set in typically English landscapes serve to emphasize this impression. The patterns in the Chinese *famille-rose* style have a skittish vitality, especially in the treatment of geese-like birds, whereas floral decoration in the Chelsea manner often has an engagingly tentative quality. The Longton Hall palette owes much to saltglaze colours and is unlike that of any other factory. Potting shapes were freely adapted from Meissen, saltglaze stoneware and, sometimes, directly from the Chinese; handle forms, in particular, were frequently of a complicated and rustic-looking double-scroll form. Overglaze transfer printing was done on a limited scale, but by Sadler at Liverpool rather than at Longton Hall. Blue-and-white was produced almost throughout the factory's lifetime, the painted patterns being almost always in the Chinese taste, as interpreted through English delftware. The underglaze blue decoration was usually executed with a pleasing freedom, though the painting had a tendency to 'run'.

The most characteristic Longton Hall figures have a delightfully fluid rhythm and are full of eccentric movement. Subjects such as flower-sellers, topers and grape-sellers lean to exuberant and unlikely angles on their slightly clumsy Rococo bases. While hardly sophisticated, this modeller developed a truly original style not seen in other English figures. More conventional models were derived from Meissen, and in some cases, directly from saltglaze. Inspiration from sculptural sources was expressed in the well-known 'Hercules and the Nemean Lion' and also in the pairs of cupids on galloping horses. The colouring on Longton Hall figures included the typical yellow-green, crimson pink and, more incongruously, the deep underglaze 'Littler's blue'. The later figures, possibly influenced by gold-anchor Chelsea models, are often much larger in size and atypical in their paste and glaze. This class of figures, some of which are marked with an impressed 'K', may await re-attribution to the Vauxhall factory.

Following the closure of Longton Hall in 1760, Littler moved to West Pans, near

LONGTON HALL
SAUCEBOAT,
c.1755–58
(H11.5cm/4½in)

A characteristically rustic Longton Hall shape, which also occurs decorated in underglaze blue. The puce veins and the distinctive tone of lime green are typical of this factory.

Musselburgh, in Scotland. There, from about 1764 until the mid-1770s, he and his wife Jane produced a range of domestic wares, often based upon earlier Longton Hall shapes, though in a much coarser, more granular body. Decoration was typically in a rich ultramarine underglaze blue, but some of the overglaze floral painting was attractively executed, in a dryish-toned palette. As at Longton Hall, no factory mark was used, though some West Pans porcelain bears an enigmatic crossed 'L's mark in underglaze blue.

LIVERPOOL

It is clear that there were at least four or five different factories producing porcelain in Liverpool between 1754 and 1799, though much research still remains to be done about their proprietors, their exact locations in the city, and in one or two instances, the nature of the porcelain they produced there.

GILBODY

Samuel Gilbody's factory, in production from about 1754–1761, was responsible for some of the most attractive of all Liverpool porcelain. Examples are relatively scarce and not always readily identifiable, because his products varied greatly in quality. Vases and mugs were something of a speciality and decoration commonly showed a saltglaze influence also apparent on many potting shapes, handle forms and potting mannerisms. Typical colours included a soft-toned pink, a deep yellow and a rich brown, and the decoration was sometimes of outstanding quality. Wasters excavated on the factory site testify to the production of blue-and-white porcelain, which probably accounted for at least two thirds of the output. The underglaze blue was generally a dark, slightly inky tone, with a tendency to run, thus blurring the pattern. Overglaze transfer printing was done, though evidently on a very limited scale, and most examples of this work appear on mugs. A small number of figure subjects are known, among which are a shepherd, after a Derby original, Minerva, and a version of the 'Rustic Seasons'. At its best, the phosphatic body has a smooth shiny glaze, silky to the touch. Yet such were the technical difficulties experienced, that by no means all the products attained the highest standards. As with all the Liverpool china-makers, no factory mark was used.

CHAFFERS

The Liverpool factory of Richard Chaffers belongs to the mainstream tradition of porcelain production in the city. Situated on Shaw's Brow, not far from the Gilbody site, the factory was in production from about 1754 until 1765. At first, a bone-ash body was used, but within two years or so, Chaffers adopted a soapstone recipe. The most successful and ambitious patterns tended to be chinoiserie and Chinese figure subjects and bird decoration, all seen to best effect on mugs and large cider jugs. Floral designs, though restrained in style, were less derivative than the stock Oriental

LONGTON HALL
FIGURES,
c.1756–58
(taller:H14cm/5½in)

The animated postures, cherubic faces, yellowish green scrollwork bases, are typical features of the rustic subjects that were a speciality of this Staffordshire factory. Although unsophisticated by Meissen standards, the modelling has great vitality and sense of movement.

and 'Japan' patterns borrowed from Worcester. Many shapes, too, were adapted from Worcester, yet most display unmistakable Liverpool potting features, such as the flattened strap handles on coffee pots, mugs and coffee cups, and the broad, rounded, and often upturned lips of cider jugs. Overglaze transfer prints were the work of John Sadler, characterized by their sepia tone and seen to advantage in Masonic and commemorative themes. In common with all the Liverpool factories, underglaze blue decoration formed a substantial proportion of the output, sometimes with the addition of iron-red and gilding, an embellishment with implications that were perhaps more commercial than aesthetic. Landscape designs were strongly and often simply drawn, and one, the 'Jumping Boy' pattern, occurred frequently on neatly potted octagonal tewares.

THE CHRISTIAN FACTORY

After Chaffers' death in 1765, Philip Christian, his principal partner, continued to produce soapstone porcelain on the same site. The polychrome patterns were for the most part either simple floral designs or Chinese figure motifs, very much in the manner of Worcester. Generally, the palette was stronger than in the Chaffers' period, with a vivid green, a bright yellow and a characteristic purple-mauve, together with a free use of white enamel. Overglaze transfer prints were done at the factory in a grey tone, quite unlike Sadler's work, and they occur primarily on tea wares. By comparison with Chaffers' porcelain, the blue-and-white was more carefully painted, with finer outlines and patterns often peppered with dots. The underglaze blue was a paler tone than that of Chaffers', though the later transfer prints tended to be heavy, dark-toned and less satisfactory. Moulded coffee- and teaware were a speciality, and sauceboats, jugs and some mugs had ornate handles with terminals moulded as a biting snake. The potting was thin, crisp and neat, and the moulding was also of excellent quality.

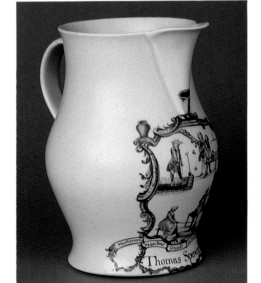

LIVERPOOL CIDER JUG, c.1762–65 (17.5cm/6⅞in)

A fine Chaffers Liverpool cider jug inscribed 'Thomas Spencer' and decorated with scenes of a potworks.

PENNINGTON BROTHERS (AND OTHERS)

The class of porcelain at present ascribed to the Pennington brothers – James, John and Seth – is so disparate in terms of paste, glaze, decoration, technical quality and general appearance, that it seems almost certain that it will ultimately be subdivided into at least three separate factories. Of the three Pennington brothers, one continued the factory at Shaw's Brow, vacated by Philip Christian in 1776, while another, possibly James, occupied a factory on Brownlow Hill. From this confused situation, it is possible to isolate provisionally three distinct groupings of Liverpool porcelain, all of bone-ash type. The earliest of these groups, which includes the most characteristic Liverpool shapes and decorative idioms, would seem to span a period of about 1765–1780. This group cannot have been produced by the Shaw's Brow factory, however, because it was occupied by Philip Christian for most of this period. Instead, another class of wares notable for polychrome floral and Chinese figure patterns, is a more likely candidate for the Shaw's Brow location. Still later in date is a group of poorly potted Liverpool wares, many of them transfer-printed in underglaze blue with debased versions of the 'Quail' and 'Fisherman' patterns. Many dated examples from this grouping suggest that they were made during the last two decades of the eighteenth century.

LOWESTOFT

The Lowestoft factory, situated in a small fishing port on the Suffolk coast, was isolated from the main centres of the ceramic industry in England. This contributed to the individual nature of its products and also to the relatively slow pace of its stylistic development. Founded in 1757 by four partners – Philip Walker, Robert Browne, Obed Aldred and John Richman – it was Robert Browne who emerged as the leading figure and the manager of the factory. By the standards of the period, it was a small factory, employing no more than 70 workers, and at times, fewer, yet its comparatively long history accounts for the abundance of its surviving products. The recipe used was a bone-ash body, similar to that used at Bow and was probably obtained from a workman at that factory.

For the first 10 years, the Lowestoft production was entirely devoted to underglaze blue decoration. Patterns were in the Chinese style, showing a delightfully inventive delftware influence, and generally painted in a dark, inky tone of underglaze blue. Moulded decoration was used on such shapes as cider jugs, sauceboats and sometimes, teaware, with charming miniature Oriental landscapes, painted within oval and circular panels. Potting shapes were often derived from saltglaze stoneware, but until the 1770s the decorative impact of other porcelain factories was muted. Throughout the factory's lifetime a special feature was made of pieces which bore inscriptions and dates relating to births,

marriages and East Anglian towns and villages. These dated pieces, of which more than 200 examples are known, provide a crucial framework for the chronology of potting shapes, styles of decoration and the variations and alterations to the porcelain body over a period of more than 40 years.

From the 1770s onwards, the blue-and-white decoration lost much of its freshness and individuality. Among the range of shapes more or less unique to Lowestoft were pap warmers, feeding cups, flasks, preserve pots, and most distinctive of all, birth tablets. Made in both colour and underglaze blue, these were inscribed with a child's name and date of birth, though their exact function is uncertain.

Coloured decoration, first used on a restricted scale in the late 1760s, gradually became an important part of the Lowestoft production. Floral and Chinese figure subjects predominated, alongside the 'Redgrave' patterns, in underglaze blue and

LOWESTOFT MUG, c.1762–65 (11.5cm/4½in)

This bell-shaped mug, illustrating the unpretentious almost childlike painting seen on so much Lowestoft porcelain, bears the painter's numeral. On later examples, the underglaze blue becomes brighter and the decoration more stylised.

LOWESTOFT TEAPOT, 1774 (H14.5cm/5¾in)

Inscribed 'Maria Hoyle' and 'Norwich 1774', this teapot exemplifies the slightly naïve style of painting typical of this relatively small East Anglian factory, supplying primarily a local market. The majority of the decoration was in the Chinese taste.

overglaze iron-red and gilt. For a brief period in the 1770s, the accomplished but anonymous 'Tulip painter' produced outstanding floral designs, which often featured a large full-blown tulip. For the most part the factory's polychrome painting was mundane and repetitive. By the late

1780s patterns in the Chinese export taste, and a little later, French sprig designs had been introduced alongside the still popular Mandarin patterns. A small number of figure models, mainly from the 1780s, included pairs of musicians, dancing putti, sheep, cats, pug dogs and swans.

Viewed dispassionately, much of the Lowestoft production, especially from 1770 onwards, has little to commend it artistically, yet its local interest, reflected in inscribed pieces, its varied range of potting shapes and the unpretentious nature of its decoration, lend it the appealing simplicity of folk art, an impression emphasized by the factory's dependence upon an essentially parochial market.

CAUGHLEY

The Caughley factory, situated on the River Severn some 64 kilometres (40 miles) upstream from Worcester, began producing porcelain in 1772. One of the Caughley partners, Thomas Turner, reputedly worked at Worcester, and it is understandable that the influence of that factory was widely evident, and its soapstone recipe closely followed. Indeed, during the 1770s and early 1780s a high proportion of the Caughley output imitated Worcester shapes and patterns, the 'Pine cone' and 'Fisherman' patterns being among the many underglaze blue printed designs that were 'borrowed'. Apart from some high quality blue-and-white patterns, confined to the earliest period, much of the hand-painting was of floral decoration in the manner of Chantilly, a factory much admired by Turner, executed in a bright tone of underglaze blue. Turner's main source of competition was the imported Chinese blue-and-white 'Nankin'-type porcelain, and these densely complicated chinoiserie designs were copied at Caughley on a large scale during the 1780s and 1790s. Nonetheless, although these Chinese wares were, perforce, imported from the other side of the world, they were still cheaper than the Caughley imitations, a vivid commentary on the economics of porcelain manufacture of that time.

This concentration on blue-and-white wares derivative of other porcelain makers was alleviated only by some commemorative pieces, mainly mugs and cider jugs, and a range of dessert wares with finely painted landscape and architectural scenes, after watercolours by Paul Sandby. The potting at Caughley was of a high standard, resembling and ultimately excelling contemporary Worcester wares. A wide range of shapes was produced including 'toy' tea services and such forms unusual in early English porcelain as flower pots, monteiths, sorbet cups, vinegar bottles, artichoke cups and even buttons.

Coloured wares were produced on a far more modest scale, many of them being simple underglaze blue designs embellished with gilding, often in a Neoclassical style. Floral patterns were less sophisticated, though some ambitious compositions were probably decorated at Chamberlain's Worcester factory. Unlike most other eighteenth-century English factories Caughley was frequently marked, either with a 'C', an 'S', or, on flat wares, with the impressed word 'Salopian'. In 1799, the Royal Salopian Porcelain Manufactory, as it was by then styled, was taken over by the proprietors of the nearby Coalport factory.

PLYMOUTH
AND BRISTOL

After numerous experiments over more than 20 years, the first commercially successful English factory of hard-paste, or 'true' porcelain, was established at Coxside, Plymouth in 1768. The proprietor William Cookworthy, a Quaker chemist, had been engaged since the 1740s in the search for a viable recipe for hard-paste porcelain. Understandably, the early products were of an uneven technical standard, and displayed such faults as smoke staining and kiln warping. Cookworthy had particular difficulty in firing plates and even saucers, yet, conversely, he was able to make figures and large ornamental vases. Certain overglaze colours persistently misfired and the underglaze blue was characteristically an unintended blackish tone. Oriental designs of flowers, figures and landscapes provided the main decorative idioms, although some typical bird decoration, loosely inspired by Sèvres, appeared on mugs, vases and cider jugs. Shapes, like the bulk of the painted designs, tended to follow Worcester prototypes, though some harked back to the Vauxhall factory. Shell salts and centrepieces encrusted with seaweed and shells were produced in colour, blue-and-white and also, as at Bow, 'in the white'. Figures, usually on high scroll bases picked out in brown-crimson, were sometimes of imposing size, as in the case of the 'Four Continents', but these were much prone to distortion in the firing, which caused them to lean slightly from the vertical. Most Plymouth models were Rococo in spirit, though less pretentious and overblown than their late Chelsea and Bow counterparts.

In 1770, Cookworthy transferred his factory to Castle Green in Bristol, a city with a deep-rooted potting tradition. By this time in his mid-sixties, Cookworthy took a less active part in the management of the factory, and by 1774 Richard Champion, a Quaker merchant, was in sole control. By comparison with Plymouth, Champion's porcelain was more conventional in its output, based primarily on tea and coffee services, and both shapes and decoration were inspired by Meissen and Sèvres rather than by Chinese porcelain. Neoclassicism, entirely alien to the backward-looking Plymouth style, was a fundamental theme in much of Champion's production. A far younger man than Cookworthy, he was quick to assimilate this new decorative idiom, which found expression in the Bristol 'named' services made for his special friends and customers. Gilding of superb quality was a feature at Bristol, and to obtain the finest effects it was 'laid on' a vermilion base which greatly enriched its tone. It was no coincidence that this device appeared mainly in conjunction with Neoclassical designs in the Sèvres taste, whereas the simpler Meissen compositions had plain brown-red borders. Alongside these prestigious Neoclassical wares, Champion

PLYMOUTH SAUCEBOAT, c.1768–70
(L14cm/5½in)

A distinctive Plymouth Rococo form, recalling a silver prototype. The piece bears a tin mark. (ABOVE)

CAUGHLEY JUG, c.1775–78 (14.6cm/5¾in)

Known in the eighteenth century as 'Dutch jugs', these cabbage-leaf moulded jugs were made at most of the principal factories. This piece bears a 'SX' mark. (TOP)

CHAMPION'S BRISTOL TEAWARES,
c.1775–76

A coffee cup, saucer and cream jug from the Leinster service, marked with a blue 'X'. Neoclassical decoration and gilding of superb quality, are characteristics of the more ambitious Bristol styles. (TOP RIGHT)

CHAMPION'S BRISTOL FIGURE, c.1775
(25.5cm/10in)

This figure is emblematic of 'Autumn', from a set of the 'Classical Seasons'. Bristol figures tend to be large in stature. (ABOVE)

found it necessary to produce humbler, less costly, domestic china, often decorated with simple green swags and presumably intended to subsidize his more ambitious endeavours. Yet perhaps the most individual component of the Bristol output was the series of biscuit plaques framed with decorative borders modelled in relief with festoons of flowers.

Whereas some Bristol figures resemble the earlier Plymouth models, many show the influence of Derby, and in particular, of the modeller Pierre Stephan. Figures tended to be large, a little wooden in their modelling, and often on either rock-work or rectangular bases. Classical subjects such as 'The Seasons' and 'The Elements' were vigorously modelled in the Sèvres style, while the massively conceived figures of 'The Goatherd' and 'The Milkmaid' evoke the sentimentalized world of Boucher. Yet alongside these derivative subjects were smaller, more original models, such as the 'Boy frightened by a Dog'.

A significant proportion of Plymouth porcelain was marked with the alchemist's sign for tin, either over the glaze or in underglaze blue. The majority of Bristol porcelain also bore a factory mark, a plain cross or, less often, a capital 'B'. Financial problems obliged Champion to close down the factory in 1781, and the patent rights were purchased by the founders of the Newhall factory in Staffordshire.

ENGLISH AND WELSH PORCELAIN 1780 TO 1820

The period covered in this chapter is the most important in the development of that most British of ceramics — bone china. In the late eighteenth century porcelain production was still dominated by various forms of soft-paste or soapstone porcelain made outside the Staffordshire area. By 1820, bone china predominated and its manufacture was largely concentrated in the Staffordshire Potteries set up in the latter part of the period.

The change was revolutionary. The production centres moved, the materials altered and the shapes and styles of decoration changed. These evolved from the Neoclassicism of around 1780 to the exuberance of the Regency, which ended in 1820.

By 1780, London had lost its pre-eminent position in porcelain manufacture. William Duesbury of Derby purchased the Chelsea factory in 1770 and, though some wares were produced in London until the final closure in 1784, its great days were over. In 1776 he bought and closed the Bow factory. Vauxhall had long vanished by 1780, as had Limehouse and the mysterious Girl-in-the-Swing factories.

In the provinces some centres of production, such as Bristol, were in decline, Lowestoft had some 20 years life left, and the old Liverpool stalwarts had been succeeded by the Penningtons. Derby and Worcester, however, flourished during this period. South Derbyshire had its time of glory, as did the Shropshire concerns at Caughley and Coalport, at times almost matching the achievements of Worcester.

COLLECTION OF ENGLISH PORCELAIN, 18TH TO EARLY 19TH CENTURY

Staffordshire plate, c.1810; Flight, Barr and Barr Worcester vase, 1813–40; Chelsea figure, gold anchor period, 1757–69.

LOWESTOFT

Unlike most other factories, Lowestoft remained true to its soft-paste formula until its closure *c*.1799, probably caused by growing financial difficulties, exacerbated by competition from Staffordshire. Interestingly, though, the later Lowestoft body contained about 30 to 45 percent of bone ash. This does not make it a bone china, however, because the other ingredients did not match those of the Staffordshire formula.

The inclusion of bone ash gave the late Lowestoft paste a very clean white appearance, though, typically, where the glaze is thin and the body is uncovered, a slightly brown discoloration can often be seen. On foot-rims and other exposed areas this is a particularly helpful aid to identification. The wares were not normally marked, except for painters' tally marks (from 1 to 8 are recorded) frequently found under foot-rims. Occasionally a crescent mark, presumably in emulation of that of the Worcester factory, is encountered.

There is a wide diversity of shapes but table wares predominate. A very few figures – either human or animal – are known. The most celebrated products are the various table wares decorated with 'A Trifle' from Lowestoft (or, more rarely, Bungay). These were painted either in underglaze blue or in *famille-rose* enamels, with patterns akin to Staffordshire designs known generically as 'New Hall', but which owe their origin to Chinese export porcelain. It should be pointed out that the terms 'Chinese' or 'Oriental Lowestoft' used in old reference books are erroneous – there is no such product and the wares illustrated are Chinese export pieces.

However, Lowestoft did produce imitations of Chinese Mandarin-type patterns, usually with pink-scale borders, including some very handsome vases.

As with every other English factory of the period, Lowestoft underglaze blue was competing with the vast quantities of imported blue-and-white Chinese porcelain. Lowestoft's later blue-and-white lacks some of the liveliness and vigour of the early pieces and its printed patterns were mainly emasculated versions of Worcester wares. Moreover, its Oriental-style decoration was out of tune with the Neoclassical style of the last quarter of the century. In the late 1780s and 1790s the factory did produce, somewhat belatedly, wares with classical outlines.

A number of Lowestoft pieces bear dates: every year from 1780 to 1799 is recorded (except 1785), and the factory was unique in producing rare named and dated birth tablets.

Never one of the foremost factories, Lowestoft produced pieces which have a special charm in their middle-class, somewhat provincial, naïveté. Norwich Castle Museum houses a splendid collection.

LOWESTOFT PEAR-SHAPED JUG,
c.1780–1800 (19.2cm/7½in)

The painting, typical of the factory during this period, is attributed to Robert Allen. The identity of Jeremiah Warner is not known. On the reverse is the verse: 'Success to the miller, Likewise to his wife, May they live happy, All days of their life.'

THE WORCESTER FACTORIES

After Dr Wall retired from the Worcester factory in 1774 it continued with little alteration under the management of William Davis. The wares are almost indistinguishable from those of the Wall period. The same marks were used with the addition of printed pseudo-Chinese characters containing disguised numerals. The wares on which they appear are inferior to earlier examples.

In 1783 the factory was purchased by John Flight, the firm's London agent who worked the factory with his sons Joseph and John producing mainly tea wares. The old styles and marks continued although, occasionally, the word 'Flight' is found. In 1792, after the death of his father, Joseph Flight formed a partnership with Martin Barr; the firm traded as Flight & Barr (from 1792 to 1804), and as Barr, Flight & Barr until Martin Barr's death in 1813. It then became Flight, Barr & Barr, continuing much as before. During this last period the quality of the wares was outstanding. They ranged from simply decorated tea wares of the 1790s to superb Regency vases and ornaments. The factory employed some of the leading painters of the period including Samuel Astles, Henry Stinton and Moses Webster (flowers), John Barker (shells), Solomon Cole, Thomas Lowe and John Pennington (figures), William Doe (insects), Jon Pitman (animals and game), Samuel Smith (shells and landscapes), Charles Stinton (fancy birds and flowers) and, most important of all, Thomas Baxter.

It is reported that the directors toured the factory exhorting the painters to treat their pieces as jewels and that they paid them by the hour and not by the piece – a rare practice in the industry. They did not need to advertise – the name and address in painted script was all that was needed.

The wares were finely enamelled, usually in panels on coloured grounds applied by the oil and dusting process which gave a smoother, deeper result than the brush. The gilding was applied with mercury and burnished to produce a hard, bright finish. The hand-rolled 'pearls' are far more effective than the moulded beads used by most factories. The body, although hard in appearance, was a soapstone formula with a rather grey tint.

The Davis/Flight/Barr factory was soon to have a rival in Worcester. Robert Chamberlain, who had been the chief decorator at the factory, left in 1786 and started up on his own as an independent decorator, mainly of Caughley wares. In about 1791 he began to manufacture on his own account using a hybrid hard paste. Chamberlain was soon producing a wide range of tea, dessert and ornamental wares to a high standard. Among the most attractive are those decorated with local scenes such as Malvern Abbey or views of

CHAMBERLAIN WORCESTER inkstand, c.1815 (H8.9cm/3½in)

A typical example of the fine Regency-style decoration for which the factory was famous. The potting, gilding and painting are all of the highest quality. (BELOW)

Worcester and its cathedral. Most pieces are marked and always include the firm's name. Many wares bore pattern numbers; by 1820 these had reached 860.

The third factory in Worcester was that of Thomas Grainger. There is some doubt as to the precise nature of Grainger's early business but it seems likely that he started by decorating Coalport blanks. In about 1805 he began manufacturing on his own, and like Chamberlain used the hard-paste body. Grainger had several partners, and traded variously as Grainger & Wood, Grainger Lee & Co., and Grainger & Co.

In the early years of Grainger's factory few wares were marked and their identification is somewhat tentative. The wares are of a good standard if not quite of the superlative quality of the other two Worcester concerns. It is likely that Grainger sought a slightly lower level of the market than his two local rivals. From the evidence of the firm's pattern numbers, which had reached about 1350 by 1820, much of the production was concentrated on useful wares, more so than Chamberlain's, but good, well-decorated ornamental wares were also made.

THE SHROPSHIRE
FACTORIES

It is geographically appropriate to consider next the wares made in Shropshire. In 1775 the Caughley porcelain factory was established about a mile south of Broseley, by Thomas Turner and Ambrose Gallimore. It quickly commanded a market for medium-priced blue-and-white porcelain table wares, very close stylistically to those of nearby Worcester. Indeed, many of the wares bore the mark of a capital letter 'C' which could be – and still can be – easily mistaken for the Worcester crescent mark. 'S' for Salopian was also used. The wares were decorated with painted and printed underglaze blue

FLIGHT, BARR AND BARR vases, c.1810–40

The superb quality of this Worcester decoration is evident in the various scenes. The large vase is Barr, Flight and Barr of c.1810. (ABOVE)

chinoiseries and specimens are not uncommon. The soapstone body often has an orange translucency (compared with the Worcester body, which generally shows green), the glaze fits well and the whole effect is of neatly potted, trim wares.

In the late 1780s and through the 1790s much Caughley porcelain was decorated with enamels and gilding at Chamberlain's establishment in Worcester. For a brief period, from about 1795 to 1799, the factory turned to producing a hybrid hard paste, but surviving examples show a surprising number of faults and clearly the experiment was unsuccessful. In 1799 Turner sold his rights to the Coalport partnership who continued on the Caughley site until 1814 when all production was concentrated at Coalport.

closed the Caughley works, thus concentrating production on the one site.

Both John Rose and the Anstice partnership made hybrid hard-paste porcelain, but some time after the two were united John Rose appears to have changed to making a bone-china body. The wares of the two concerns are not easy to separate and it seems clear that there was much plagiarism between the two. Shapes are almost identical and the patterns strikingly similar, though each company maintained a pattern book, which enables the products of the two enterprises to be identified. The John Rose factory patterns had reached 999 by about 1818, and thereafter used fractional numbers – for example, 2/123. The Anstice concern produced more than 1400 patterns by the time it closed.

COALPORT
HARD-PASTE
DISH, c.1810
(26.3cm/10⅜in)

This typical Imari decoration is executed in the conventional palette of underglaze blue and on-glaze red and green with gilding.

The Coalport site, the surviving buildings of which house a fascinating ceramics collection as part of the Ironbridge Gorge Museum, was an important potting centre from the mid-1790s to 1926. The various partnerships are too involved to quote here, but in essence there were two factories side by side separated only by a canal: the John Rose Coalport china factory and, for the period 1803–14, the works of Anstice, Horton and Thomas Rose. In 1814 John Rose took the Anstice factory and

The standard at both factories was high and both made well-potted and heavily decorated tea wares. John Rose supplied the London decorating trade, including, notably, Thomas Baxter, with blanks.

Anstice wares carry no factory mark. At Coalport, in this period, marks are rare but the script 'Coalbrookdale' has been noted occasionally, though this mark and all others normally relate to the period after 1820. It is in this latter period that some of Rose's finest work was done.

DERBY

The factory that consistently attained the highest standards was located in Nottingham Road, Derby. In 1780 William Duesbury I was still in charge; on his death in 1786 his son William Duesbury II inherited a thriving factory. In 1795 he took Michael Kean into partnership; after Duesbury's death two years later Kean married his widow Elizabeth and continued to run the firm until 1811. In that year Robert Bloor, the firm's clerk, bought the entire concern, which he managed until mental ill-health forced his retirement in 1828. Throughout these changes of ownership and management the firm prospered.

Many factory records have survived enabling us to attribute wares to individual artists. They include Richard Askew, James Banford, William Billingsley, Zachariah Boreman, Thomas Brentnall, John Brewer, Robert Brewer, William Coffee, George Complin, Richard Dodson, Jockey Hill, William ''Quaker'' Pegg, George Robertson, Thomas Steel, Moses Webster and Edward Withers. This incomparable group of artists decorated the soft-paste Derby body with a wonderful array of flowers, fruit, and landscapes that often depict Derbyshire beauty spots. Shipping and camp life, country houses, literary episodes and mythological scenes were embellished with brilliant gilding. The primary drawback is that the creamy-coloured, finely crazed body is prone to some discoloration, particularly during the late Bloor period. Apart from cabinet pieces the firm produced everyday wares, especially in the Bloor period, though generally speaking their clientele was the upper-middle and aristocratic classes.

Figures, too, were produced, particularly the renowned biscuit figures, including shepherds and shepherdesses modelled by J.J. Spangler and William Coffee on copies after Sèvres. The City Museum and the Works Museum, both in Derby, have comprehensive porcelain collections.

The saga of William Billingsley begins at

DERBY PLATES, *c*.1790–1820

This display shows the remarkable range of the factory's output during the Regency period. The picturesque landscapes, flowers (by Billingsley) and figure subjects are enhanced by gilding of the highest quality. (RIGHT)

PINXTON TEAPOT, *c*.1800 (H15.3cm/6in)

A New Oval shaped teapot, decorated with a simple French sprig pattern. The shape is not dissimilar to one made by Flight Worcester. (BELOW)

BRAMPTON TEAPOT FROM THE 'DR. BOOT' SERVICE, *c*.1805

Made from hard-paste French porcelain from La Courtille and decorated at Brampton in Torksey, most of the pieces in this service are decorated with local Derbyshire views, including the factory site. (BELOW RIGHT)

Derby where he was one of the chief flower-painters. He left in 1795 to set up a porcelain factory at Pinxton. He had long been experimenting with porcelain bodies and believed he could produce a material equal, if not superior, to Sèvres soft paste. His stay at Pinxton was short, for he left in 1799. The wares manufactured there have a remarkably fine body; it is decorated, as might be expected, in styles reminiscent of Derby, with flowers and landscapes possibly by Billingsley himself. Many pieces, which were mostly table wares, had simple floral sprig patterns or gilt motifs. They were rarely marked, though pattern numbers are found occasionally. After Billingsley's departure the factory continued, possibly only decorating blanks until it closed in 1813. These rare Derbyshire wares represent something of a last stage – or even a lost cause – for the old eighteenth-century soft-paste porcelains. Pinxton porcelain was totally uneconomic; the future lay with Spode and his fellow Staffordshire producers of bone china.

From Pinxton Billingsley moved on to Mansfield where he bought porcelain to decorate from a variety of sources including France. He stayed in Mansfield for two years, from 1799 to 1801, and then moved to Brampton in Torksey where again he decorated wares bought in the white, some of which he inscribed 'Billingsley, Mansfield'. His next move was to Nantgarw and Swansea (see page 147).

HERCULANEUM
TEAPOT, c.1805
(L25.5cm/10in)

Attractively painted with a monochrome scene, this teapot is of Old Oval form. The shapes of the knob and handle are specific to the Liverpool factory.

THE LIVERPOOL
FACTORIES

By 1780 the early factories of Chaffers, Christian and Gilbody had all closed. From this date until 1820 there seem to have been four major sites producing porcelain. On Shaw's Brow, Seth Pennington and John Part occupied the old Chaffers and Christian factory from 1778 to 1799. Pennington continued with other partners until 1805. The wares attributed to Seth Pennington cover a very considerable range, but modern research has begun to throw doubt on some traditional attributions, and it seems likely that some of the wares should more correctly be assigned to John Pennington, who occupied the Folly Lane or Islington Pottery from 1779 to 1786 and was succeeded by his widow Jane until 1794.

Much underglaze-blue printed ware, often of a relatively poor quality, is attributed to the Penningtons, in particular badly modelled jugs with a biting snake handle. So too are polychrome wares that range from delicately potted tea wares with Chinese figures, to large vases decorated with scale patterns and floral and figure subjects. They hardly seem to have come from the same factory, and it may be some time before we can accurately attribute to individual potters the large production from these later Liverpool factories.

The situation is further complicated by the fact that there is strong documentary evidence of a porcelain factory on the Haymarket, which was run by Zachariah Barnes from 1783 to 1796. However, no wares can currently be reliably attributed to him. As the wares are unmarked from whatever source, the problems are intractable, if not totally insoluble.

Two classes of Liverpool porcelain of the period are more amenable. From 1795 to about 1800 the Islington site was occupied by Thomas Wolfe & Co. His hard-paste wares are also unmarked, but sherds of underglaze blue patterns have been excavated from the site and matched with complete pots. These pieces are extremely rare, and so far are confined to tea wares.

The second group is that associated with the Herculaneum Pottery established at Toxteth by Samuel Worthington in 1796. The workforce was largely recruited in Staffordshire and thus the wares have a distinct Staffordshire flavour. The principal products were various earthenwares with porcelain added only after 1800, but probably before 1805. Marks are few and far between; the word Herculaneum is occasionally found, and even more rarely an impressed capital 'L' would seem to be an authentic mark.

The earliest wares seem to be of a good-quality bone china with a glaze that has a slightly oily feel. They are mainly useful wares decorated with simple floral sprigs in the New Hall manner. Later wares include vases in the Paris style with excellent gilding and accomplished painting. There are also characteristic tea wares, some with shapes unique to the factory decorated with finely painted landscapes, floral studies and, on one service, superb mythological scenes. High-quality 'bat'-printed wares are not uncommon but the production of these pieces seems to have ceased some time in the late 1820s to early 1830s. Much further research is needed on this important aspect of the factory's production, which has tended to be overshadowed by the great creamware jugs and bowls that were exported to the United States and elsewhere in considerable quantities. The porcelain wares, usually unmarked, often carried pattern numbers and these seem to range from 1 to about 1400.

NEW HALL

Like Liverpool, Bristol had for many years been an important potting centre, as well as a major port. There, Richard Champion produced hard-paste porcelain to William Cookworthy's formula. But Champion made substantial losses on his wares and in 1781 he visited Staffordshire with the object of either moving his factory there or, more likely, in

order to sell his patent. The outcome was the setting up of a company of Staffordshire potters, eventually to be known as New Hall. They operated in Shelton and manufactured a slightly modified form of hard-paste porcelain distinguishable by its somewhat grey tone, a lack of crazing in the glaze (though minute gas bubbles can sometimes be discerned), and its dense compact body. For the New Hall partnerships, it was a profitable venture. From 1781/2 wares were manufactured in hard paste, but, in about 1814, they changed to bone china.

The vast majority of examples are tea wares, with a few dessert wares, attractively decorated jugs and punch bowls, but virtually no ornamental pieces. They were aimed at a middle-class market. In the early days, wares were classical in shape and decoration (although this ran side by side with Chinese-style decoration usually of *famille-rose* flower sprays, or bold Mandarin patterns). Until well into the nineteenth century the wares carried no factory mark, but the large items found in a service often bore a pattern number. For hard-paste wares, these ranged from 1 to approximately 1000, though patterns both above and below this may be found in both bone china and hard-paste porcelain.

In the early period the rarest and most sought-after wares are those painted in a very characteristic style by the French artist Fidelle Duvivier. In the middle

period of the factory some fine services were decorated with overglaze bat prints of named country houses. These were sometimes left uncoloured, but the more favoured are those with additional overglaze enamel colours. This same technique was used for some prints after George Morland, fruit and flower groups, and attractive studies of women and children in the style of Adam Buck.

In the bone-china period, after about 1814, the silver-shape (or more correctly commode-shape) tea wares gave way to the New Oval shape and its several derivatives. These late wares have been far less studied than the early hard-paste pieces. They sometimes, but rarely, bear the printed

NEW HALL HARD-PASTE TEA WARES, *c*.1782–87

This fluted drum-shape is extremely rare. It is a fine example of the restrained nature of Neoclassical design. (ABOVE)

NEW HALL CHOCOLATE CUP AND STAND, *c*.1815–25 (H7cm/2¾in)

The piece is decorated with a bat print which has been coloured. It is one of many Adam Buck-type prints used by New Hall. (TOP)

NEW HALL HARD-PASTE TEA WARES, *c*.1795–1800

A typical Old Oval shaped teapot. These tea-ware shapes in hard-paste porcelain were closely copied by contemporary factories. (TOP LEFT)

factory mark of "New Hall" within concentric rings. According to the authority, Holgate, the pattern number sequence may have reached 3600 by the time of the factory's closure in about 1835.

To complicate matters somewhat, in the period from about 1790 to 1810, several factories, almost certainly in Staffordshire, made hard-paste wares in emulation of New Hall. These unmarked wares are still unidentified and have been arranged in several groups designated Factory X, Factory Y and Factory Z. It was, however, a tribute to the success of the New Hall factory that others copied both their material (the hybrid hard-paste porcelain) and their shapes and forms of decoration.

Not all such imitators are anonymous. There are rare examples from the Turner factory (from the period 1790–1795), and more plentifully from Davenport, Coalport, Anstice, Horton & Rose, Miles Mason, Chamberlain's and Grainger's Worcester, and from the mysterious and unidentified factory whose wares are marked with the impressed "W(***)". Most of these hybrid hard-paste wares are of good quality and are for the most part well made, such as the Coalport dish, the Chamberlain inkstand and the Davenport bulb pot (illustrated on p. 146). But even while these fine pieces were being potted, the most significant of all developments was taking place at the Spode factory.

SPODE

The Spode Pottery was established on its present site in 1770. Shortly before the death of the founder Josiah Spode I, experiments had been conducted in porcelain production. These were brought to fruition by Josiah Spode II some time between about 1797 and 1798. Recent research suggests that Spode had produced some examples of hard-paste porcelain, and it was by using the basic ingredients of hard paste – china clay and china stone – to which was added calcined

JAMES NEALE & CO. JUG AND COVER,
*c.*1785–95 (11.5cms/4½in)

Neale's rare tea wares are beautifully potted in prototype bone china. The decoration is invariably restrained and classical.

animal bone (from 33 per cent to as much as 50 per cent of the mix), that bone china, the material that was to revolutionize the industry, was produced. The addition of bone ash to the body was well known at Bow and Lowestoft – both used it, for example – and indeed it seems that James Neale of Hanley had produced a prototype of bone china in the late 1780s. The potting and decoration of his very rare wares are of outstanding delicacy. But if the Spode Pottery did not invent bone china, it certainly perfected it and marketed it supremely well, to such an effect that by 1820 it had ousted all the old eighteenth-century soft pastes as well as the New Hall-style hard pastes. That development has provided the basic material for English porcelain for nearly two centuries. It works well in the clay and has a lower firing temperature than hard paste, which saves fuel. It is stable in the kiln, and has a marvellous (some say too perfect), clean white finish, excellent translucency and a close-fitting glaze which takes all types of decoration with the minimum of difficulty. Spode's triumph set the seal on Stafford-

shire's pre-eminence as the centre of porcelain production in England.

Spode not only developed bone china, but also set a standard of excellence in both potting and decoration that others strove hard to equal. Almost from the first, Spode's china was devoid of any of the faults that occasionally beset its competitors. The Spode glaze does not craze, the ware does not go creamy, the enamel colours do not flake and the gilding is rich and glowing. From about 1800, when production got into full swing, until the end of the Spode period in 1833 (the firm became Copeland & Garrett at that date), Spode was the foremost Staffordshire porcelain producer. Its output spanned the entire range of tea, dessert and dinner wares, and the whole gamut of useful objects such as inkwells, pen-trays, incense burners, ornamental vases, pot-pourris and cabinet pieces. The wares were marked with the family name and more often than not with a pattern number. These advanced from 1 in about 1800 by annual steps of approximately 150 new patterns, thus reaching more than 1500 by 1810, 3000 by 1820 and in the region of 4700 by 1833.

Spode's blue-printed earthenware was probably the best in the industry, and its printing was carried through to the porcelain, where many items were decorated with attractive overglaze bat prints with scenes that were derived from Bartolozzi, George Morland, Richard Westall, Samuel Howitt and others. Prints can be found in grey, red, blue and even gold, but black is by far the most common. Being of overglaze the prints have occasionally become thin through use and wear.

Spode's polychrome painted and gilded wares from about 1805 to 1822 were the work of Henry Daniel and his team of artists and gilders. Uniquely in the industry, they were entirely separate subcontracted decorators working on the Spode site. Thus much of the credit for the consistently high quality and standard of Spode's decoration belongs by right to Daniel. After Daniel left to establish his own factory, the quality of decoration remained excellent, probably

because many of the workmen remained behind with Spode rather than following their old master. The range of decoration comprised the full gamut of taste with chinoiserie, Japan patterns, flower and fruit studies, picturesque landscapes and scenes from rural life, copies of contemporary paintings, designs inspired by literature and other sources, many richly finished in burnished and tooled gilding. Spode's wares are the epitome of the best of Regency taste.

MINTON

Within Staffordshire many other potters were quick to follow the lead of Spode. One of the first in the field was Thomas Minton. Established in 1793, Minton began producing bone china in about 1800. For some reason not yet fully understood, it was abandoned in about 1816 to be resumed in about 1824. During the first 16-year period more than 900 patterns were produced, some in the New

MINTON BONE CHINA TEA CUP AND SAUCER WITH MATCHING PATTERN BOOK, *c*.1802–05

Illustrating here pattern number 85, the Minton pattern books are useful for identifying pieces. (ABOVE)

SPODE BONE CHINA OLD OVAL TEA WARES, *c*.1806

Decorated with pattern 857, these pieces display typical Spode shapes; note especially the handle forms. Other contemporary factories, however, made very similar shapes. (TOP)

Hall *famille-rose* style, others with Chinese figures. Bat prints of shells occur rarely, and geometric patterns are plentiful. A few landscape patterns and fine flower subjects are also known. Most of the production was of tea wares, primarily in three main shapes – the Old Oval, the New Oval and the London. Dessert wares are also recorded, and a few large punch bowls and some rare ornamental items occur occasionally. The factory seems not to have marked its earliest wares, though the pattern number alone may occur. After about 1805 a device akin to the Sèvres mark of crossed 'L's was used, usually above the letter 'M' and the pattern number. These rare, early wares are well potted and handsomely decorated.

DAVENPORT HARD-PASTE BULB POT, c.1810–12 (H15.3cm/6in)

This bulb pot is one of a garniture of three, with monochrome figure painting and gilt enrichments. No source for this depiction of Britannia has yet been found. (LEFT)

DAVENPORT

An important factory already mentioned, that of John Davenport, was founded in 1794 and it too was remarkably successful until its decline in the 1870s, and closure in 1887. Early Davenport porcelain can be in either hard paste or bone china. The hard paste, which probably was not made after 1812, seems to have been used almost exclusively for bulb pots. Other than these a tea service is known, as are a few dessert wares and rare vases. These pieces are marked with the name Davenport impressed over an anchor. It has not been conclusively established when Davenport first produced bone china, but 1800 seems a reasonable date. Certainly, it was of the highest standard by 1806 when the factory was visited by the Prince Regent, for whom it made wares and who pronounced them the deserving equal of ''old Seve''.

Although the bone china of this period is prone to crazing and has often changed to a not unattractive pale cream colour, the factory had clearly established itself among the market leaders. The bone-china wares were at the outset apparently unmarked, but later the word ''Longport'' in red script was used, and around 1812 variants of

MILES MASON COVERED BOWL, c.1805–10 (10.4cm/4in)

Decoration is printed overglaze with a bat print of infant putti in the manner of Bartolozzi. Bat printing was especially popular in the Regency period, depicting a great variety of landscape and figure subjects, as well as shells, fruit and flowers. (LEFT)

printed marks that incorporated the family name Davenport became standard. Like their competitors Davenport maintained pattern books, now alas lost. The teaware patterns had reached about 1000 by 1820, but the dessert wares reached only about 400. The many types of ornamental ware made in the bone-china body were not allocated pattern numbers. The patterns are quite distinctive and the factory seems to have made a speciality of landscapes in the picturesque style painted in both monochrome and polychrome by several very accomplished artists. Their names and those of the skilful flower and fruit painters are unknown to us.

MILES MASON

The cessation of trade in Chinese export porcelain from 1791 by the English East India Company led Miles Mason, a Chinaman, into becoming a manufacturer himself. He first operated in Liverpool with Thomas Wolfe and then worked on his own account in Lane End, Staffordshire, from about 1802, and later at the Minerva Works, Fenton. His early porcelain wares are a hybrid hard paste, but in about 1806 he changed to the standard bone-china body. Mason's wares are very well decorated; the patterns include flowers and landscapes in colours and gilding. His wares are rarely marked, though occasionally the name is impressed in the foot-rim of the tea pots, vases and the like. A printed mock Chinese seal mark is also found both with and without the name 'M. Mason'. Tea wares predominate, with a range of fashionable shapes and decoration that include bat-printed patterns, several Mandarin patterns with typical pink-scale borders containing vignette landscape scenes, and many lavishly gilded specimens. Pattern numbers are used somewhat erratically, the recorded range being 1–986 by 1813, when Miles Mason retired. Mason's sons Charles James and George continued the business for many years, but the huge success of their Patent Ironstone China meant that less attention was paid to porcelain production. Their bone china, which was manufactured until the 1840s, was not marked and it is only recently that examples have been matched with their ironstone counterparts and their identification authenticated. Nevertheless, there is still a great deal more to be learned about the bone-china production undertaken by Miles Mason's sons.

NANTGARW AND SWANSEA

Welsh porcelain was made only for the wealthy and the aristocracy who could afford it. As Samuel Johnson remarked at the Derby factory, 'Porcelain is more expensive than silver' – this dictum certainly applied also to Welsh porcelain.

At the end of the Napoleonic wars came a boom: the demand for high-quality goods was matched by the affluence to buy them. The London china dealers were selling fine porcelain from all factories and the Welsh Nantgarw and Swansea porcelains were among the most beautiful. Mortlocks, the retailers, were pleased to announce in the *London Courier* in July 1816 that they 'were

supplying beautiful Swansea cabaret teasets to the Royal Princesses'.

The creative and driving force behind Welsh porcelain was William Billingsley, a gifted ceramic artist from Derby, whose ambition was to produce a porcelain equal to that of France. To achieve this, he carried out experimental work. In 1775 he left Derby and after much wandering and many abortive efforts at Pinxton, Torksey and Worcester, he finally arrived in Wales in 1813 with his two daughters and his son-in-law, the potter Samuel Walker.

With the financial assistance of William Weston Young, a wealthy Quaker and entrepreneur, he set up a porcelain factory at Nantgarw, near Cardiff, and produced a beautiful translucent porcelain which is very close to Sèvres in appearance. Unfortunately, the 'glassy' nature of the body and the limited safety margin of the temperature necessary to vitrify it resulted in unacceptable losses in the kilns. The venture failed and, in 1814, Billingsley was persuaded to enter into an arrangement

with Lewis Weston Dillwyn of the Cambrian pottery for the manufacture of porcelain at Swansea.

Dillwyn soon found to his cost that the Nantgarw formula was not viable and between 1814 and 1817 he experimented with the recipe. It was unlikely that Billingsley was involved with this experimentation except for the early firings, as he

SWANSEA DESSERT PLATE, EARLY 19TH CENTURY

Like much of the output of this factory, the painting is of a high standard. The design is distantly influenced by Japanese Imari porcelain.

was interested only in the Nantgarw formula. He therefore once again became the master painter and Samuel Walker became the master potter.

Swansea porcelains fell into three main categories. Firstly, there was the 'glassy' variety. This had a fritted body of great beauty and its translucency has often been described as 'sodden snow'. Its thin glaze has the appearance of French hard-paste porcelain of the period. Secondly, there was the variety known as 'duck egg' porcelain. Its white translucency was sometimes tinged slightly with green. It had a thick creamy-white glaze which enhanced the painting. Thirdly, there was also the 'trident' body, referred to by Dillwyn as 'a good sound tolerable body', a description which must surely damn it. The body had an olive-brown translucency and a thin grimy-looking pitted glaze which was wholly unacceptable to the London china dealers.

As well as the high quality of the finer Swansea porcelain, there were two other factors that made it attractive – the shapes and the decoration. The modeller was Isaac Wood, and he, under the creative genius of Billingsley, produced shapes of great charm which have rarely been surpassed by any British factory. These included dinner and dessert services with elegant tureens, ice pails and dishes; fine tea services with attractive teapots and sucriers; inkwells and other shapes, mostly in the Empire style.

Swansea, unlike Nantgarw, set out to have its wares decorated locally as well as to supply the London china dealers with porcelain in the white. Billingsley gathered around him some of the most talented ceramic artists and gilders of the time and made Swansea one of the finest artistic centres. The quality of the gilding, the careful flower painting, particularly the groups of wild flowers, and the high standard of the freely painted set patterns all combined to set Swansea porcelain apart from the majority of British factories.

Marks include an impressed 'DILLWYN & Co', 'SWANSEA', 'BEVINGTON & Co' (rare) and crossed tridents. 'SWANSEA' appears also as transfer-printed or painted in red; *Swansea* appears in red, gold and other colours.

By 1817, Billingsley had become increasingly dissatisfied with his status at Swansea and he returned to Nantgarw, followed shortly afterwards by Walker. Between the years 1817 and 1820 he produced quantities of a beautiful translucent soft-paste porcelain with a pure white glaze which was in demand with the London dealers. Unlike Swansea, the whole output was sent in the white to London for decoration and sale.

The principal output of Nantgarw was plates. Dinner, dessert and tea services were produced but the range of shapes in the services was limited. Other products included pen-trays, tazza vases, inkwells and cabinet cups. A feature of all Nantgarw porcelain is that the body is generally more thickly potted and is heavier in weight than Swansea porcelain. Nantgarw plates and most of the flatware have the impressed mark of 'NANTGARW' over a 'CW'.

In 1820, Billingsley, defeated by the wastage in the kilns and his financial losses, was persuaded by John Rose to take employment at Coalport where he and Walker remained until his death in 1828 and where he was buried. William Weston Young took over the factory at Nantgarw and employed the accomplished artist Thomas Pardoe to decorate the porcelain.

NANTGARW
TEAPOT, EARLY
19TH CENTURY

The service from which this teapot comes was painted with Regency-style scenes by Thomas Pardoe.

NANTGARW
DINNER PLATE,
EARLY 19TH
CENTURY
(D24cm/9½in)

This view of Cowbridge church was painted by the artist William Weston Young.

OTHER FACTORIES

The Trade Directories of the period reveal that, by 1820, upwards of 70 china manufacturers were listed. We have reasonable knowledge of only a few of the major firms of the period. Consequently attribution of early nineteenth-century unmarked bone china is far more difficult than is the case with the comparatively fewer porcelain factories of the eighteenth century.

Space precludes more than a mention of certain other Staffordshire porcelain makers, such as Machin or the various Ridgway concerns of Charles Bourne who began making fine-quality bone china in 1817, or of Hilditch, Hicks & Meigh, Mayer & Newbould, Peover, and Rathbone. Their wares are rare, difficult to attribute correctly, and often unmarked.

One major Staffordshire name has not been mentioned – Wedgwood. Astonishingly, the great firm and its founder Josiah fought shy of porcelain production. Though Cookworthy had approached him in 1781,

Wedgwood had passed the poisoned chalice to some of his fellow Staffordshire potters. Far too much money had been lost in the making of porcelain for the now middle-aged entrepreneur to risk a venture into 'this gulf', as he termed it. After Josiah's death in 1795, the firm entered troubled water, and it was not until 1812 under Josiah Wedgwood II that bone-china production began at Etruria. Although these rare wares are now much sought after they do not seem to have been successful commercially; production declined after 1820 and ceased altogether by 1829.

The wares are, however, of excellent quality. The decoration is good with the

RIDGWAY BONE CHINA TUREEN AND COVER, c.1815–20 (H15.3cm/6in)

The coloured landscapes are painted in pattern 562. (LEFT)

WEDGWOOD BONE CHINA SUCRIER WITH PATTERN BOOK, c.1815–20

This decoration is attributed to John Cutts. (BELOW LEFT)

usual Japanese and Chinese figures, flower and bird studies and landscapes executed by John Cutts. The pattern range is from about 470 to 1052, and the pattern books still exist at the Wedgwood Museum, Barlaston. The bulk of production was tea wares, although a few smaller ornamental items are known, and helpfully, many of the wares are marked with the word Wedgwood, usually printed in red.

To end this section with Wedgwood is not inappropriate, for though their bone china was not very successful commercially, their adoption of the material is symbolic of the old guard having eventually capitulated and accepted that the future lay not with soft paste or hard paste or variants thereof. Bone china was the porcelain for the future and the Staffordshire industry in the remainder of the nineteenth century and beyond was to be based upon its commercial success.

CONTINENTAL

PORCELAIN

1780 TO 1930

The eighteenth-century Continental porcelain factories were established as a source of interest and prestige for monarchs and aristocrats. Money was lavished on the factories and the quality of the end product was more important than the cost of its production. From 1760 to 1830, however, porcelain can generally be said to have been in a state of transition from a precious material developed under courtly patronage to a material that enabled factories to make a profit. As technology advanced the ability to produce good-quality hard-paste porcelain became widespread and a multitude of new factories sprang up throughout Europe. Nevertheless, the less expensively produced items had a huge, new market in the rising merchant and middle classes. The negative result of this new production was that artistic standards fell.

MEISSEN GROUP, c.1880

This piece was originally modelled by Acier from March to April, 1777, with help from Schönheit and named 'The Broken Eggs'. The background is a Berlin Plaque, c.1880, painted by Knoeller, with a full-length portrait of Princess Louise.

VIENNA PLAQUE, *c.*1819 (H27.4cm/10¾in)

This plaque was painted by Joseph Nigg. (BELOW)

**SORGENTHAL
COFFEE CANS
AND SAUCERS,
VIENNA, *c.*1800**

*The first can and
saucer* (BELOW
LEFT) *was painted by
A. Kothgasser in
c.1804. The shield
marks are executed in
underglaze blue with
impressed date code
and numerals, and the
painter's numeral, 96,
is in purple. The other
pieces have similar
markings. The second
set* (BELOW CENTRE) *was
painted after a picture
by Sir Thomas Lawrence
in c.1799; the final
set* (BELOW RIGHT)
*was painted in
c.1800 with the rich
blue colour invented
by Joseph Leithner
in 1792.*

NEOCLASSICAL
AND EMPIRE STYLES
1760 TO 1830

The Neoclassical style was inspired by the art of ancient Greece and Rome, and more directly by the excavations of the ancient Roman towns of Pompeii and Herculaneum in the mid-eighteenth century. These rich cultures were emulated first by Sèvres and later by all the major European factories. The style they developed employed classical motifs including scrolling acanthus, draperies, palmettes and cherubs. Sumptuous painting and gilding with complex formal borders set with medallions is also typical of the style. The ensuing Empire style shares many of these decorative elements, but whereas Neoclassical shapes were characterized by simple, square-sided or conical cups with angular handles, and vases *à la grecque*, the Empire-style cups became wider with paw feet and caryatid handles and the vases became more complex using Egyptian and Etruscan shapes. It was a more elaborate style that indulged in imitating rare stones, gems, mosaics and arabesques.

VIENNA

In 1718 the Vienna factory was founded by Claudius Innocentius du Paquier. By the 1760s, after an innovative beginning and having produced hard-paste porcelain only eight years after Meissen, the factory was largely imitating the products of others, especially Sèvres. However, with the appointment of Konrad Sörgel von Sorgenthal as Director in 1784, began what was perhaps the factory's most glamorous period. From 1783 he introduced a date-code system which until 1799 used the last two numerals of the year and the last three from 1800. Many pieces were also marked with the painter's numerals, inscribed in enamels on the base or foot-rim. In 1785 he appointed as a master modeller Anton Grassi, who visited Rome in 1792 for several months taking careful notes of all the classical forms excavated at the time. The finest painters Sorgenthal employed were often masters in other fields: Anton Kothgasser (1769–1851) for example, was a well-known painter on glass, and Moritz Michael Daffinger (1790–1849) was a famous portrait miniaturist.

Typical Viennese porcelain of the so-called Sorgenthal Period (1784—1805)

included cups and saucers for *déjeuners* or for display in cabinets. The richly gilded, hand-painted products were embellished with classical subjects as well as Greek red-figure painting, wares in imitation of red or black Chinese lacquer, and numerous panoramic views of towns. Many new coloured grounds were developed and refined by Joseph Leithner, the most distinctive of which were known as 'Leithner blue' and 'Leithner gold'.

The Demise of Vienna

After the death of Mathias Niedermeyer in 1827, his replacement, Benjamin von Scholz tried to revive the factory's flagging fortunes. He introduced cheaper-quality porcelain, piece-wages and reduced the number of staff. His successor in 1833 was Andreas Baumgartner who continued the policy of making a larger number of lower-cost items, even introducing printed decoration. His successor was the chemist Franz Freiherr von Leithner who died shortly before the introduction of the gloss-gilding process and the use of chrome green as a ground colour, around 1853. Regrettably these developments came too late and the factory went into terminal financial decline; production slowed down to a

trickle by 1863 and the Royal Vienna works finally closed in 1866.

Despite Vienna's move towards mass production, high-quality works were produced up until the factory's closure. The flower-painter Joseph Nigg (fl. 1800–1843), who occasionally worked on canvas, was primarily a painter on porcelain, and his studies, both copies of Old Masters and his own compositions, demanded the large surfaces that plaques, trays and vases provided. Eduard Pollack and others, including F. Poppel, W. Herold, M. Fromhold, A. Doring, J. Geyer, and A. Peil continued to paint for the Vienna factory until 1864, producing high-quality exhibition pieces, Royal commissions (although they were, by then, infrequent) and, especially, cabinet cups and saucers.

It is a testament to the great influence and standing of the factory that its designs, especially in the form of cabinet plates and vases, were continued by a number of other firms until the end of the century. For example, the Hungarian Herend factory, established by Moritz Fischer in 1839, bought some of the Vienna factory's moulds. Like Samson, Herend's speciality was reproducing Chinese porcelains, but it made wares in the style of all the leading European factories at the time. In the case of its 'Vienna' porcelains the shield mark was sometimes used as a backstamp.

BERLIN

The Berlin ceramicists, like those at Vienna, used porcelain essentially as a canvas for paintings, creating works of the highest technical and artistic standard. The Berlin Königliche Porzellan Manufaktur (KPM) was founded by Johann Ernst Gotzkowsky in 1761 and was subsequently taken over after bankruptcy in 1763 by Frederick the Great. He participated in the factory's overall management and commissioned many services and large decorative pieces for his various different castles. Between 1770–1780, despite the

GARNITURE OF THREE VIENNA-STYLE VASES, *c.*1880 (56cm/22in)

These German vases imitate pieces produced by the Royal Vienna Factory during the early part of the nineteenth century.

King's preference for German Rococo, the factory developed classical forms and decorations.

Frederick the Great's successor, Friedrich Wilhelm II (1744–97), showed little interest in the factory and it was not until Friedrich Wilhelm III (1770–1840) came to the throne that strong royal patronage emerged once again. Moreover, the beginning of the nineteenth century saw a great expansion of the bourgeoisie who bought single, purely decorative, cabinet cups and saucers, as opposed to complete services in large quantities.

The defeat of Napoleon in 1815 was followed by many years of lavish decoration synonymous with the elaborate Empire style. This period also saw a move to employ contemporary artists, the most famous being Karl Friedrich Schinkel (1781–1841), Friedrich von Gärtner (1792–1847) and Johann Gottfried Schadow (1764–1850). These men, who were also architects and sculptors, developed in conjunction with the KPM painters the so-called 'Berliner Vedutenporzellan', which depicted detailed architectural and town views, framed by complex tooled gilding. The production of painted vases greatly increased, reaching a peak in the 1830s and 1840s. Concurrently, less expensively produced pieces such as lithophanes and pipe bowls were created, in addition to the single cabinet cups and saucers.

THE NINETEENTH CENTURY

Berlin from the 1820s to the 1850s can be applauded as having a rich, innovative and stylish output or criticized for continuing a long-outdated tradition of using porcelain primarily as a medium for painting. At a time when most of the other factories were manufacturing Neo-Rococo and Neo-Renaissance styles, Berlin continued to produce Neoclassical wares even into the 1870s, but the painting on them was of a very high quality. However, innovations were made, although rarely, in the early nineteenth century, as illustrated by Karl Friedrich Schinkel's 'Lalla Rookh' Persian-

BERLIN PIPE BOWL, *c.*1840

BERLIN PLAQUE, 'THE RAPE OF THE DAUGHTERS OF LEUCIPPUS', *c.*1850 (H54.5cm/21½in)

This plaque is impressed with 'KPM' and sceptre marks. (LEFT)

style vases made in 1821 to mark the visit of the Russian crown prince and princess.

The majority of Berlin porcelain plaques were not painted in the factory but were sold as white blanks to outside workshops. The painting on these plaques was of a higher standard than other factories' plaques. The subject matter evolves throughout the century. The period from 1840 to 1860 predominantly features copies after the Old Masters and the famous depictions of the Virgin of the Immaculate Conception, the Penitent Magdalene, Holy Night and many others, several of which were being exhibited at the Dresden, Munich, Berlin and Florence galleries at the time.

A number of painted pieces were exhibited in the Great Exhibition of London in 1851; the work of R. Dittrich, Gaude Derounier, A. Lutz, and the Wagner family is acknowledged as among the finest.

Later in the century the subjects became more lighthearted, with scantily clad nymphs standing among flowers, or harems and Middle-Eastern girls in traditional costume holding jugs or standing by wells. Production continued into the early twentieth century, some with a distinctly Art Nouveau feel. However, most of the paintings echoed the fashion of revivalism and provided a safe alternative to the more avant-garde Jugendstil or Art Nouveau style that emerged from the 1890s.

In the 1860s, Berlin started to experiment with Neo-Renaissance pieces, and copies of Italian maiolica and German stoneware were made. But by then the style was already becoming unfashionable. In the 1870s, Berlin (KPM) was facing financial difficulties which led to the appointment of Hermann Seger as technical director and Louis Sussmann-Hellborn as the first artistic director. Hermann Seger was a man of great talent and he was responsible for reviving the factory with his series of new glazes and other technical innovations.

hand, Brongniart contributed to the revival of stained glass, to which he allocated a special workshop (which worked on projects by Ingres, Delacroix, etc.)

Shapes and decoration generally followed the styles of the period. Under the Empire, architects such as C. Percier or T. Brongniart produced classical, pure, almost severe, lines. When the French monarchy was restored, historical influences were

SÈVRES HARD-PASTE VASE, c.1810

The painting on this vase by J. Georget is taken from a painting by David. (FAR LEFT)

SÈVRES HARD-PASTE PLATE, 1823

This plate is from an 'industrial arts' service and depicts the atelier *of the painters and gilders at Sèvres. The painting is by J.Ch. Develly.* (BELOW LEFT)

SÈVRES BREAKFAST SET BY H. RÉGNIER, 1832

This illustration is taken from the catalogue of the 1862 Paris International Exhibition. (BELOW)

SÈVRES

In 1800, Louis Bonaparte, Minister of the Interior, put a young mining engineer, A. Brongniart, in charge of production at Sèvres. Brongniart was the son of a famous architect and moved among the intellectual and artistic circles of his day. He also proved to be a remarkable administrator. He began by restructuring the company's finances, though at a heavy cost: most of the workers were forced into early retirement, and outdated stock was sold off at low prices. Sèvres could no longer afford the luxury of being unprofitable and had to produce sumptuous pieces for royalty, official residences and diplomatic gifts, as well as simpler ware. Technical progress was deliberately restricted. Engraving was used only for repetitive designs (friezes) and only the large plaques were made from poured slip. On the other

drawn from Medieval and Renaissance themes as well as exotic designs inspired by Egyptian, Chinese or Turkish motifs.

The same developments occurred in decoration, which was dominated by framed miniatures painted in reverse on ground colours, which masked the luminous white of the paste entirely. In the days of the Empire, these pieces were decorated with portraits of Napoleon and members of his family, as well as scenes of landscapes which evoked his military victories; later, cameo-style painting made its appearance. Subsequently, decoration was inspired by the same sources as the shapes (Gothic, Chinese, etc).

A wider variety of wares was now produced, including vases, tableware, toilet sets, as well as more ambitious pieces, such as copies of paintings on large plaques, boxes, tables and even desks.

Traditional biscuit sculpture concentrated mainly on likenesses of the royal

family or famous people. Small, decorative items disappeared almost completely, while under the Empire grandiose table centrepieces were created which were gradually supplanted by elaborate baskets.

The management of the factory changed much more frequently during the second half of the nineteenth century. The directors were generally scientists supported by brilliant chemists; however, some excellent artists were in charge of the decoration, such as J.P.M. Diéterle (1840–52), J. Nicolle (1856–71), and A. Carrier-Belleuse (1875–87). It was a time of important technical advances, such as trials of various soft-paste formulae and the introduction of a pouring technique for very thin or very large pieces. Most important of all was the perfection in 1884 of a new paste which was fired at 1280°. This degree of heat enabled the colours to fuse better and exploit the decorative effect of flame-shaped spots in the glaze and crystallization. Two short-lived workshops opened. One produced enamelled metal and the other, faience and glazed earthenware. In 1877, the factory abandoned the old building to occupy its present premises.

After a brief predominance of shapes and designs inspired by reinterpreted classical forms, the Second Empire witnessed the triumph of a 'Louis XVI-Empire' style (this had been easy to introduce because the factory had retained its old moulds), which led to a revival of small decorative sculpture. Simultaneously, pâte-sur-pâte decoration became popular. As soon as the Second Empire ended, baroque shapes and the decorative device of framed miniatures were abandoned in favour of outlines and designs that were Japanese-inspired.

The arrival of A. Sandier as artistic director in 1897 marked the true beginnings of Art Nouveau at Sèvres. All the shapes were redesigned, displaying a preference for sinuous but smooth contours. The decorative designs concentrated on stylized flower motifs in pastel shades, the stems and flowers subtly following the contours. Biscuit sculpture was almost entirely devoted to graceful female forms. By the end of the first decade of the twentieth century, there was a powerful move towards the style which triumphed under the name of Art Deco. The new shapes designed by the architects H. Patou, J. Ruhlmann and H. Rapin were geometrical and angular, and bright, even violent, shades were used in decoration which the director, G. Lechevallier-Chevignard, commissioned from several outside artists.

PARIS

By the 1820s Paris supported a large number of porcelain factories as well as freelance painters who worked on white porcelain obtained from various sources. Their wares tend to be more sparsely decorated than those of the truly great Neoclassical factories of Sèvres, Berlin, Vienna and St. Petersburg.

Although the factories continually faced financial ruin except for a few years around the 1820s, many of their productions are of a high quality. Before 1820 the Napoleonic Wars and the dominance of Sèvres were to blame and afterwards many factories were forced to move outside Paris as labour costs increased and land was unavailable for expansion or too expensive. By 1850 most of the Parisian factories had moved to Limoges and only a small quantity of Limoges-decorated porcelain was still being produced in Paris.

The best-known factories in Paris in the first half of the nineteenth century are those of Dagoty and Honoré, Dihl and Guérhard and Darte. On occasions they all produced pieces of an equally high standard to those of Vienna, Sèvres and Berlin, but the majority of pieces are simply decorated with sprigs of flowers and gilded borders.

THE NINETEENTH CENTURY

By 1830 there were no major porcelain manufacturers left in Paris, with the exception of the Jacob Petit factory on the outskirts of Fontainebleau, which was established in 1834. Petit was a master of historicism, echoing the style of other factories, especially Meissen and Sèvres, without directly copying from them. His products were often embellished with encrusted flowers, jewels, elaborate relief moulding, large painted areas with bright colours and lavish matt and burnished gilding. The bulb pots he produced are a particularly good example of this mixture of styles: the shape was inspired by Chinese crocus pots, the ground colour was taken from Sèvres and the painted panels with gilded Rococo swag borders were lifted straight from the eighteenth century.

CHARLES HAVILAND DISH, 1876 (25cm/9¾in)

This plate was designed by Felix Bracquemond, and draws definite stylistic influences from 'Japonisme'. (ABOVE LEFT)

PAIR OF JACOB PETIT NEO-ROCOCO VASES, 1840 (H23cm/9in)

These elaborate vases have a 'JP' mark in underglaze blue. (LEFT)

Another famous manufacturer also working near Paris at this time was the infamous Edmé et Cie., Samson works, founded at Saint-Maurice in 1845. This firm became noted not merely for taking its inspiration from a variety of other factories, but for copying their products directly. The firm's variety of output is astounding, with hundreds of different copies of seventeenth- and eighteenth-century Chinese export pieces, scores of models from Meissen, Nymphenburg, Ludwigsburg and Höchst, as well as copies of Italian maiolica.

The glaze of the porcelain pieces has a glassy appearance and there is a tendency to stiffness in the modelling, which separates Samson wares from the originals.

LIMOGES

After 1830 Limoges developed into the major centre for French porcelain. Factories sprang up in the area taking advantage of cheap labour costs, local raw materials and space for expansion. Many of these concerns developed into well-managed and well-run modern workplaces with the latest technology and an efficient workforce.

The Haviland concern was the most successful, with other major names including Gibus et Cie.; Pouyat; Gérard, Dufraisseix and Abbot, and Henri Ardant. Haviland and Co. was founded by the Haviland Brothers who were New York importers of ceramics. David Haviland settled in Limoges in 1842, and carried on exporting the products of factories such as Gibus et Cie. and Pouyat. He then set up a decorating workshop and finally founded the Haviland and Co. factory, producing his own porcelain for export along with that of other factories.

Most of these factories produced domestic china, although each one was capable of producing luxury wares of high quality. This production of mainly domestic wares interspersed with the occasional more ambitious piece was also a hallmark of the provincial factories outside Limoges. For example, in 1851 Charles Pillivuyt established a factory in Mahun-sur-Yèvre, Cher, which mostly produced table wares except for special pieces designed for the great international exhibitions. The Pillivuyt factory's attempt at Japonisme was less successful, for although the decoration was asymmetrically placed in a Japanese manner, the shape of the porcelain blank used was a traditional scroll-edge dinner plate.

RUSSIA

The main Russian factory, the Imperial Porcelain Manufactory in St. Petersburg, was reputedly founded in 1744. After 1800 it concentrated on Neoclassical wares, stimulated by Count D.A. Guryev who re-organized it in that year. New kilns and other technical improvements ensued and several porcelain artists from the leading European factories,

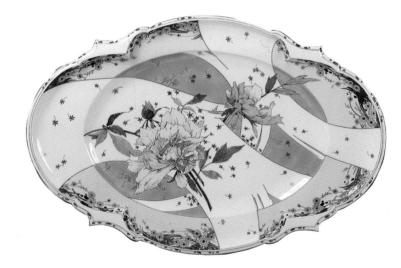

PAIR OF FRENCH COLOURED BISCUIT GROUPS, *c.*1870 (27cm/10½in)

These beautifully painted pieces draw upon historical themes and touch upon contemporary morality. (See page 6)

CHARLES PILLIVUYT DISH, *c.*1888 (W56.8cm/22¼in)

This dish is typical of the pieces produced by Pillivuyt's Mahjun-sur-Yèvre factory. A traditional, Western-style plate is decorated in a highly exotic, eastern manner.

including from Sèvres and Berlin, were employed. The appointment of the French potter Adam as manager in 1808, and Franz Gartenberg from the Gardner factory as the chemist in 1803, put St. Petersburg at the forefront of Neoclassical and Empire design. Elegant shapes which imitated Greek, Roman, Etruscan and Egyptian forms were painted with gilded bands and eagle, lion and swan motifs. The service created for Count Guryev, begun in 1809, was perhaps one of the factory's greatest achievements, taking several years to complete and comprising some thousand pieces. It is decorated with gilded borders of laurel wreaths, acanthus leaves and other foliage on a magenta ground and painted with views of St. Petersburg and scenes of its inhabitants, peasants and craftsmen at various pursuits. The sculptural supports for the baskets, vases and cups in the service were conceived by Stephan Pimenov. Portraits of the war against Napoleon celebrating the victors of the battles in 1812 and military motifs in general were a strong favourite on many of the products created in the first part of the nineteenth century.

ST. PETERSBURG

The St. Petersburg factory, unlike other factories, did not need to make financial considerations its main priority. After Alexander I, Tsar Nicholas I took control, and the factory's style began to move away from the Empire style. In the 1830s, a variety of ornamental pieces, such as clocks, baskets and candlesticks were made in the German style, their Neo-Rococo decorations and subjects stemming from a much wider range of sources, in particular Sèvres, Meissen, Oriental porcelain and Russian antiquities. Many of the services commissioned by Nicholas I illustrate the Sèvres and Meissen Rococo influence. Royal patronage continued to flourish until the end of Nicholas I's reign with no shortage of large presentation wares being requested. At the same time figurative groups were being produced in biscuit, often portrayed in Russian costume.

MEISSEN VASE, COVER AND STAND, *c.*1860 (71cm/28in)

After an eighteenth-century original by J.J. Kändler, the piece has the crossed swords mark in underglaze blue.

Under Alexander II (1855–1881), the factory appointed new managers and the porcelain painter Lippold and the master modeller August Spiers were employed. However, they were not great innovators and although St. Petersburg won prizes in 1862, 1867 and 1873, one can only assume this was for technical excellence rather than for originality.

GARDNER

This was the most successful of the privately owned factories established at Verbilki, North of Moscow, by an Englishman called Francis Gardner. He employed technical experts from Meissen, including the painter I. Kestner. In common with St. Petersburg many of the commissions copied originals from Meissen and Sèvres; this was evident in the display services made for Catherine the Great in 1777.

Antoinette Fay-Hallé and Barbara Mundt note in *Nineteenth-Century European Porcelain* that 'an important expansion of [Gardner's] repertoire of figures followed publication of the almanac *Laterna Magica*, or Petersburg Tradesmen, Craftsmen and other workers, with drawings by Zelentsov'. These figures, which were produced from the early nineteenth century onwards, were brightly glazed, and stood on mottled circular or rectangular bases. Biscuit porcelain figures of craftsmen were made in the mid-nineteenth century. The standard remained high until 1891 when the concern was taken over by Kuzactov who subsequently concentrated on mass-produced transfer-printed porcelain until the factory's nationalization in 1917.

MEISSEN

Europe's oldest porcelain factory, established in 1710 near Dresden, was comparatively inactive in the early nineteenth century, having been the major innovator and manufacturer throughout the eighteenth century. Sèvres, Vienna and Berlin all produced Neoclassical porcelains in larger quantities that were often, although with notable exceptions, of a superior standard to those made at Meissen between 1774 and 1814 when the factory was under the management of Count Camillo Marcolini.

1780 TO 1830

In the 1780s, Meissen employed Johann Gottlieb Matthai and Christoph Gottfried Jüchtzer who produced many pieces after classical originals. The factory had a number of other Neoclassical modellers including Johann Daniel Schöne, Christian Karl Schiebel, Michel Victor Acier and Johann Carl Schönheit. Judging by the rarity today of Neoclassical table-ware, cabinet cups, presentation pieces of all kinds and figural groups (compared with the large number of Rococo designs modelled by J.J. Kändler and P. Reinicke in the eighteenth century), it would appear that there was considerable resistance to change by the management of the factory. Furthermore, Meissen's market share was diminished in the late eighteenth century as Austria and Prussia banned its imports and England, France and Russia placed a high tariff on all pieces entering their countries.

By the time Marcolini retired in 1814 production was almost at a standstill, largely owing to the Napoleonic Wars. The new manager, Carl Wilhelm von Oppel and his assistant Heinrich Gottlob Kühn, modernized the factory with a round kiln and developed the green underglaze and gloss-gilding processes.

Perhaps the greatest achievement of the Meissen factory in the early nineteenth century was the dessert service, started in 1819, produced for the Duke of Wellington to celebrate his victory at Waterloo. The service compares favourably with those also made at Sèvres, Berlin and Vienna.

1830 TO 1870

The mid-nineteenth century witnessed the industrial age, an era of mass productions when economies of scale and meeting popular demand became more important than aristocratic and royal patronage.

The world exhibitions from 1851 onwards brought about a rapid expansion in the dissemination of styles, industrial techniques and knowledge of the material culture of past civilizations. Exhibitions in London, Paris and Vienna in 1851, 1862, 1867, 1873 and 1889 inspired manufacturers throughout Europe to copy, combine and generally imitate what they had seen. The medal-winning exhibits and the government commissions that followed set standards for factory managers to emulate. In this competitive environment every historical style was revisited – no technical challenge was too great.

In general terms, during the 1830s Empire porcelains developed into the elongated forms synonymous with the Biedermeier period and the revival of Rococo

MEISSEN GREEN-GROUND PART DINNER SERVICE, LATE 19TH CENTURY

Each piece of this service has a crossed swords mark in underglaze blue.
(LEFT)

IMPERIAL PORCELAIN FACTORY VASE, ST. PETERSBURG, c.1834 (H73cm/29in)

This Russian Palace vase is painted with an Alpine lake scene.
(BELOW)

designs. Shortly after this, Gothic designs became fashionable as did imitations of Limoges enamels, and the 1860s and 1870s saw a resurgence of interest in classical and Renaissance designs. The historicism of the nineteenth century was not a neat progression from one stylistic revival to another: many of the styles were produced at overlapping times by most of the major factories. Furthermore, if one style consistently proved its saleability it would be continued for an indefinite period, as was the case with the Neoclassical and Rococo revivals produced by Meissen from the 1840s into the early twentieth century.

TECHNOLOGY

There is probably no better example of Meissen's ability to produce commercially viable mass-produced products than the lithophanes that were made from 1829.

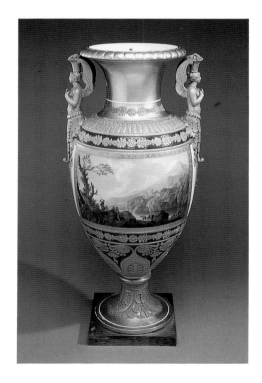

Tens of thousands of them were made between 1830 and 1850. When they are held up to a bright light or candle they reveal a picture in contrasting lights and darks. The religious subject matter of these objects is typical of the painting found on porcelain of the period, such as Raphael's depiction of the Sistine Madonna or Madonna della Sedia, or Correggio's Holy Night. The genre scenes included a variety of sentimental subjects such as children, dogs and maternal images. Copies of Dutch, French and Italian School painting from the seventeenth and eighteenth centuries were also popular. Lithophanes were also made in equal numbers by Berlin and, in smaller quantities, at Sèvres, Plaue, Volkstedt, St. Petersburg and Royal Copenhagen.

blue and gilt is the most common.

From the late 1840s Meissen revived many of the decorative cabinet pieces that were painted with typical merchant and harbour scenes in the manner of Christian Friedrich Herold, the Rococo porcelain models first produced by J.J. Kändler and T. Reinicke, and the Neoclassical porcelain figures first produced by Acier and Schönheit. Ernst August Leuteritz who was the head of the modelling department from 1849 was chiefly responsible for the figures. These products include romantic figures of a gallant and his companion, a shepherd and shepherdess, ladies in crinoline dresses, allegorical groups of the seasons, continents and elements, mythological groups, putti, animals, clocks, tables, mirrors, chand-

MEISSEN LITHOPHANE, 19TH CENTURY

This lithophane depicts Cologne, a bustling port at the heart of the German industrial revolution. (BELOW LEFT)

PHOTOGRAPH OF THE LONDON EXHIBITION, 1862

A large quantity of Berlin porcelain was on view at this important exhibition of international manufacturers. (BELOW CENTRE)

MEISSEN PRESS-MOULDED DISH WITH GLOSS-GILDING, c.1850

This dish epitomizes the mid-nineteenth century taste for the elaborate. (BELOW RIGHT)

The gloss-gilding process perfected by H.G. Kühn in the late 1820s was another significant step in reviving the factory's flagging finances at the time. It allowed gold to be mixed in solution and painted or mechanically applied to porcelain, which saved labour costs and time and reduced the amount of gold needed. Moreover, elaborately moulded plates could now be inexpensively produced by pouring liquid clay (slip) into glass moulds instead of the former time-consuming process of hand-pressing clay into each half of a mould. These elaborately moulded plates were decorated in a variety of colours, although underglaze

eliers, large vases, monkey bandsmen, muses, musical groups, tradespeople and dinner services with moulded borders and flower sprays. The popular snake-handled vases in Neo-Renaissance style were made in large quantities from the mid-1860s. Meissen also made Neo-Renaissance Limoges-style pieces copied from the Royal Worcester examples that were displayed at the London Exhibition of 1862. From 1878 the pâte-sur-pâte technique invented earlier in France was developed at Meissen; it involved laying small amounts of slip on top of each other and carving them to produce contrasting areas in diaphanous relief.

BOHEMIA

In general, the Bohemian factories of Schlaggenwald, Pirkenhammer, Klösterle and Elbogen, and the scores of smaller firms operating in this area, took their stimulus from the larger European factories such as Berlin, Meissen and Vienna. In the early nineteenth century they produced wares in the Neoclassical and Empire styles with the familiar painted copies of Old Masters, allegories of Love, Hope and Friendship, as well as views of towns. From the second quarter of the century until 1850 they found their market niche by making display pieces of a fair quality, with printed rather than hand-painted decoration, which enabled them to be sold at accessible prices. They followed fashions generally, leaping from the Neo-Rococo to the Neo-Renaissance, at the same time copying the highly popular decorative wares of the other factories, especially those of neighbouring Vienna.

THURINGIA

Meissen's influence was as important as Vienna's in the growth and development of the scores of factories that proliferated in the Thuringian duchies. Sitzendorf, Gotha and Volkstedt are among the most well known factories. But there was also C. Teichert in Meissen and Thieme in Potschappel, the latter established in 1850 by William Liebman. Both these factories produced many similar items, the latter specializing in 'Crinoline' groups. These figures were made by dipping real lace into porcelain slip which was applied to the figure. When the lace was burned in the kiln its skeleton remained.

Kloster Veilsdorf was established in 1760 by Friedrich Wilhelm Eugen, and produced some much-admired porcelain in the Neoclassical style. In 1797 it passed into new ownership and from then on concentrated on domestic wares, figures and vases in Meissen style. These Neo-Rococo wares, painted with panels of Watteauesque lovers in eighteenth-century gardens and bordered with lavish gilding and flowers, ensured good sales. In 1863 the factory was purchased by Eduard Albert Heubach who, while largely extending the industrial ceramics side of the firm, made bisque dolls' heads and bisque figures. These were also produced from the 1830s by Königliche Porzellan Manufactur (KPM) in Berlin, who were among the first to manufacture porcelain dolls' heads, and Armand Marseille and Simon and Halbig, who both continued to operate until the 1920s.

ROYAL COPENHAGEN VASE, 1885 (H57cm/23in)

This 'Royal Presentation' vase was designed by C. F. Hetsch and painted by E. Orth.

STYLES

1860 TO 1930

In 1860 porcelain products still relied largely on the mixing of various historical styles precipitated by the international exhibitions, and 'Eclecticism' or 'Historismus' was in many ways to remain the dominant style well into the twentieth century, providing a comfortable, easily understood alternative to the newly emerging movements. This is particularly true in the case of Art Nouveau, or Jugendstil, a

stylistic movement which most contemporary commentators regarded as a rather unpleasant novelty.

In 1862 the principal impetus for change came from Japan which, after a long period of isolation, showed a number of pieces at the International Exhibition of 1862. Western spectators saw a style of decoration and form that had no parallel in the artistic production of Europe. The extravagances of the Rococo, with its elaborately decorated panels enclosed with gilt swag borders, and the symmetry inherent in Renaissance design, disappeared and were replaced by simpler shapes with sparsely decorated areas and asymmetrically placed motifs. Hugh Wakefield in the book *World Ceramics*, describes the change in style as allowing '. . . the freedom to leave ground surface unadorned; and it meant eventually the freeing of form from many deeply ingrained conventions of classical origin. The idea of moving away from a western sense of balance produced refreshingly simple new designs. The new style was made more distinctive by modern developments in materials, glazes and manufacturing techniques.'

Glaze effects were another important facet of the influence from the Far East. A number of collections of Chinese, Japanese and Korean porcelain had been formed by this time in all the major European museums and attempts were made to reproduce many of these glazes, which included celadon, sang-de-boeuf, flambé and crystalline effects.

Developments in new glaze techniques inspired by the Oriental monochromes and celadons were not limited to France, although the earliest experiments were made at Sèvres. At the same time that Théodore Deck was experimenting in France, so too was Hermann Seger working in Berlin. Seger more than justified his position as head of the Royal Porcelain Manufactory's 'Techno-Chemical Research Institute' in Berlin when he developed the famous 'Seger cones' that allowed the accurate control of firing temperatures.

After the flambé glazes were developed

ROYAL COPENHAGEN CUP AND SAUCER, c.1886–88

These pieces, from the Reiherservice (Heron Service), were designed by Pietro Krohn and are decorated in underglaze blue and gilding.

ROYAL COPENHAGEN PORCELAIN VASE, c.1900 (10cm/3⅞in)

This piece was glazed by the chemist Valdermar Engelhardt, after a design by Arnold Krog.

at the Berlin factory, other glaze colours and combinations of colours were created. The Meissen factory, under the head chemist Julius Heintze, also experimented in the late 1870s and he made the first red monochrome vases in 1883, extending the range to include crystalline and multi-coloured glaze effects by the 1890s.

The Royal Copenhagen Porcelain Manu-factory in Copenhagen had something of a renaissance from 1883, when it was sold to the Alumina earthenware company. It had in previous decades been rather undyna-mic, but was now completely turned around by Philipp Schou who was in charge at Alumina. He invested in new technology and in 1885 employed Arnold Krog, an architect whose new ideas in glaze techno-logy and painting produced a new style.

In 1885 Krog toured Holland, Belgium, France and England viewing not only contemporary work but also coming into contact with Japanese Art. In 1886 he visited the well-known Paris dealer in Oriental porcelain, Siegfried Bing.

The subtle greys and blues in Krog's

work can be found in the work of Japanese potters such as Miyagawa (Makuzu) Kozan or Fukagawa. Krog decorated porcelain between 1886 and 1916 and although the colours and arrangement of the painting were heavily inspired by Japan the motifs were often very European in flavour. Towards the end of the century he forsook the Oriental flowers and animals for Danish examples. Besides Krog many other talented painters were employed at Copen-hagen including Erik Nielson, Christian Thomson, C.J. Bonnesen and F.A. Hallin, to name only a few. Each piece produced was signed by the artist.

This new form of decoration, which covered the whole surface of the vessel rather than just a part of it, was clearly the antithesis of the formal designs that had dominated the preceding 200 years. When shown at the World Exhibition of Paris in 1889 they were awarded the *Grand Prix* and it was not long before most other European factories attempted to make porcelain in the new Copenhagen manner.

Krog also can be given the considerable

credit of developing the modern style of figure-making. As has already been seen, the majority of the nineteenth-century makers were concerned with replacing Rococo or classical figures whether in porcelain, biscuit, parian or pottery. Copenhagen left all these formalities behind, concentrating on animal models with a naturalistic feel yet at the same time distinctly stylized in both shape and glaze.

Bing and Grondahl in Copenhagen pro-duced the famous Heron Service designed by Pietro Krohn who was a Japonisme enthusiast. Rörstrand in Sweden, Meissen and Nymphenburg all followed suit and produced pieces not only in the Japanese style but also used the blue and grey glaze effects synonymous with Krog's work.

ART NOUVEAU

All the factories previously mentioned in connection with Japonisme were to a greater or lesser degree influenced by Art Nouveau, which had its heyday from the early 1890s to the early twentieth century.

The movement took its root from the nineteenth-century writers on aesthetics such as John Ruskin and William Morris in England and Leon de Laborde and Eugène-Emmanuel Viollet-le-Duc in France. They rejected revivalism and instead sought to obliterate the distinction between so-called Fine Art and Applied Arts. They stated that the importance of art was not the medium used but that it should be a reflection of the age in which it was made. Art Nouveau certainly had few antecedents; and its sinuous style so heavily influenced by nature freed design from its links with the past.

Art Nouveau was regarded by many, however, as an unpleasant novelty, against the more familiar eighteenth-century style. The major outlets for Art Nouveau were, therefore, somewhat limited. The main shops included Siegfried Bing's 'L'Art Nouveau' Gallery, which started in 1895, and La Maison Moderne, which opened in 1898, both in Paris. Siegfried Bing's gallery

was an extension of his love for Oriental art and Japonisme in general. He sold the best examples of Art Nouveau: his ceramics included pieces from The Royal Copenhagen Factory, Rörstrand, and Bing and Grondahl, and notably the designs produced by Eugène Colonna and George de Feure executed by Gérard, Dufraisseix and Abbot (G.D.A.) in Limoges.

With the exception of Sèvres, perhaps the greatest exponent of the sinuous Art Nouveau style was the Rozenburg factory in the Hague, established in 1883 by the German potter Wilhelm Wolff Freiherr von Gudenburg. In collaboration with T.C.A. Colenbrander, who was artistic director between 1884 and 1889, some Japonisme designs were developed. After Colenbrander left, the new director J. J. Kok, aided by S. Schellink, eventually introduced in 1889 the unique, fine egg-shell porcelains that encapsulate the Art Nouveau style in both form and decoration.

ROYAL COPENHAGEN CHRISTMAS PLATE, 1926 (17.8cm/7in)

Christmas plates were made each year by the factory. (BELOW)

COLLECTION OF ROZENBURG EGG-SHELL PORCELAIN VASES, *c.*1900

Many of these vases were designed by J. J. Kok and painted by S. Schellink.

THE MODERN MOVEMENT

Art Nouveau continued into the early twentieth century. However, after the International Exhibition in Paris in 1900, the style deteriorated as manufacturers attempted to synthesize the design for mass-production. Its place was taken by the Modern Movement and the group of styles termed Art Deco, which reached its peak at the Paris Exhibition of 1925. Modernism concentrated on form rather than decoration, in contrast to Art Nouveau.

The Modern Movement reached its height at the Exposition des Arts Décoratifs et Industriels Modernes in Paris in 1925, but carried on into the 1930s. The inspiration for the modern style came from a variety of sources, including Cubist painters, architecture, Central America, tribal art, Egyptian art as well as modern industrial designs encompassing such diverse things as trains and aeroplanes. The style was designed to be new, dynamic and, where appropriate, functional.

Germany and Austria were the leading countries to develop the modern style. The movement was based on the conviction that design of modern forms was determined by function. Combined with the new materials of the time the result was something ordered, functional and not frivolous. The root of the concept, that applied arts should be uncluttered and functional, came from the concepts behind the British Arts and Crafts Movement and notably C.R. Ashbee's Guild of Handicrafts. This was based on the principles of a medieval guild system, whereby the values of good design and integrity of production outweighed the material concerns of economic gain.

German factories were particularly good at producing wares in this modern style, combining technical know-how with innovative and distinct design. Many artists and designers connected with the Darmstadt group were involved with ceramics. This artists' colony, supported by the Grand Duke of Hesse, was founded in 1901. Peter Behrens and Hans Christiansen both produced table services that were manufac-

ROYAL PORCELAIN FACTORY, BERLIN, 'THE BRIDE AS EUROPA ON THE BULL', c.1910

This piece was designed by the sculptor Adolf Amberg for the wedding of the German Crown Prince in 1905 to form part of a procession of figures.

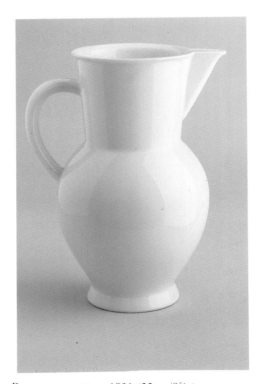

BAUHAUS JUG, c.1931 (22cm/8⅝in)

This Hallescheform jug was designed by Marguerite Wildenhain Friedlaender.

tured by the Bauscher Brothers and Weiden and Krautheim & Adelberg of Selb. Other manufacturers who worked with the Darmstadt group included Meissen, Ohme, Serapis and Waechtersbacher Steingutfabrik.

At the Royal Porcelain Factory in Berlin the arrival of Theo Schmuz-Baudiss in 1902 resulted in new designs. Perhaps his most distinctive work can be seen on his *sgraffito* pieces, where the engraved outlines are especially effective on his stylized shapes. He also developed some distinctive rich, floral linear compositions. Other modellers include E. Rutte and Adolf Flad.

The newcomer to the porcelain world was Philipp Rosenthal, whose factory was founded in Selb, Bavaria in 1880. There he produced some important dinner service designs, most notably the 'Darmstadt', 'Donatello' and 'Isolde' designs which between 1904 and 1910 were produced in white, but in later years were given additional pâte-sur-pâte and underglaze designs. Form and shape were of primary importance and were much emulated by other porcelain manufacturers.

ROSENTHAL
COFFEE POT, CUP
AND SAUCER,
1954

*These pieces, designed
by Raymond Loewy
and Richard Latham,
exemplify the purity of
line and sparseness of
decoration in the
middle of the
twentieth century.*
(RIGHT)

DESIGN FOR A
TEAPOT, JOSEF
HOFFMANN,
*c.*1920

*This teapot has
moulded organic
decoration and is
signed with the
monogram 'JH'.*
(BELOW RIGHT)

students to reduce design to all that was needed for basic, functional and utilitarian products. In 1923 the designers Otto Lindig and Theodore Bögler were given their own studio where they could design pieces for major porcelain factories such as the Staatliche Porzellan-Manufaktur of Berlin.

The Austro-Hungarian Empire was similarly active from 1903 with the founding of the Wiener Werkstätte. This workshop was established by Joseph Hoffmann who, in conjunction with Gustav Klimt, Koloman Moser and other architects, painters and sculptors had previously formed the 'Secession' Movement in 1897, Vienna's version of Art Nouveau. In 1905 the 'Wiener Keramik' workshop was established by Michael Powolny and Berthold Löffler. Ernst Wahliss's 'Serapis-Fayence' factory, also in Vienna, made some notable abstract figures from 1911.

In Prague a group of architects, heavily influenced by the Wiener Werkstätte,

Figure-making saw something of a revival following the example set at Copenhagen. The glazes used became part of the piece, unlike the less flowing style of the preceding two centuries. Some of the most distinctive designs were created by the sculptor Ernst Barlach, who modelled a series of Russian figures that were manufactured between 1908–1913 by Schwarzburg-Rudolfstadt.

Joseph Wackerle's figurative work is also worthy of note: he trained as a woodcarver in Partenkirchen before 1904, and worked for Nymphenburg, Meissen and Berlin between 1906 and 1925. Adolf Amberg produced some striking figures too, in particular the series of 16 wedding procession figures made for the German Crown Prince in 1905 at the Berlin factory.

Meissen saw something of a revival from 1900 as a result of employing a number of new designers, including Paul Scheurich, Max Esser, Paul Borner, Paul Walther, Otto Pilz and Hermann Fritz. Paul Scheurich's figures, made from 1914 and based on dancers in the Ballets Russes, are among the

best-known creations. Meissen also commissioned the architect Henri van de Velde in 1905 to make his now-famous dinner service, painted with floral motifs in a geometric arrangement. In 1906 Richard Riemerschmid, the Belgian painter, architect and designer, also designed a porcelain table service for Meissen, with moulded rims, painted in underglaze blue and gilded.

Ceramics were taught at the newly created Weimar Art School commonly known as the 'Bauhaus', which was the brainchild of Walter Gropius. Architects, painters, craftsmen and sculptors united under one roof, and 'minimalist' and 'functional' ceramics were developed at the Bauhaus pottery workshop in Dornburg from 1921 to 1924. The Bauhaus existed between 1919 and 1932, and attracted the radical thinkers from the art world, including Breuer, Albers, Klee, Kandinsky and Mies van der Rohe, who, among others, sought to produce good simple designs capable of being mass produced, so that they would be affordable. The tutors Gerhard Marcks and Max Krehan taught

founded in 1908 the craft workshops known as the Artel organization. The strongly Cubist wares produced by Vlatislav Hofman and Pavel Janak were inspired by their training in modern architecture rather than in ceramics. Vlatislav Hofman designed ribbed and fluted vases or vases made up of interlocking circles and triangles painted with blocks of colour to emphasize the geometric forms. Pavel Janak also designed some vases of fluted form and decorated them with plain stripes.

LATER BRITISH AND AMERICAN PORCELAIN

During the last three quarters of the nineteenth century two ceramic formulae dominated English porcelain — bone china and parian. These home-grown bodies spearheaded the move away from Regency or Neoclassical forms and decoration to a freer Victorian style which embraced the designs of Gothic, Rococo, Renaissance and many other periods, and gave them all a unique twist.

Some companies found it very difficult or even impossible to make the transition from Regency to Victorian. Firms such as Derby, Rockingham and two of the Worcester factories — Flight, Barr and Barr, and Chamberlain — remained solidly Regency, and even when they tried to update their designs in the 1830s and 1840s the Georgian influence persisted. The result was the creation of some monstrous hybrids, typical of which were Rockingham's 'Rhinoceros' vase and Chamberlain's desk ink set in the form of King John's tomb.

The china mania of the eighteenth century spread downwards through the social strata. By the nineteenth century the new ceramic bodies and mechanical inventions could give the growing middle class what it wanted — well-made porcelain at reasonable prices.

COLLECTION OF MINTON CLOISONNÉ WARE AND WORCESTER VASES, c.1870

The influence of Japan on English ceramics was very strong at this time.

MINTON(S)

Minton, founded in 1793, became Europe's leading ceramic factory during the Victorian era. Historical styles were interpreted by the factory in a new and often dramatic way and new techniques were constantly being sought after. Herbert Minton said 'to stand still for a moment, is to lose our foothold in the market place'.

REVIVED ROCOCO STYLE

Early bone-china production concentrated on tea wares decorated in the restrained Regency style, with delicate florals, idealized English landscapes and chinoiserie predominating. These were gradually overtaken by the revived Rococo, a style well suited to the Minton china body, which appealed to the emerging middle classes.

Ornamental wares of the 1830s were dominated by curvaceous shapes adorned with a profusion of flower encrustations. Minton ornament books show pot-pourri, Dresden vases, extinguisher stands, watch frames, thermometers, note racks, and clock cases, which were not only painted but also embellished with flowers applied in relief. Should that not suffice, some were further adorned with lace. Tea wares, too, were produced in flamboyant shapes with moulded embossments; bisque or enamel-painted figures were either flower-encrusted or used flowers as accessories.

Artists of this period rarely signed their work, but attributions can often be made through style and specialization – Steel in fruit and flowers, Tatler in flowers and landscapes, Bancroft in feathers and flowers, Smith and Wareham in birds. Wareham painted the birds on a *déjeuner* service commissioned by Queen Victoria in 1840. Simpson was Minton's leading figure painter and later became Head Designer at Marlborough House and miniature painter to Queen Victoria. Pratt painted heraldic devices, and Beard executed landscapes. Till specialized in gilding.

The open pattern book shows patterns 700, 701 and 702 of the second period with a corresponding cup and saucer (702). (BELOW)

Early tea wares, ornaments and figures depend for their attribution on the Minton pattern books. From 1842, a series of impressed year cyphers was introduced.

SÈVRES STYLE

In 1849 Léon Arnoux, a multi-talented master potter from Toulouse, joined Minton as 'ceramic technical director with freedom of initiative'. He was responsible for the improved whiteness and translucency of the Minton body, the lustrous glaze and the development of the colour palette. He perfected Minton *bleu-céleste*, a vibrant heavenly blue, and *rose du Barry* (synonymous with *rose Pompadour*), the ground colours used for the Sèvres style porcelains produced throughout the remainder of the century. Many of these were painted by Thomas Allen.

GOTHIC INFLUENCE

A.W.N. Pugin, the leading exponent of the Gothic style, and Herbert Minton, the son of the factory's founder, had, during the 1840s, worked together on major architectural schemes, notably the interiors of the

MINTON VAISSEAU À MAT, c.1900 (43.5cm/17in)

This Minton bone china version of the Sèvres model demonstrates the technical skills achieved at this time. The whiteness of the body, the clarity of the ground colours and the painting and gilding were thought to surpass the original. The rustic scene is painted by J.E. Dean. (ABOVE)

new Houses of Parliament. Their association led Pugin to comment 'I think my patterns and your workmanship go ahead of anything'. Although many of Minton's Gothic-inspired designs were intended for tile or earthenware manufacture, in the 1860s Pugin's 'Fleur de Lis' and 'Blue Gothic Border' decorated bone-china tea wares. The first Minton ornamental shape influenced by this style was Shape No. 8, 'Gothic Pedestal Vase', *c.* 1830.

PARIAN

At the Great Exhibition of 1851, when he was asked the controversial question, 'Who was the first inventor of the parian material?', Herbert Minton replied, 'I believe my nephew, Mr Hollins, and Mr Copeland both claim it. I will not, however, undertake to decide who did first make it, but it is very easy to prove'. The controversy still rages. Parian, named by Minton after the white marble from the Greek island of Paros, was a porcelain-like body of feldspar and china clay introduced in 1845. It was an ideal material for producing scaled-down models of large classical sculptures, along with subjects from literature, history, politics, sport and religion and many contemporary figures of the day.

Minton adapted some of its earlier bisque moulds for its parian wares, but many new models came into production mainly through Herbert Minton's association with Sir Henry Cole and his Summerly's Art Manufactures. *Dorothea*, and *Una and the Lion* were modelled by John Bell, with other important sculptors and modellers being Jeannest, Carrier, Klagman, Redgrave and Sir Richard Westmacott.

The Minton parian catalogue, published in 1852, lists 226 parian figures which range in price from two shillings (approximately £5 today) for a 'greyhound' to six guineas (approximately £300) for *Theseus*.

A method of tinting the parian body was patented in the 1850s, and figures were produced with contrasting drapery in dark chocolate, terracotta, salmon or celadon. It could also be gilded.

PARIAN FIGURES, 1874 (34.5cm/13½in)

At the Great Exhibition Queen Victoria purchased various parian figures and a dessert service designed by Jeannest, which was an unusual combination of parian and bone china. Costing 1,000 guineas, it was presented to the Emperor of Austria.

Minton was awarded the bronze medal for 'beauty and originality of design' at the Great Exhibition and the gold at the Paris Exhibition of 1855. In 1856 Queen Victoria granted the factory its first Royal Warrant of Appointment.

PÂTE-SUR-PÂTE

'Pâte-sur-pâte' (paste on paste, or clay on clay) was the technique of building up successive layers of 'slip' on a tinted parian body in its clay state. These layers of white or polychrome slip had to be applied to the pot when it was 'workable', which meant that it had to be kept overnight in damp lead-lined boxes while in the process of decoration. One of Minton's most significant contributions to Victorian ceramics, the technique was developed by Marc Louis Solon, who came to Minton in 1870 and had

worked on the process at Sèvres. Solon skilfully built up his subjects, exploiting to the full the technique's ability to render the translucency of drapery, water and other materials. His themes were maidens plagued by mischievous cherubs who were imprisoned, chained to railings, whipped, or fed as a sacrifice to an 'eternal flame'!

Solon's shapes were of classical inspiration or totally new, and with the most complex handles. His choice of ground colour was unique, his 'changing pink' (*pâte changeante*) varying from strawberry to mushroom, depending on the light. A pair of these pink ground shapes was exhibited at the Paris Exhibition of 1878.

Pâte-sur-pâte was laborious, time-consuming and expensive to produce, but Minton allowed Solon to devote all his time to this type of decoration over a long period. He trained a number of apprentices

MINTON PÂTE-SUR-PÂTE VASE DEPICTING THE SPARTAN GIRLS WRESTLING BEFORE LYCURGUS, M.L. SOLON, 1903 (87cm/34½in)

– A. Birks, L. Birks, Mellor, Rhead, Hollins and Bradbury – who were responsible for the more repetitive work while Solon himself would execute the main figures. Each piece signed by Solon is unique. The largest pâte-sur-pâte vase produced by Minton was commissioned by Queen Victoria to commemorate her Jubilee of 1887. Solon spent seven months on the decoration alone.

Pâte-sur-pâte continued to be produced until 1937, when it was used to create royal profiles on commemorative wares and to decorate Art Deco-style cigarette boxes.

Minton was fortunate in securing the services of Dresser, who provided a series of dramatic designs using the Minton turquoise and strong pink as grounds for stylized Japanese motifs painted in enamels and outlined in gold. These were not replicas and, in some examples, were more adventurous than the originals. Arnoux himself, along with Kirkby and Reuter, also produced work in this style.

In the Minton archives are books of Japanese bird and flower paintings by Tsunenobu and Maikawa of Kyoto, the source for many porcelains of the 1870s.

wonderful concoctions. New cults such as the Aesthetic Movement, the Pre-Raphaelites and the realism of the Renaissance directly influenced Minton earthenware production but had a less aggressive effect on its porcelains.

The large earthenware plaques and moonflasks, freely painted at Minton's London studio under the supervision of William Stephen Coleman, were excellent vehicles for the Aesthetic style of decoration. On china, however, the painting was more restrained – to fit a smaller surface area and to allow for the additional

MINTON DESSERT PLATES, 1879
(24cm/9½in)

This bone china part dessert service shows Oriental, Moorish and Venetian influences. Other pieces in the service represent German, Indian, Austrian and French themes. The containers are painted in E. Reuter's precise style, and the flowers and foliage in the free style of R. Pilsbury. (LEFT)

MINTON ADULT'S TOY TEA SERVICE, c.1871

This French inspired bone china service (pattern A 501) has printed and enamelled rose festoons, turquoise enamelled bands and gold-printed decoration. It was used for display rather than as a child's tea service. (OPPOSITE)

ORIENTAL INFLUENCE

Chinese figures in landscapes and richly gilt and coloured Imari patterns feature strongly in the earliest Minton pattern books of the 1800 period, and the delicate chinoiserie designs remain popular to this day. A further stimulus was provided by the first major showing of Japanese artifacts at the London Exhibition of 1862.

Cloisonné wares attracted the interest of a progressive group of young designers which included Christopher Dresser. Dresser had spent time in Japan studying Japanese artifacts and this interest, together with his training as a botanist, inspired many of his designs.

Japanese-style figures, such as *Japanese Lady* and *Japanese Lady and Gentleman* were also produced. These Japanese influences were long lasting. At the Paris Exhibition of 1878 a flask was exhibited decorated in coloured clays in relief with flying storks and circular patches by Toft, and new tableware patterns were named 'Hollins Japan' and 'Connaught Japan'.

ECLECTICISM

Throughout the Victorian era, Minton used a glorious pot-pourri of styles – Rococo shapes with Oriental motifs, Classical shapes with Medieval designs and Art Nouveau borders were among the many

embellishment of gold – but female heads and semi-nude maidens against a background of peacock feathers, Japanese prunus, and sunflowers, decorated many dessert services and flasks into the 1880s.

It is important to stress, however, that throughout the life of the factory 'traditional' patterns retained their popularity. These were given a new dimension by the introduction of the acid gold technique in 1863 which enabled gold ornamentation and borders to be given a textured finish in bas-relief. This technique lent itself particularly to special commissions, and to the crested and badged services which were supplied to the Royal Family and the aristocracy worldwide.

ART NOUVEAU

Minton was influenced by the Viennese Secession Movement. Elongated shapes were introduced, with strap-like or sinuous handles with plant-like or stylized floral motifs in enamel colours of lilac, turquoise, green and crimson, outlined in raised paste gold. Other exaggerated shapes were decorated traditionally with Adam-style swags or classical figures in pâte-sur-pâte. Table wares were also decorated with Art Nouveau borders richly gilt and intended for the luxury market.

ART DECO

Stylish figures of the 1930s were designed by Doris Lindner. A particularly daring example, *The Bather*, wears a jazzy two-piece swimsuit. Another fashionable figure evocative of the period, *The Hikers*, was produced in two colourways (variations).

New tea- and coffeeware shapes were introduced, notably the cube-shaped 'stacking sets' supplied to Lyons Coffee Houses and the Cunard Steamship Line. Tulip-shaped cups were introduced with angular handles, and favoured decorative motifs were squares, diamonds, crescent moons, stars, oblongs and polka dots.

Lustre wares are associated with this period, the earliest examples appearing around 1916. John Wadsworth, Art Director of the factory from 1902, designed a range of shimmering fruit bowls, rose bowls, vases and tazzas, in iridescent colours, of blue/purple/turquoise, peach and green. They were painted with stylized cockerels, birds of paradise, or flower baskets, and had borders of dragons, pines or fruit. China lamps were produced in strong colours of orange, green, silver and crimson, decorated with polka dots, swirls, stylized leaves, waves and stripes. Silk shades were supplied to co-ordinate with the bases.

CHAMBERLAIN

Robert Chamberlain's factory, on the Diglis side of Worcester Cathedral, was the deadly rival of the other Worcester factory, that of Joseph Flight. Starting in the 1780s, it was well established by the 1820s, and had produced some famous services by then, such as those made for Admiral Nelson and the Prince Regent. It had even flirted with a highly translucent frit body which it called 'Regent China', an attempt to rival the fine Welsh porcelains.

Chamberlain had a number of highly talented painters. Apart from Thomas Baxter, who was employed there after his return from Swansea, these painters included Humphrey Chamberlain junior who, unusually, was allowed to sign some of his superb figure subjects; Walter Chamberlain, his brother, who also painted figure subjects; George Davis, the Flight factory painter of 'fancy' birds, known as 'Doctor' Davis by his colleagues; and Enoch Doe and George Rogers who painted flowers and landscapes for the factory and set up their own decorating establishment.

There was a sizeable quantity of decorating done outside the factory in Worcester,

MINTON TABLEWARE PATTERN BOOK, c.1930

This open new pattern (NP) book of the 1930s shows designs of the period. Among these designs by John Wadsworth and Reginald Haggar are stylish hand-painted geometrics, printed and enamelled florals and the more traditional patterns which remained popular. (RIGHT)

CHAMBERLAIN WORCESTER BASKET
AND INKWELL, c.1845 (basket: L21cm/8¼in)

Examples of how fine craftsmanship can become
ludicrous. Both pieces have well modelled and
finely painted shells that swamp the vessels they are
meant to embellish. The beautifully painted dog
appears encaged in seaweed and shells.

either by painters from the factory who were also moonlighting, as Doe and Rogers were, or by decorating establishments proper, such as that of Conningsby Norris and Sparkes. Naturally, the main factories were not keen to allow these independents to have factory-made ware on which to work, so most of it was bought from Coalport, which specialized in supplying glazed bone-china blanks for outside artists. Sparkes' shop in Broad Street, Worcester, claimed the patronage of Queen Adelaide, the widow of William IV, who lived for some years at Witley Court, a few miles from Worcester. Its advertisement in Lascelles Gazetteer for Worcester of 1851 is an interesting social comment on china-buying at that time:—

'Dinner, Dessert, Tea and Coffee Services
always in stock from the lowest description up
to the most costly patterns upon the fine old
Dresden and Sèvres shapes, so much admired
by connoisseurs of really fine transparent
porcelain. The Nobility, Clergy and Gentry,
are respectfully informed that orders are taken
at this Establishment for Services got up with
Arms, Crest, Mottos etc., on the most reason-
able charges – crests from sixpence each.'

Chamberlain's factory did its best to bring the new middle-class buyers of

porcelain into its net from the 1820s to 1840s, mainly by producing relatively inexpensive tea, dinner and dessert sets. The sets, comprising about 42 pieces, cost upwards of two guineas (about £150 today) for simple printed patterns without gilding. The constituents of a tea set at that time included coffee cups which shared the same saucer as the tea cup. There were no small tea plates, which did not come in until the late nineteenth century. A great number of dessert services were made, as it was the custom to finish dinner with fruit eaten from a separate service comprising plates and dishes or comports.

While Flight, Barr and Barr clung to the vanishing market making wares for the nobility, and died in the attempt, Chamberlain tried to produce both fine wares for the wealthy and simpler wares for customers of more modest means. It even moved into the production of cheaper, opaque earthenware or vitreous bodies. Unlike Flight, it threw itself into producing figure subjects and ornaments: small animal models, sets of five figures of the Rainer family of Tyrolean dancers who toured England in 1827, milkmaids and theatricals. A growing number of cottages made as pastille burners and night lights show that

Chamberlain was trying to cope with the change of mood in porcelain in the 1830s. However, its attempts at walking the delicate and dangerous tightrope seem stilted and old-fashioned, a half-hearted compromise. An extreme example is the series of superbly painted plaques with scenes of the Houses of Parliament or Brighton, which were 'modernized' with borders of porcelain shells. Although finely made and naturalistically coloured, these 'shells' serve only to lower the pieces to the level of cheap seaside souvenirs.

The Chamberlain factory's attempts at producing flowered vases and ornaments in the 'Coalbrookdale' style were also unsatisfactory because the basic shapes still clung to a Georgian grandeur.

At the 1851 Great Exhibition, Chamberlain was damned with faint praise, the critics liking only the double-pierced vessels that were based on Sèvres, for their technical ingenuity. The china of this last period is generally poor, heavy and crazed, often marked Chamberlain & Co., sometimes with a top-heavy '2'. Chamberlain and Company, as the firm was known from 1840 to 1851, gave up the struggle and a new partnership took over in 1852.

KERR AND BINNS

This partnership brought fresh life back to the Worcester factory. W.H. Kerr, an Irishman, was joined by R.W. Binns (in 1852), and their first task was to restore the qualities that had made Worcester porcelain famous in the past. The 1853 Exhibition of Art and Industry in Dublin presented them with the perfect occasion to display Worcester's revived spirit.

Kerr and Binns asked an Irish modeller, W.B. Kirk, to produce a special dessert service based on Shakespeare's play *A Midsummer Night's Dream*. The body was a daring combination of bone china and unglazed parian, and used the same feldspar stone from County Fermanagh as was used at Belleek. Worcester had finally discovered parian, which was to stand it in good stead for another 80 years.

The Shakespeare service, which had especially lively modelling, was a considerable success. Queen Victoria requested a special viewing and this probably led to Kerr and Binns' greatest commission, a royal dessert service that Her Majesty desired should have her favourite ground colour of *bleu celeste*, in the Minton style.

Several skilled new painters were taken on, chief among them being Thomas Bott, who specialized in what he called 'Limoges Enamel'. This was a white enamel on a dark blue ground which imitated the medieval enamels on metal that were the speciality of Limoges. The work was very time-consuming and it is said that his masterpieces, a ewer and basin and two vases made to commemorate the 800th anniversary of the Norman Conquest, took him two years to create, the strain of which was so great that he died shortly after their completion. His son, T. J. Bott, continued the work and was joined by other fine artists such as John Hopewell, who painted birds, and David Bates, who painted flowers at the factory, but left in 1880 to become an oil painter.

The factory did not concentrate just on elaborate pieces, but also produced quantities of relatively inexpensive small ornaments. Many of these had a useful purpose as well: humorous animals were in reality match pots, and hollow figurines became the first of a series of candle extinguishers. These figurines included monks and nuns, abbots and abbesses.

Much Kerr and Binns ware was not marked but where a mark did appear it was generally a circle which contained four scrolling 'W's, a crescent (one of the early marks) and the number 51 (this related to 1751, when the factory was founded). When impressed this mark sometimes looks like a circle with a cross inside it. The mark used on the finest wares was a shield with the initials 'K & B', the word Worcester, and sometimes the last two numbers of the years, e.g. 58 for 1858, and the initials of the painter.

CHAMBERLAIN WORCESTER INKWELL OF KING JOHN'S TOMB, *c.*1846–50 (L22cm/8½in)

This inkwell was made following the opening of the real tomb in Worcester Cathedral in 1846. (LEFT)

ROYAL WORCESTER 'AESTHETIC' TEAPOT, 1882 (H15cm/6in)

This teapot is a skit upon Oscar Wilde and the Aesthetic Movement. (BELOW)

WORCESTER ROYAL PORCELAIN

In 1862 the Worcester factory changed its name yet again and became a new limited company which has continued to the present day. It is often referred to as Royal Worcester.

At first the factory was thoroughly Victorian in outlook and it slowly overtook the lead that Minton had established. It kept in step with fashion by producing unglazed and glazed parian figures and busts, 'Capo di Monte' Italianate figures which were freestanding or moulded on vessels, 'Henri Deux' based on early French ceramics, and Victorianized versions of medieval German, Italian and Persian styles. The trade names chosen by the Victorian manufacturers to evoke earlier styles rarely related closely to the finished article, if at all.

One style the company specialized in was 'Japanesque', a westernized form of Japanese art that was extensively copied by everyone, even the Japanese themselves. The popularity of 'Japanesque' or 'Japonaise' swept the country: ladies wore kimonos and carried fans or a Japanese lap

dog; houses were lined with Japanese-style wallpaper and filled with bamboo furniture.

Gilbert and Sullivan also poked fun at the concurrent Aesthetic Movement, in their operetta *Patience*. The piece that is most evocative of the derision that met the Aesthetic Movement is Royal Worcester's Aesthetic teapot, a skit on Oscar Wilde and the Aesthetic Movement. The lid of the pot is male on one side and female on the other; the figures wear large flowers like a brooch and are dressed in the 'greenery-yallery' colours favoured by the supporters of the Grosvenor Gallery, the London art centre of the cult. The tea pours out of the palm of

ROYAL WORCESTER VASE BY GEORGE
OWEN, LATE 19TH CENTURY (22cm/8¾in)

*George Owen is rightly regarded as the greatest of
all reticulators.* (RIGHT)

ROYAL WORCESTER CANDLESTICKS,
LATE 19TH CENTURY (27cm/10½in)

*This beautiful pair of glazed parian candlesticks
was modelled by James Hadley. The figures are in
the style of Kate Greenaway.* (BELOW)

GRAINGER WORCESTER BOWER
GROUP, *c.*1830 (H25cm/10in)

*This beautiful group is made of unglazed biscuit
china, the gentle colours on some of the flowers
having been touched by a brush loaded with
ceramic colour and frit.* (BELOW)

one hand, the other arm 'bent in the Aesthetic stance' is the handle, and underneath is the peculiar inscription 'Fearful consequences through the laws of Natural Selection and Evolution of living up to one's teapot'. This is a reference to an exhibition held at the Grosvenor Gallery at which visitors were shown one piece only – a beautiful Chinese blue-and-white teapot. They were asked to contemplate this and go home and try to live up to it. It encapsulates also the debate on Darwin's evolutionary theory which was raging at the time.

The chief modeller at this period was James Hadley, later to leave and form his own company (1896–1905), who had a sure touch with shapes of vases and especially with the modelling of human figures. Large numbers of different figure subjects were made in the beautiful glazed parian body,

either sold in the white or with simple or elaborate decoration. Fine painters and gilders were employed to do this work, the very best being known as 'decorators', who were capable of all the decorating processes. Chief among these were James and Thomas Scott Callowhill. Among the painters who worked on vases, plates and plaques were John Hopewell, who specialized in birds; Charles Palmere, who painted peasants in the Teniers style; Robert Perling, who concentrated on Landseer subjects; Edward Raby senior, who modelled flowers; Edward Raby junior, who painted flowers; and Josiah Rushton, who painted figures. Signatures did not become common until about 1900 and then only for the top painters.

In 1893 Royal Worcester, in common with many leading British companies,

mounted impressive stands at the Chicago Exhibition, following up its many successes at art fairs in such cities as London, Paris, Vienna and Philadelphia. Fairs were an opportunity to impress by showing the most elaborate pieces. Worcester's two major *tours de force* were shown at Chicago and are now in the Dyson Perrins Museum in Worcester. They epitomize High Victorian craftsmanship, the desire to impress and the urge to lavish an enormous amount of time and expense on a single piece. The first piece, the huge Chicago Exhibition Vase, 133 cm (52⅜ in) high, is typically eclectic, with modelled cupids on an ivory ground combining Italian Renaissance and Indian styles. The main body is painted with flowers of the four seasons by Raby and heavily gilded with raised gold and bronze. It took a year to make.

The second piece is totally different. It is a glazed parian covered vase, hand-reticulated (pierced) with more than 5,000 holes by George Owen, the master of this incredibly difficult craft. The holes are complicated geometrical shapes which give the appearance of lace, and had to be cut out of the raw clay while the pot was in a 'green' state, that is while the body still had moisture in it. The difficulties of this technique are indescribable and the method died with its chief exponent.

ROYAL WORCESTER PLAQUE, PAINTED BY HARRY DAVIS, EARLY 20TH CENTURY (W23cm/9in)

Harry Davis, probably the finest ceramic artist of the twentieth century, is represented here by his most famous of subjects, sheep in a Scottish Highland setting. This plaque is one of a pair.

In 1902 Royal Worcester acquired the Grainger factory, which had been formed in about 1806. Grainger had absorbed Victorian Rococo better than the other Worcester companies and produced lively porcelain in the 1820s and 1830s to rival even Minton and Coalport. Many of these pieces are not marked, with the result that Grainger porcelain has received scant attention from collectors who attribute examples to other factories.

In the second half of the nineteenth century the chief painters were the Stintons – John senior and junior, and the latter's brother James and son Harry. In 1902 the remaining Stintons moved across town to Royal Worcester where John junior and son Harry painted Highland cattle studies, and James concentrated on game birds, all of which are now highly collectable. It is a

salutatory fact that neither John nor Harry had ever been to Scotland in their lives and painted all their work from imagination and postcards. The Stintons joined a talented group of painters that included Richard Sebright, who specialized in fruit, William Hawkins, the foreman, who concentrated on flowers and copies of famous paintings, and Harry Davis, perhaps the finest ceramic painter of this century. A great range of superb paintings poured from Davis's brushes – copies of paintings by Claude and Corot, Highland sheep and English landscapes, and especially fine London scenes of the 1920s. He fired his pieces more than the other painters – sometimes the metallic oxides would be fired in the kilns up to a dozen times, which gave them an extraordinary depth of colour and perspective.

Financial problems beset Royal Worcester in the 1920s and 1930s when only the money of the collector Dyson Perrins kept them afloat. It introduced a highly successful hard-porcelain body and attempted to compete with the popularity of Doulton's ornamental figures by creating numbers of figurines modelled in the Art Deco style by freelance artists. Most of these were unpopular and few were sold. Inevitably, however, they are now highly sought-after.

The public demanded naturalism and the only two modellers whose work was popularly accepted were Doris Lindner, who created dogs, farmyard animals and horses, and Freda Doughty who produced studies of children. Freda Doughty introduced her sister Dorothy's bird models to the factory and in 1935 there began a long series of naturalistic birds perched on foliage made for the American market in limited editions. These were followed by a series of equestrian and bull models by Doris Lindner, starting with the model of Princess Elizabeth on Tommy at the Trooping the Colour in 1947, in a limited edition of 100 pieces. These bone-china creations are among the great porcelain achievements of the twentieth century but have suffered a decline in popularity due to quantities of so-called 'limited' editions which are sold as potential investments.

DERBY

The original Derby factory was purchased by Bloor in 1811 and continued until 1848. This is usually known as the 'Bloor Derby' period and has a poor reputation among collectors because the quality of the bone-china body declined and the pieces of this period tend to stain yellow or brown. However, the standard of decoration that was such a feature of late eighteenth-century Derby continued, and the famous Japan or Imari patterns that were introduced in the eighteenth century have continued in production to the present day. A great number of figures were produced, mostly subjects which were introduced in the eighteenth century, and although not as fine as the earlier examples, they are still worthy of attention. Marks used were a printed crown and 'D', often transferred via the printer's thumb, and the name 'Bloor Derby'.

The company closed in 1848 when a new factory was established in King Street, Derby until 1935; this factory specialized in copies of earlier Derby wares. From 1862 the mark used was a copy of the crown, batons and 'D' mark, with the initials S.H.

DERBY IMARI CUP AND SAUCER, 1890

Pattern number 383 was one of the most popular of the Royal Crown Derby designs. Imari, or Japanese style patterns normally have underglaze blue and onglaze red and gold decoration. (BELOW)

for Stevenson and Hancock and, after 1866, for Sampson Hancock. The production had little to recommend or condemn it.

In 1876 a new factory was established, the Derby Crown Porcelain Co., until 1890, when it was continued by the Royal Crown Derby Co. Derby Crown used a printed crown and cypher mark and the words 'Royal Crown Derby' were added in 1890. A date-code system was introduced so that it is possible to date the piece to the year of manufacture. Large quantities of the Imari pattern were produced, then, as now, enormously popular. But it was the superbly strong ground colours and outstanding gilding and jewelling which set the Royal Crown factory apart. Finest of all the decorators was Desiré Leroy, a Frenchman who had worked at Sèvres and who specialized in meticulously accurate painting and gilding. Other skilled painters included Rouse and Dean. Their works stand viewing under a magnifying glass and rank with other Victorian masterpieces by such great craftsmen as Owen of Worcester, but overall Derby's painting did not reach the height attained by the other factories.

SPODE COPELAND

Spode is usually credited with the invention of the classic English bone-china formula by the end of the eighteenth century, and although porcelain played a relatively small part in comparison with its huge production of printed earthenware, ranges of tea and table wares were made, from the simple to the elaborate, and fine ornaments were produced.

Unlike many of the Staffordshire factories, a fairly high proportion of Spode's porcelain is marked, usually with the word 'Spode' and the pattern number in red. One of the most elaborate of these patterns is number 1166. Spode's pattern numbers run in a progression from 1 and had reached over 5,000 by 1833 when it entered a partnership with Copeland and Garrett.

William Copeland took sole charge of the factory in 1847, by which time it had introduced its parian porcelain body for figure subjects and busts. Parian ware, or statuary porcelain, was meant to look like marble and the title was taken from Paros,

PAIR OF DERBY VASES DECORATED BY D. LEROY, 1906 (H13.5cm/5½in)

These superbly jewelled and painted trophy vases were decorated by Desiré Leroy in 1906 and are shown by the original Derby pattern book. Leroy's virtuosity and skill in such difficult and time-consuming processes are breathtaking when seen at close quarters. (ABOVE)

the island where Greek and Roman marble was mined. Most busts were classically inspired copies of ancient marbles or mythological, historical and present-day figures presented in classical dress. Famous sculptures of the day, admired at the various exhibitions, were used, reduced in size by a pantograph which reproduced every nuance of the original. The busts and complicated figures were, of course, much less expensive than the original marble sculptures and brought fine art into the homes of the general public. If you could

COPELAND PARIAN FIGURE OF 'DANCING GIRL REPOSING', BY W.C. MARSHALL, 1849 (47cm/18½in) (LEFT)

COPELAND GILDED AND JEWELLED PLATE, c.1865 (22.5cm/8⅞in) (BELOW)

COPELAND VASE, PAINTED BY HÜRTON, 1862 (70cm/27½in)

This vase was made for display at the 1862 Exhibition in London. Many factories made special pieces for exhibitions as a means of showing off their finest skills. (BELOW)

the best. The bodies were slightly different in tone; Minton's was whiter than Copeland's, which has a creamier look. Much parian is unfortunately not marked.

Apart from parian, Copeland produced some superbly crafted services and vases; some of the latter painted by C.F. Hürton could hardly be bettered. Copeland's factory still continues today, but under the name of Spode. It has merged with Royal Worcester in one of those apparently ever-changing ceramic conglomerates.

afford a guinea or two you could have your own copy of Hiram Power's *Greek Slave* in your drawing room. Or you could buy tickets in the draws organized by the Art Union of London and hope to win, for example, a copy of Copeland's *Dancing Girl Reposing*, sculpted by W.C. Marshall and commissioned by the Art Union in 1849.

These works by Copeland had an enormous success at the Great Exhibition of 1851. Although Copeland was not alone in the manufacture of fine parian, its busts and figures, along with Minton's, were among

COALPORT

By the late 1790s John Rose had established a porcelain factory on the banks of the River Severn at Coalport near Ironbridge, and by 1799 had taken over the Caughley factory. Coalport had developed into a large factory by the 1820s, making mainly tea and table wares, most of which are not marked except for pattern numbers. Their series ran from 1 to 999 and was followed by 1 again with the next series number over it – thus 999 was

followed by 2/1; 2/999 by 3/1, etc. The factory produced good white wares, quantities of which were sold to independent outside decorators, many of them in London. The firm discovered its strength in the 1830s with flower-encrusted pieces in the Rococo style. A few of these pieces were marked with the word 'Coalbrookdale', 'CD' or 'C. Dale' which has given the title of Coalbrookdale to these wares. Not all pieces attributed to Coalbrookdale were made at the Coalport factory, however; flower-encrusted works were produced by

COALPORT
DESSERT SERVICE
AT BRIGHTON
PAVILION, EARLY
19TH CENTURY

*This service, of an
Imari design in blue,
pink and gold, was
presented by George III
to his physician Dr.
Willis.*

many other porcelain factories, such as Minton, Alcock and Grainger's Worcester.

Flowers and leaves are the very embodiment of Victorian Rococo and were applied abundantly to a wide range of objects. They smothered pairs of vases or garnitures of three – a larger one in the middle – displayed on mantelpieces; they covered desk sets in libraries and pot-pourris. Even tea wares were encrusted, making them almost unusable. Flower-making is a highly specialized craft and only the nimblest, smallest female fingers could fashion the single petals, stamens and stems which were joined with liquid slip to build the flower. Many flowered pieces were glazed and coloured; some were left unglazed but have colours mixed with frit touched onto a few key flowers to make them more prominent. A few examples are adorned with modelled fruit as well as flowers, but they do tend to be far less attractive.

From the 1830s Coalport began to produce vases and ornamental dessert ware with strong ground colours in imitation of the two famous ground colours of Sèvres, *bleu celeste* and *rose Pompadour*, or *rose du Barry*. There was considerable Sèvres influence at Coalport at this time, especially in the painting of two artists, Cook and Randall. Cook's speciality was flowers and Randall's fancy birds. As well as work for Coalport Randall decorated a vast number of Sèvres blanks or added grounds to simply decorated pieces. In the 1860s and 1870s Randall changed to painting real tropical birds, which are very fine.

Coalport left its original home in the village of Coalport to go to Stoke-on-Trent, where it is now part of the Wedgwood group. Two of the great bottle kilns at Coalport are still preserved as part of the Ironbridge Gorge Museum, and Randall's work can be seen on display in the kiln in

COALPORT FLOWERED VASE, *c*.1835
(H28.2cm/11⅛in)

This vase is a fine example of the neo-Rococo style of the 1830s.

WEDGWOOD BONE CHINA VASE, c.1885–90 (22cm/8¾in)
*Although the Josiah Wedgwood factory seemed to be happiest making pottery,
they did make some good bone china. This vase is in Victorianized Regency
style.* (RIGHT)

COALPORT DESK SET, c.1835 (L31cm/12¼in)
The bleu céleste *ground contains panels painted with fancy birds and flowers
by Randall and Cook. The set is in the style of mid-eighteenth century Sèvres,
but was made at Coalport almost a century later.* (BELOW)

which it was originally fired. Since 1875 the Coalport mark has included the date AD1750, the inaccurately claimed date of the factory's founding. It is a common misconception that this represents the date when the piece was made.

WEDGWOOD

Josiah Wedgwood & Sons produced the finest and most original earthenware created in England from 1759, but made porcelain for only a short period (from about 1812 to 1829) in the early nineteenth century. The factory then began to produce porcelain once more, from 1878 onwards.

Their early bone china is very white and often simply and tastefully decorated. Josiah the first seems to have had a dislike of porcelain and although Josiah the second made his token amount, he did not fling himself wholeheartedly into the making. In the last hundred years great quantities of bone china have been made and Wedgwood also produced a parian body, which it called Carrara after the famous Italian marble. However, it was still a drop in the ocean compared with its more substantial production of pottery.

The most spectacular wares made in the twentieth century were the so-called 'Fairyland' lustre wares – bowls, vases or plaques painted and printed with gold and decorated with elves and fairies in moonlight scenes, designed by Daisy Makeig-Jones from 1914. These were inspired by the Art Nouveau movement and it was not going to be long before Art Deco and the jazzy designs of skilled designers such as Clarice Cliff were to take over Stoke-on-Trent.

ROCKINGHAM

Pottery had been made on the estate of Earl Fitzwilliam (later to become Marquess of Rockingham) in Yorkshire from about 1745, but in 1825 the owners, the Bramelds, became insolvent. The earl gave them financial assistance and by 1826 porcelain was being produced, but the financial management of the business was badly handled and the firm struggled on until 1842, when it closed. Like Flight and Chamberlain of Worcester, Rockingham remained solidly Regency and its attempt to move with the times were almost risible. At its best Rockingham produced superb tea and dessert wares, vases and well-modelled animals and figures. Few pieces were marked except for the saucers of tea services, which have the Griffin mark with various wordings under the base, printed in

red until 1830 and in puce thereafter. Pattern numbers from 1 up to about 1586 and then from 2/1 up to 2/220 were used; a red painted class number 'C L 1' to 'C L 14' or so was sometimes used under some ornamental pieces.

There are three things of which Rockingham collectors should be aware. The first is that many reproductions were made in glistening hard-paste porcelain in Paris bearing the Griffin mark. The second is that many genuine contemporary pieces are attributed to Rockingham through ignorance. The third is that, as far as is known, Rockingham never made animals such as sheep and poodles with added scraps of clay to simulate wool or fur.

OTHER FACTORIES

There were many factories producing porcelain in the nineteenth century. Many lasted only a few years and few warrant serious attention – with the exception of those discussed below.

ROCKINGHAM 'RHINOCEROS' VASE, 1830s (H98cm/3ft 2½in)

The peculiarity of this vase stems from a Victorian misunderstanding of the qualities of the Rococo. (TOP)

PART OF A ROCKINGHAM TEASET, 1830s

A slightly unhappy mixture of Regency and Rococo styles. The only pieces to carry the griffin mark are the saucers. (ABOVE)

CHARLES BOURNE

This Staffordshire firm made some very superior porcelain between 1817 and 1830, of such a high standard that the wares are usually confused with better-known firms. The patterns were frequently floral and Imari types and are best recognized by their system of putting 'CB' above the pattern numbers, which range from 'CB 1' to at least 'CB 1017'.

SAMUEL ALCOCK

Also a Staffordshire firm, from about 1826–1859 this factory made some very good tea wares which have only just been identified. It used a pattern sequence of 1 to 9990, then fractional numbers with 2, 3, 4, etc. as the numerators. They are best known for their ornamental wares, especially elaborate parian vessels and busts, but they also made beautiful animals on bases, such as poodles. Pottery vases decorated in the Greco-Roman style with classical subjects are more likely to be marked 'S.A. & Co'. The factory continued to produce porcelain under the direction of Sir James Duke and Nephews until 1864.

H. AND R. DANIEL

The Daniels, who had previously supervised the decoration of Spode, ran their own business from about 1826 to 1846. They specialized in tea services in the Neo-Rococo style, with highly eccentric handles and feet and also finely decorated dessert wares. These tea services are rarely marked but carry a pattern number series that runs from 3,500 to 8,844.

DAVENPORT

More famous for its earthenware, this Staffordshire factory made bone china from about 1808 until 1887, happily making the transition into the Victorian era. Wares are often marked with the word Davenport, or an anchor, or sometimes both are shown together on the same piece.

MILES MASON

Originally a dealer in Oriental porcelain, Mason began as a manufacturer when stock became difficult to obtain in about 1800. At first he produced high-fired hard-paste porcelain but moved on to bone china until 1830. Tea- and dessert-ware shapes were unique to the factory, with thumb rests on cups, which point backwards. Marks are rare; 'M. Mason is usually impressed into the foot-rims of teapots only. Mason's fame rests with its ironstone body.

RIDGWAY

Various partnerships in Staffordshire produced porcelain. The most important were John and William Ridgway, in partnership from about 1814 to 1830. Very fine tea and dinner wares were made, some of which had elaborate marks incorporating the Royal Arms. But the most helpful form of identification is the pattern number series of 2/1 up to 2/9999 followed by a 3 series on ornamental wares, a 5 series on tea wares, and 6 on dessert wares.

DOULTON

One of the most famous firms in the field of stoneware and earthenware, Doulton, did not start production of fine porcelain until 1882, in Stoke-on-Trent. In the last years of the nineteenth century some fine ornamental ware and finely painted services were produced, and in the twentieth century a flood of figures has been issued by the factory. These figures range in subject matter, the most contemporary-looking models being perhaps the bathing girls, synonymous with Art Deco style.

SMALL FACTORIES

There were hundreds of small factories which made porcelain in Stoke-on-Trent during the nineteenth century and up to the First World War. Among those whose work stands out are: John Bevington (1872–1892), which produced porcelain figures and wares in the Dresden style; W.H. Goss (1858–1944) which manufactured parian busts and figures which inspired a market for mass-produced commemorative souvenir mementoes of either miniature vases with coats of arms or famous buildings; George Jones & Sons, from 1861, whose pâte-sur-pâte was produced in the 1870s by Frederick Schenk; Hicks and Meigh who produced bone china (from about 1816–1835); Hilditch (about 1811–1867); Machin (about 1803–1848); Mayer and Newbold (1817–1833); Moore Brothers (about 1872–1915) who employed some fine artists such as Boullemier and Sieffert; and Robinson and Leadbeater (1864–1924).

Last, but not least, is Belleek in County Fermanagh, Northern Ireland, which was established in 1863 and continues production to the present day. It produces glazed parian that has not changed much in composition or form over the whole period of its existence. Some pieces are highly sculptural in form. Belleek wares, especially those of the so-called First Period, without the words 'Co. Fermanagh Ireland', are now highly collectable.

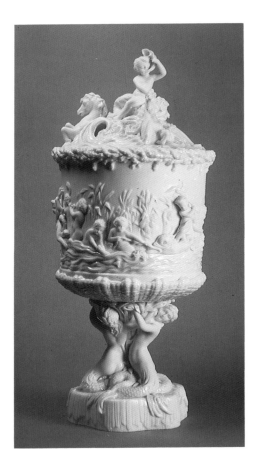

ROYAL DOULTON BATHING GIRL FIGURINE, *c.1930 (12.7cm/5in)*

A cheeky and humorous figurine made in the Art Deco style. The quality of modelling and painting of these charming pieces was at its finest in the 1920s and 1930s.

STAFFORDSHIRE TEASET, FOLEY, *c.1900* (ABOVE)

BELLEEK PARIAN VASE, LATE 19TH CENTURY (47cm/18½in) (TOP)

AMERICAN PORCELAIN

The identification of American porcelain requires familiarity with the chinaware of other countries, for many American shapes and decorations are derivative and difficult to distinguish from English, French, German or Italian forms.

Since most techniques used by American potters had been perfected earlier, outside America, the easiest way of identifying American from English or Continental porcelain is by its paste. By strict definition, all American porcelain is soft paste or artificial porcelain, but some looks like hard paste and its makers claimed it to be 'true' porcelain, though analysis inevitably reveals the presence of an ingredient such as ball clay or bone ash. Late nineteenth-century attempts in America to imitate Sèvres or Paris porcelain, in particular, might therefore be better described as 'adulterated hard paste'.

Most clays and feldspar found in the United States did not behave predictably when used in the recipes proven in England or France. Some kaolin, for instance, contained large amounts of water-soluble iron, an unknown substance to the early American potters, which was ruinous to any porcelain body. So early American ceramicists sometimes preferred to depend wholly or partly on imported materials, and indeed, the practice was maintained by a few into the twentieth century.

However, a fine bed of kaolin was discovered during the eighteenth century in South Carolina. Together with clays from Delaware and other American materials, this was utilized by Gousse Bonnin and George Anthony Morris to produce porcelain in Philadelphia, Pennsylvania, between 1770 and 1773. The paste was remarkably similar to that made by Bow, and the shapes and chinoiserie decoration in blue were so much like those produced at other English factories of the period, that several years ago an eminent English cera-

mics expert refused to believe the examples shown to him had not been made in Britain. Scientific analysis later revealed in them the presence of a type of quartz unknown in British porcelain.

Porcelain was produced in English shapes but with a body and glaze similar to those of French porcelain, by Dr. Henry Mead of New York City. This output began in 1816, and continued at the same factory under the management of Louis Decasse and Nicholas Louis Edouard Chanou in the mid-1820s. A gilded tea set bearing the mark of Decasse and Chanou and an American eagle stamped in red is the most important surviving product from there. A factory was also built in nearby Jersey City, but all that remains which is attributable to

BONNIN & MORRIS PICKLE STAND, PHILADELPHIA, 1770–72 (H14.3cm/5⅝in)

this effort is one small bowl. Such early ventures failed partly because of the problem of trying to harness native materials, but also because of the economic climate of the time. Businesses rose and fell rapidly on the waves of financial panic that plagued the new Republic. Meanwhile,

porcelain of equal if not preferable quality to the local product could be obtained more cheaply from abroad.

America's first successful porcelain factory, founded in Philadelphia by William Ellis Tucker, started its kiln in 1827 and remained in production for 12 years, turning out a great volume and variety of wares. The majority of Tucker porcelain has a greenish translucency, though later examples are orange or straw-coloured, which indicates that at least two glaze formulae were used and possibly more than one body. One vasiform pitcher and a gilded design normally found on tea and coffee services appear to be unique to Tucker. The latter, commonly called 'the spider pattern', more closely resembles a line of squid swimming sideways across the hollow pieces. Otherwise, it is difficult for most people to detect Tucker porcelain from French or especially Italian porcelain of the same period. However, a test using an ultra-violet light was developed by the American Phillip Curtis for questionable pieces which are gilded. Under shortwave ultraviolet light a halo effect appears around the gold. A similar effect can sometimes be produced around decorative details on nineteenth-century French and German porcelain, but not around the gilding.

Although Tucker wares of the late 1830s have a Victorian appearance, it was the next generation of porcelain-makers in the 1850s that would go a step further and begin creating truly American shapes and decoration. Others had painted American designs and slogans on their products, but Charles Cartlidge of Greenpoint, New York, made hotel ewers or pitchers with moulded eagles under the spouts and representations of the Charter Oak on the sides. He also produced an eagle paperweight and plaques with relief portraits of famous Americans. His creations were copied by other American manufacturers such as the brothers Boch, also of Greenpoint, and the American Porcelain Manufacturing Co., of Gloucester, New Jersey.

The fascination with American shapes and symbols persisted until the time of the

Centennial Exposition in Philadelphia in 1876, when the newly formed United States Potters Association determined to show the world what could be done in the United States. Some extraordinary objects were produced for the event, including a pair of monumental vases by the Union Porcelain Works of Greenpoint, New York, with handles in the form of bison heads, a relief portrait of George Washington on either side surrounded by illustrations of important American inventions in polychrome enamels, and moulded and bench-carved highlights of American history around the bases. The firm of Ott & Brewer of Trenton, New Jersey, displayed parian sculpture created especially for the occasion by Isaac Broome. His most am-

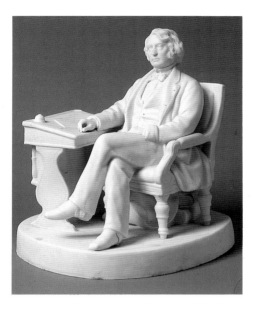

Philadelphia Exposition, particularly those from Japan, France and England, while the public revealed that its taste had not retreated from the Neoclassical. Why else would parian busts continue to be produced in America into the first decade of the twentieth century? The preference for foreign designs led many manufacturers in the United States in the late 1870s and early 1880s to produce Belleek-style wares, ivory bone china in imitation of Royal Worcester, and copies of Sèvres and other fine products from abroad. Trenton, New Jersey became the headquarters of this phenomenon until its capitulation to the plumbing industry.

An influx of imported porcelain, notably from Austria and Japan after World War I,

bitious achievement was a vase, 86.3cm (34in) high, circled by free-standing figures playing the American national game of baseball. James Carr of New York City displayed large parian busts of Jesus Christ, George Washington, Ulysses S. Grant and others, together with a figure of the abolitionist Senator, Charles Sumner.

Unfortunately, Americans were less impressed by these efforts than were visitors from abroad. American ceramic scholars praised the foreign exhibits at the

DECASSE & CHANOU GILDED TEA SERVICE, NEW YORK CITY, 1824–27 (ABOVE)

PARIAN FIGURE OF SENATOR CHARLES SUMNER, NEW YORK CITY POTTERY OF JAMES CARR, 1875 (H32.9cm/13in) (TOP)

CHARLES CARTLIDGE & CO. PRESENTATION PITCHER, GREENPOINT, NEW YORK, 1853–56 (H30cm/11¾in) (ABOVE RIGHT)

brought a halt to the manufacture of fancy porcelain in America and reduced the industry to turning out table china and products for restaurants and hotels.

The depression of 1929 further reduced the number of companies producing porcelain. Of the firms important at the turn of the century, only Lenox, Inc. continues to be a significant porcelain manufacturer in the United States, and much of its ceramics production today takes place overseas.

FAKES AND FORGERIES

Fake: to tamper with, for the purpose of deception.

Forgery: the making of a thing in fraudulent imitation of something; that which is forged, counterfeited or fabricated. *Oxford English Dictionary*

To collect porcelain is to select one of the most difficult areas on which to lavish your love and money. From its earliest beginnings the field has been muddied by objects that range from honest imitations to blatant forgeries. The Chinese, creators of true porcelain in the eighth century, continually looked back to earlier styles, reproduced them and paid homage to the reign in which the originals appeared by applying the original mark, where appropriate. For the Chinese at that time, this practice posed no problem, but for later European collectors it has proved a source of some confusion.

Once trade with China and Japan developed in the seventeenth century, designs that would satisfy European demand were made to order and the Japanese Imari palette of underglaze blue, iron-red and gilding was copied in China. These designs were copied, in turn, by the early European factories such as Meissen and Worcester. Chinese blue-and-white and Japanese Kakiemon were copied by Meissen, Chantilly, Chelsea and Bow.

But it was not only Far Eastern designs that were copied. Chelsea, Bow and Derby also copied Meissen, the last two even borrowing the Meissen crossed-swords mark, as did Worcester and Lowestoft, among others. There is little doubt that the crossed swords were used as a deliberate attempt to deceive: the early English factories were forgers. Sèvres began at Vincennes with a charter which stated that it was to make porcelain in the manner of the Saxe (in other words Meissen).

Time has now pardoned these misdeeds: these deceptions are now looked on as 'influenced' wares, and the pejorative term 'forgery' has been quietly forgotten. Indeed, such is the strange world of collecting, that many eighteenth-century 'forgeries' are more desirable and expensive than the very originals they copied. For example, Lowestoft, Worcester and Derby interpretations of the Chinese blue-and-white are 10 times more expensive than the originals. A Longton Hall or Chelsea copy of a *blanc de Chine* figure will be twice as expensive as its precursor. A Lund's Bristol *famille-verte* tea bowl and saucer will outstrip its parent by a factor of three or four, as would a Meissen 'Imari' teabowl and saucer. Despite the strong demand for Kakiemon wares in its native Japan, copies by Meissen, Chantilly and Chelsea can still approach or overtake their source in value.

In all probability, copies of eighteenth-century wares made in the nineteenth century by manufacturers such as Samson, or in the twentieth century by Newland, will eventually be collected in their own right. Indeed, Samson's beatification has already begun. Time also changes our perspective and the Imari porcelain made in Japan in the last century can now be seen simply as a continuous production.

How can we determine whether the object we are holding is a forgery? The most reliable way is to assume the object is wrong and then try to prove to yourself that it is right. There are several questions you should ask. The first should be: 'Why make a forgery of this?' If the answer comes back 'Because it is, or once was, worth a considerable sum of money', then ask a second question: 'Does the amount of effort put into the forgery represent a healthy profit for the maker?' Almost every forgery has been made for financial gain.

The materials needed to make porcelain are inexpensive: clay costs little; water, the enamels and gold can be had for pence; the fire, kiln and wheel involve no great investment. But materials vary from place to place and time to time, and it is from these, often subtle, variations that the forgery or fake can be detected.

The following mnemonic covers all the points which will help you when considering the legitimacy of an object – every one should be considered.

F *Faces, fingers, flowers, factory mark*: Are all the details consistent with the period the work purports to be from?

O *Overfill*: Is this decoration too much of a good thing?

R *Reason*: Why would anyone fake this?

G *Glaze*: Are the colour, texture, firing faults, thickness, consistency, and tightness of the body correct for the factory/country/period of the piece? Are there any signs of the glaze having been tampered with? Also *Gilding*: Is the colour, mercury/honey, tooling right for the period?

E *Era*: Is the style of the piece consistent with the period? Are the details of the iconography possible?

R *Rough Treatment*: Is the wear/scratching/chipping consistent with the age and function of the piece? Could it be artificial?

I *Ingredients*: Are the body, weight, colour, translucency, thickness, shape, form, method (casting, moulding, hand-modelling) correct?

E *Enamel colours*: Did the factory/country use this palette at the time? Do the colours have the correct density/surface appearance? Do they sit on the glaze/body correctly?

$ Is the price right?

FORGERY OF A DERBY SQUIRREL BY REGINALD NEWLAND, TORQUAY, *c.*1955 (17.5cm/7in)

The piece has all the naïvety one might expect from an early experiment. The figure bears the red anchor and dagger mark of the Bow factory.

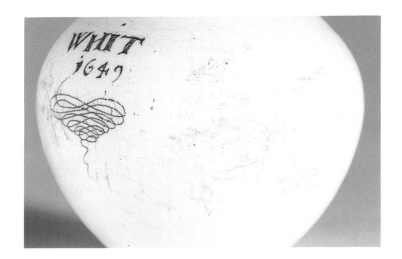

ENGLISH TIN-GLAZED EARTHENWARE WHIT BOTTLE, probably early 20th century (19cm/7½in)

Although pottery, this piece displays very clearly the forger's lack of foresight in his application of false wear.

It is not suggested that every one of these questions will always be answered satisfactorily; what is needed is a balance of probability. If there is still doubt then another question could be posed: 'When?' There are fashions in collecting, and what might be worth forging or faking at one time would not be worthwhile at another: a knowledge of collecting history is therefore a distinct advantage.

RE-DECORATED MEISSEN PLATE, ORIGINALLY PAINTED WITH FLOWERS, (22.5cm/8¾in)

This plate has been stripped and re-decorated with a chinoiserie scene. The plate dates from around 1740, but the decoration is twentieth century.

DETECTING A FORGERY

The hardest forgery to detect is not the almost exact copy of a known example – there will always be enough differences on comparison to make rejection of an attempted duplication relatively easy. Clever forgers get their materials and style right and then fill a gap – they produce an object which *might have been*. Collectors will be all too happy to slot this missing link into the genre, ignoring their disbelief in a wave of self congratulation.

PAINTING

Ceramic painters who set out to produce a pastiche have an immediate decision to make: do they aim for the maximum return on their effort by producing an object which will sell for a large sum, or lower their sights and make something simpler? Most, naturally, opt for the former and because on the whole, the more complex the decoration is, the higher the price, many porcelain forgeries have over-elaborate decoration.

Collectors must not only satisfy themselves that the overall picture 'works' but that every individual component does too. Constant study of the genuine article is the only way to get the eye attuned.

At most periods, certainly in the early years, porcelain decorators have likened their white background to the artist's canvas/paper and have not been afraid to allow it to show as part of their composition. Forgers, on the other hand, are usually terrified of a vacuum and fill every part of their 'canvas', often producing far too solid a design.

WEAR

As objects are handled, used, washed and moved they scratch, chip and wear, and a close examination may disclose valuable evidence. Plates are usually stacked one upon another, so the well of one will show wear where the foot-rim of the one above has rested on it. Knife scratches may appear on the well, rarely the rim, and the gilding will be worn. Under a magnifying glass, later decoration will show enamels flowing into old scratches. Vases will tend to be scratched round their maximum diameter where they have rubbed against walls or companion pieces. Damage is most likely to handles, knobs and feet and signs of restoration should be looked for here.

RESTORATION

Modern techniques have brought restoration to a high degree of sophistication. Glues, modelling materials and paints can be cured in an oven (the pieces are not refired) and do not deteriorate or discolour, which makes their detection difficult. Nevertheless, the restored portion is still going to present a slightly different surface from the original and will always be softer. You can either run a pin round the suspect area, where it will slow on its travels (there is no need to scratch the surface) or touch the piece with your teeth. Porcelain will give a sharp click, whereas the restored area will return a dull thud.

HOMEWORK

Forgers have to contend with innumerable technical problems which range from ingredients to kiln temperatures, but these difficulties are nothing compared to the pyschological barrier. It is a fact that artists cannot divorce themselves completely from their own time: what they create will include some subtle hint of their era and no amount of research will enable them to recreate an earlier age totally. This anachronism is, unfortunately, not detectable immediately and becomes apparent only with the passing of a decade or two. Newland's forgeries are all too obvious now, but they deceived the best eyes of the time when they were created in the 1950s.

Each element must be looked at with a view to faulting the originator. Clothing, tools, ship rigging, weapons, flowers, all these can be inappropriate to the design under discussion and show that the forger has not done his or her homework.

PRICE

Buying from a reputable auction house or dealer is obviously the best safeguard against purchasing a spurious piece. But dedicated collectors also comb antique markets, fairs and minor country shops.

Firstly, always ask the owner. Most will find it difficult to state a bare-faced lie, and any evasion or disclaimer will immediately arouse suspicion. Secondly, knowing what an object should be worth will prevent you from falling for the 'come-on' price. This price will not be at the level of an amazing bargain but will be still too cheap by half. The former implies that the dealer has failed to recognize the object for what it is, the latter suggests that you are being tempted with something suspect.

TYPES OF
PORCELAIN

Under the following headings are some of the more common forgeries and the problems that can be encountered by collectors.

CHINESE PORCELAIN

The earliest Chinese porcelain, the *yinqing* and *ding* wares, are being reproduced today, probably in Taiwan and/or Hong Kong and are reported to be very good reproductions indeed. Their appearance coincided with the fall in market prices for porcelain as recently excavated wares of all kinds began to be smuggled out of China. It seems unlikely that the more common kinds of moulded *yinqing* will be worth reproducing. However, the more expensive *ding* wares are likely to continue to be copied, particularly since the cleaner body is easier to reproduce than the slightly brittle *yinqing*. However, the calligraphic freedom of incised decoration on *ding* wares is difficult to reproduce and modern copies should be easy to detect.

A surprising number of genuine pieces of both types bear little or no sign of wear but nearly a thousand years of burial and exposure will have softened the glaze. Modern examples may have characteristic artificial wear but care should be exercised when judging by this criterion. There has been noted a perfectly genuine *yinqing* bowl which had apparently falsified signs of wear. It was an example of a recently excavated piece but the peasant removing the adhering clay, unaware of what he was doing, had roughly abraded it.

COPY OF A CHINESE YINGQING DISH OF THE SONG DYNASTY, *c.*1920–30 (19cm/7½in)

The forger has produced a far too crisp and deep mould from which to press the dish. The piece is also hemispherical rather than sharp-sided and too heavily potted.

Chinese blue-and-white porcelain is an area of considerable difficulty for the general collector and even the experts have problems. The wares of the Late Yuan and early Ming dynasties were admired throughout the Qing dynasty and were even reproduced then, see Chapter 2. Where there were reign marks, these too were copied, but just as handwriting from the Tudor period can be distinguished from that of the eighteenth century, so too can fifteenth-century reign marks be distinguished from those of the eighteenth century. The vigorous abandon of the Ming was replaced by an attention to detail in the Yongzheng, for example.

The difficulty starts with the superb copies of early eighteenth-century copies of the Ming mark and period wares. Meticulously copying a meticulous copy is easier than copying a vigorous original. The paste and glaze too, had by the early eighteenth century been refined to a point of absolute purity, just as they are today, whereas the Ming paste and glaze has flaws and individuality which is uncopiable. However, Ming blue-and-white is being reproduced with varying degrees of success in large quantities. The shapes are quite good but the blue is far too pale and flat.

The marks and period pieces of the Kangxi, Yongzheng and Qianlong dynasties are all now of sufficient value to reproduce and are already being circulated. In addition, throughout the nineteenth century huge quantities of blue-and-white vases, dishes and jars were made for export in the styles of the Kangxi and Qianlong, bearing reign marks of both dynasties and also others, particularly Chenghua. In the last few years, manufacturers in China and Portugal have been making reproductions of Ming, Qing and Canton decorated pieces with varying degrees of success. The Portuguese copies are of a far higher standard, expensive and sold only in the better retail outlets. They bear printed factory marks which will no doubt be eventually erased by the unscrupulous. Often a brown smear of clay is wiped over the body and base of the Chinese pieces where it sticks to the outlines of the design, presumably to give a semblance of age. However, it acts only as a pointer to a dubious pedigree.

From the earliest enamelled decoration in the reign of Xuande, palace bowls and cups have been made in the same style for a period of 400 years. So identifying a chicken cup with a Chenghua reign mark to a particular reign, for example, is a job for an expert. Authentification of even the simpler enamelled cups and bowls is difficult since they are being reproduced extremely well in Taiwan.

In the second half of the last century Samson and other Paris makers, as well as Herend in Hungary, reproduced armorial dishes and the finer *famille-rose* plates and vases. Samson certainly marked many of his reproductions but these marks can be erased on a wheel. Herend used impressed marks as well as painted ones and these cannot be removed.

The greatest problem to collectors is recent fakes with finely enamelled or black-pencilled decoration after the more desirable eighteenth-century patterns. These include the Jesuit wares, armorials, Cape of Good Hope and large figure subjects. Elephants and riders for the Indian market have also been seen. These are all enamelled and gilt, usually extremely skilfully, on genuine undecorated eighteenth-century blanks or plates which have had scant decoration removed on the wheel or by hydrofluoric acid. But, however skilfully done, there is usually some trace of the original decoration left which can be detected by turning the plate in a raking

MODERN COPY OF A CHINESE XUANDE PERIOD (1426–1435) VASE (24cm/9½in)

Possibly made in Taiwan or Korea, this piece is decorated in underglaze blue in fifteenth-century style and bears a Xuande six character mark. Although the form is too squat and the decoration is a little stiff and overstated in parts, it would warrant careful attention to condemn it. (LEFT)

SAMSON COPY OF A CHINESE EAST INDIA COMPANY ARMORIAL PLATE, *c.*1880 (23.2cm/9¼in)

The underglaze blue Samson mark of two interlaced 'Ss' on the foot rim bears scratching which indicates that at some stage an attempt was made to erase it. (ABOVE LEFT)

The Kakiemon wares of the late seventeenth century were immediately successful in Europe and many factories copied them. They were copied again in the nineteenth century by the likes of Samson when they returned to favour. The recent strength of the yen has led to a great increase in prices paid for Kakiemon by the Japanese, with the result that reproductions, some more successful than others, are pouring into the market.

The Dutch painted Kakiemon designs onto undecorated blanks at the beginning of the eighteenth century and these can be difficult for the inexperienced collector to detect. The most reliable method is to look for the characteristic Dutch iron-red. Nabeshima-style wares were made in the nineteenth century and are being made now. As there is some argument among experts over the dating of Nabeshima wares, the tyro should tread extremely warily. Spurious Imari wares are now being produced in China in large quantities and suffer the same artificial ageing as described above under 'Chinese Porcelain'.

DETAIL OF RE-DECORATED CHINESE EXPORT PLATE WITH NEW ENAMELLED DECORATION OF SCOTSMEN

In all probability the plate was originally painted with a simple flower spray. Its value has been increased a hundredfold by 'doctoring'. The occidental who painted it has given the soldier eyes which are too European and the fingers are poorly painted – often the sign of an unskilled painter. (RIGHT)

light. This will show matt areas or depressed areas or a ghost of the pattern.

As with the recent copies of Qing copies of Ming blue-and-white, detection is made difficult by the inbuilt problem that the original artist had. Chinese painters worked from European originals or prints and frequently misinterpreted features with which they were not familiar. This natural naïvety makes the faker's task easier, because lack of skill on his part might be put down to ignorance on the part of a Chinese artist.

The fake is frequently detectable from the features of the face. The Chinese artist trying to reproduce a European face usually failed to de-Chinese the eye but a European faker trying to reproduce the same subtle error usually fails by making it too Chinese or too European. Fingers executed by Chinese artists also have something of the quality of anemone tentacles whereas modern copies simply look badly drawn.

The enamels used for many fakes are not quite correct in colour and most lack density, appearing as a rather speckled wash. They frequently have a matt or icing-sugar appearance instead of a shiny quality.

CONTINENTAL

From its very earliest days the Meissen factory sold white wares to outside decorators. These eighteenth-century *Hausmalerei* pieces can command high prices and have tempted modern fakers to decorate white or stripped original Meissen blanks. Chinoiserie associated with Augsburg has been attempted, but in gilding only; so too has black-pencilled decoration in the style of Meyer, of Preiznitz. The greatest problem comes with Meissen figures, numbers of which were left in the white. From the beginning of this century the difference in value between coloured and uncoloured wares made it worthwhile to decorate uncoloured ones in imitation of the originals. Passing judgement on pieces coloured later is no easy task, but on the whole the colours are too bright and do not harmonize well. Diaper, stripe and flower patterns on

ONE OF A PAIR OF MODERN VASES IN JAPANESE IMARI STYLE (63cm/24¾in)

Vases like this, as well as famille-rose *and* Canton *imitations, are flooding the market, mainly from South Korea.* (LEFT)

costume are distinctive, and later copyists rarely consider that something as simple as a stripe needs to be studied, which can provide for their downfall. Facial features on a forgery are rarely painted in with the same skill as on an original: the eyes should be drawn with a single fine line and the eyebrows and hair likewise finely painted. The eighteenth-century figures were far more true to life and faces are often grimacing, on the originals. But fakers fear that ugliness may put off a buyer and make their expressions far softer.

In the nineteenth century Meissen was copied by numerous factories, mainly in Germany but also in Paris and in Staffordshire. The German copies, mostly from Dresden, come closest to the originals as the body and glaze were similar. Huge numbers of vases and other wares were produced by Helena Wolfsohn in Dresden, mostly elaborately decorated and bearing the AR mark. They pose no serious problem and nor do the works of Dresden decorators such as Donath and Lamm.

MINOR GERMAN FACTORIES

These are well represented in the canon of copies although most of the problems lie with spurious markings rather than with exact forgeries. Frankenthal, Furstenberg, Ludwigsburg, Höchst and Berlin have all had their eighteenth-century figures and marks more or less loosely copied, the last also its wares. Quantities of spikily modelled Muses, Seasons and Continents, garishly coloured and gilt, can be found with a variety of German marks. Dancers and over-dressed ladies wearing layers of lacy porcelain skirts are *never* eighteenth century whatever the mark says. Their anorexic modelling means they are prone to damage and should be checked with care.

VIENNA

The Vienna factory poses something of a problem in that quantities of blanks remained after its closure in 1864, which were later decorated in the older styles.

REVERSE OF SAMSON REPRODUCTION OF A MEISSEN COMMEDIA DELL' ARTE FIGURE OF AVOCATTO, *c*.1870 (13.3cm/5¼in)

The patch at the base, where the Samson mark of underglaze blue crossed swords crossed by a line has been ground away on a wheel, can be seen clearly. (LEFT)

SAMSON REPRODUCTION OF CHELSEA RED ANCHOR PERIOD FRUIT-SELLER, AFTER A MODEL BY JOSEPH WILLEMS, *c*.1860–70 (22cm/8½in)

A gold anchor has been partially erased from the rear. (LEFT)

Many of the forged wares carry date codes back to the 1820s and most bear elaborate designs in Neoclassical style on a deep-blue ground with complex borders and gilding. Signed paintings are always later. After the

VIENNA-STYLE VASE WITH A CRUDE
NEOCLASSICAL SCENE AFTER
ANGELICA KAUFFMANN, 20TH
CENTURY (c.76cm/30in)

*Both the scene and the gilding are transfer-printed,
but the former has had touches of white enamel
added by hand to create some semblance of
originality.*

closure of the Vienna factory, other factories in Germany and Austria borrowed its
shield mark and made new pieces in the
same style. Another class, particularly
coffee sets, which is still being produced
today, bears transfer-printed Neoclassical
scenes which often incorporate the 'signa-
ture' of Angelica Kauffman. As always with
polychrome transfer decoration, the dots
that make up the image can be determined
with a glass, although the dots of modern
products are crude enough to see clearly
with the naked eye.

ITALY

No one seems to have attempted forging
Medici, but Doccia has been endlessly
reproduced and still is. The relief-moulded
and coloured wares previously attributed to
Capo di Monte were remade by numerous
manufacturers in the nineteenth century
and bear the crowned N mark. One such
manufacturer, and probably the most prolific, was at Rudolfstadt in Germany. The
Capo di Monte factory now makes highly
elaborate groups, mostly of raggedly
dressed peasants of Walt Disney cartoon
appearance. These bear the Naples mark
and are porcelain but there is also a sub-
class of earthenware pieces, mostly boxes,
of appalling quality with brassy gilding
similarly marked and sold through markets.
Forged models after Gricci are known.

SÈVRES AND VINCENNES

No Vincennes fakes or forgeries with *bleu
lapis* and gilt decoration have come to light
but enamelled decoration of both Vincennes and Sèvres is common. Most are
fakes, with later decoration on blanks sold
by the factory at the beginning of the
nineteenth century. The more complex the
subject, the easier it is to detect the later
decoration. Simple patterns such as flower
sprays within a blue-and-gilt border are
much harder to determine. When soft-
paste porcelain is refired at a later date it is
prone to eject absorbed moisture which
leaves minute black spots in the glaze. A
few of these are no indication but a shower
is a sure sign of malpractice. Quality
control at the factory would never have
allowed such a piece to escape.

The marks can provide some evidence of
forgery with a calligraphic 'L' providing a
warning sign. Many fakes have anachro-
nisms between the date letters and the
painters' marks, and the working period of
the painter should also fit with the date
letter. There are frequently discrepancies,
too, between the painter's marks and the
subject matter. Each painter had his or her
own speciality and did not paint flowers one
day and figures the next. 'Jewelled' ware
was produced in limited quantities and
should be treated with extreme caution.
Wares with painted portraits of the Louis'
and their courts are exceptionally rare and
are probably all recorded. Sèvres did not
make large vases with signed landscapes,
many of which are being produced today in
Spain. Any ormolu-mounted piece is under
suspicion unless attested for by several
independent witnesses.

CHANTILLY

The work from this factory was much loved
by Samson, who reproduced boxes, cache-
pots and other wares, almost always in hard
paste in Kakiemon sytle and marked with
his interlaced 'S's. There are some dubious
pieces of Chantilly around, apparently
made in the early years of this century of
tin-glazed porcelain, which are deceptive.
A stiffness in the handling of the flowers and
tendrils is a warning sign, although some
late original pieces leave a lot to be desired
in the quality of their painting.

OTHER FRENCH FACTORIES

Mennecy seems to have escaped the attention of forgers because it was never in such
high regard as Chantilly, but Samson
reproduced some of the white Saint-Cloud
wares. These he made in both hard paste
and a cream-coloured earthenware, neither
of which the factory employed. For Samson
they are particularly ham-fisted. A wrong,
unmarked white Saint-Cloud cachepot is
known, and a very few underglaze blue
decorated pieces have been seen. The Paris
factories of the late eighteenth and early
nineteenth centuries are also free from
copies, either because they have never
fetched a high enough price or, when
expensive, the pieces are too well painted
to make the effort worthwhile. But these

SAMSON COPY OF A ST. CLOUD POT AND COVER, *c.*1890 (11.5cm/4½in)

Compared with Samson's usual reproductions this is a very stiff and unconvincing imitation. It is made from coarse, high-fired earthenware and is incised with 'St C', 'T' and interlaced 'S's. (LEFT)

FRENCH COPY OF A CHANTILLY KAKIEMON VASE, INDECIPHERABLE PAINTED MARK IN BLACK, *c.*1930 (15.5cm/6⅛in)

The enamels are dull and the heavy-handed decoration, particularly on the swags, has an Art Deco quality. (RIGHT)

factories are now receiving more attention and it may well be that added marks will become a problem in the future because many are scruffily stencilled providing no difficulty to fake.

ENGLISH PORCELAIN

The major problem with English porcelain comes not with forgeries but with misidentification, because the factories copied each other a great deal and frequently did not apply marks. Samson made numerous copies of Bow, Chelsea and Derby figures, and wares of the first two. They are in hard-paste porcelain so should not prove too difficult to identify. Various marks including his interlaced 'S's were used and many figures bear type-impressed numerals, unlike any of the originals.

Forged Plymouth mugs enamelled with birds exist, as do tea wares from Bristol, both made from the 1930s to the 1950s when they were a great deal more collectable than they are today.

Chelsea-type figures which bear the gold anchor mark have been made on the Continent from the end of the last century

BASE OF A RE-DECORATED SÈVRES TEAPOT

The ring of 'spit-back' is clearly visible and is frequently found on refired soft-paste porcelain. The mark on the left displays the common failure of a faker to research his background fully.

MARK FROM A RE-DECORATED SÈVRES DISH

The date letter indicates that the piece was made in 1754, but the painter, François-Joseph Aloncle, did not join the factory until 1758. (RIGHT)

until the present day. Any gold-anchor marked figure should be treated with the utmost suspicion. The Chelsea 'goat and bee' jugs were copied by Coalport, among other manufacturers. But perhaps the most deceptive forgeries were those made by Reginald Newland in Torquay, in the 1950s and 1960s. A restorer, Newland was persuaded by a dealer to make a range of Chelsea, Derby and Bow figures which the dealer then sold privately and at auction. They appear to be early experimental pieces from the various factories and some bear factory marks. They are heavily potted, with a thick glaze that can pool and crackle like Chelsea. The colours are reasonable but have a smeary, thin quality.

In the early years of this century the value of Worcester coloured grounds – claret, turquoise, yellow and green – increased. To supply demand fakers added these backgrounds to white wares decorated only with gilt-edged panels of flowers and birds. All these should be treated with caution and colour encroaching on the gilding should be looked for. Green grounds are the hardest to identify as the enamel was difficult to fire and can run over the gilding. It is undoubtedly best to avoid them altogether.

The blue-and-white wares are almost unscathed. There are a few, rare examples of plates and mugs from Bow, Lowestoft and other factories, that were forged, possibly 50 years ago. Modern copies of sauceboats after Worcester originals have appeared on the market. These are over-thick and with a dead, over-refined paste of creamy rather than blue-white colour. The painting is extremely good.

WELSH PORCELAIN

Copies exist by Samson of both Nantgarw and Swansea plates and wares. The Swansea paste can be difficult to differentiate from Samson's hard paste but is creamier, more translucent and with the icing-sugar appearance of soft paste. Printed and impressed marks are known. Coalport also made copies of Swansea.

FORGERY OF A SWANSEA PLATE, PAINTED SWANSEA MARK, POSSIBLY PARIS, *c.*1860 (21.4cm/8½in) (BELOW)

FORGERY OF A PLYMOUTH MUG, BLUE ENAMEL TIN MARK, CONTINENTAL, PROBABLY EARLY 20TH CENTURY, (11cm/4⅛in) (BELOW)

SAMSON COPY OF A CHELSEA RABBIT TUREEN, BLUE ENAMEL INTERLACED 'S's, *c.*1870 (21cm/8¼in)

The copy is in hard-paste porcelain, unlike the original which would have been soft-paste.

THE NINETEENTH CENTURY

Most nineteenth-century pieces are valuable because of their highly elaborate decorative qualities, and the time needed to reproduce these does not warrant reproduction. There is one problem that is becoming more common and which traps novice collectors: the addition or alteration of marks. Impressed marks are almost unalterable but overglaze marks can be erased by acid or on the wheel and those of a more desirable factory substituted. A case is known of an Austrian copy of a Worcester vase with the Worcester crown circle mark substituted, and also spurious Belleek marks. In each case the fake mark had been subsequently 'glazed' over. A mark should be tested with a pin or blade as it may have been added on a transfer.

SELECT BIBLIOGRAPHY

DISCOVERY OF PORCELAIN

Carswell, John: *Chinese Blue and White and Its Impact on the Western World*, Chicago, 1985

Charleston, Robert (Ed.): *World Ceramics*, London, 1981

Garner, Sir Henry: *Oriental Blue and White*, London, 1970

Honey, W.B.: *The Art of the Potter*, London, 1980

Jenyns, Soames: *Later Chinese Porcelain*, London, 1971

Jenyns, Soames: *Ming Pottery and Porcelain*, London, 1953

Medley, Margaret: *The Art of the Chinese Potter*, Oxford, 1981

QING IMPERIAL PORCELAIN

Beurdeley, M. and Raindre, G.: *Qing Porcelain: Famille Verte, Famille Rose*, London, 1987

Jenyns, R.S.: *Later Chinese Porcelain*, London, 1951

Kerr, R.: *Chinese Ceramics: Porcelain of the Qing Dynasty 1664–1911*, London, 1986

Kwan, S.: *Imperial Porcelain of the Late Qing*, Hong Kong, 1983

Medley, M.: *The Chinese Potter*, Oxford, 1976

Sato, M.: *Chinese Ceramics: A Short History*, New York and Tokyo, 1981

CHINESE EXPORT PORCELAIN

Godden, G.A.: *Oriental Export Market Porcelains*, London, 1979

Howard, D.S.: *Chinese Armorial Porcelain*, London, 1974

Howard, D. & Ayers, J.: *China for the West*, London and New York, 1978

Jorg, C.J.A.: *Porcelain and the Dutch China Trade*, The Hague, 1982

Lunsingh Scheurleer, D.F.: *Chinese Export Porcelain. Chine de Commande*, English Translation, London, 1974

Sheaf, C. & Kilburn, R.: *The Hatcher Porcelain Cargoes*, Oxford, 1988

JAPANESE PORCELAIN

Jenyns, Soame: *Japanese Porcelain*: London, 1965

Porcelain for Palaces; the story of 'old japan' in Europe, catalogue of an exhibition organised by the Oriental Ceramic Society held in the British Museum, 1990

EARLY CONTINENTAL PORCELAIN

Brunet, Marcelle and Prèaud, Tamara, *Sèvres, des origines a nos jours*, Fribourg, 1978

Clarke, T.H.: *Marcolini Meissen Figures*, Engraved by Friedrich Elsasser 1785–1792, Off-print of Mitteilungsblatt 103 Journal of the Swiss Ceramic Society, 1988

Honey, W.B.: *Dresden China*, London, 1934

Honey, W.B.: *French Porcelain of the 18th Century*, London, 1950

Honey, W.B.: *European Ceramic Art*, London, 1959

Kingery, W.D. and Vandiver, P.B.: *Ceramic Masterpieces*, New York, 1986

Lane, Arthur: *Italian Porcelain*, London, 1954

Liverani, G.: *Catalogi della Porcellana dei Medici*, Faenza, Lega, 1936

Ruckert, Rainer: *Meissener Porzellan 1710–1810*, Munich, 1966

Savage, George: *Seventeenth and Eighteenth Century French Porcelain*, London, 1960

Savage, George: *18th Century German Porcelain*, London, 1958

Les porcelainiers du XVIIIe siecle francais, various authors, Paris, 1964

Savill, Rosalind: *The Wallace Collection Catalogue of Sèvres Porcelain*, London, 1988

EARLY ENGLISH PORCELAIN

Adams, E: *Chelsea Porcelain*, London, 1987

Adams, Redstone,: *Bow Porcelain*, London, 1981

Barrett, F.: *Lunds Bristol & Worcester Porcelain*, London, 1966

Bradshaw, P.: *18th Century English Porcelain Figures*, Woodbridge, 1981

Honey, W.B.: *Old English Porcelain*, London, 1977 edition

Watney, B.M.: *English Blue & White Porcelain of the 18th Century*, London, 1973 edition

ENGLISH AND WELSH PORCELAIN 1780 TO 1820

Atterbury, P. and Batkin, M.: *The Dictionary of Minton*: Woodbridge, 1990

Charleston, R.J. (Ed.): *English Porcelain 1745–1850*, Benn, 1965

Godden, G.A.: *Eighteenth-Century English Porcelain*, London, 1985

Godden, G.A.: *Encyclopaedia of British Porcelain Manufacturers*, London, 1988

Godden, G.A.: *Pottery and Porcelain of the First Period, 1793–1850*, London, 1968

Godden, G.A.: (Editor) *Staffordshire Porcelain*, London, 1983

John, W.D.: *Nantgarw Porcelain*, Newport, 1948

Jones, A.E. (Jimmy) and Leslie, Sir Joseph: *Swansea Porcelain Shapes and Decoration*, Cowbridge, 1988

Llewellyn, Jewitt: *The Ceramic Art of Great Britain*, 1878, 2 Vols. Reprint of 1883 single Vol., London, 1985

Nance, Morton E.: *The Pottery and Porcelain of Swansea and Nantgarw*, London, 1942

CONTINENTAL PORCELAIN 1780 TO 1930

Fay-Halle, Antoinette and Mundt, Barbara: *Nineteenth Century European Porcelain*, London, 1983

Garner, P. edition: *Encyclopedia of Decorative Arts, 1890–1940*, Oxford, 1978

Jedding, Hermann: *Meissener Porzellan des 19 und 20 Jahrhunderts*, Munich 1981

Kollmann, Erich: *Berliner Porzellan*, Braunschweig, 1966

Lechevallier-Chevignard, Georges: *La Manufacture de porcelaine de Sèvres: Paris, 1908*

LATER ENGLISH AND AMERICAN PORCELAIN

Barber, Edwin Atlee: *The Pottery and Porcelain of the United States and Marks of American Potters*, combined edition, New York, 1976

Barret, Richard Carter: *Bennington Pottery and Porcelain*, New York, 1958

Bertoud, M.: *H & P Daniel*, Micawber, 1980

Cox, A. & A.: *Rockingham Pottery and Porcelain*, London, 1983

Curtis, Phillip H.: *Tucker Porcelain 1826–1838: A Reappraisal*, University Microfilms, Michigan, 1972

Frelinghuysen, Alice Cooney: *American Porcelain Factory, 1770–1772*, New York, 1989

Godden, G.: *Coalport and Coalbrookdale Porcelains*, Woodbridge, 1981

Godden, G.: *Chamberlain Worcester Porcelain*, London, 1982

Godden, G. and Lockett, T.: *Davenport Pottery and Porcelain*, London, 1989

Hood, Graham: *Bonnin and Morris of Philadelphia — The First American Porcelain Factory, 1770–1772*, Chapel Hill, 1972

Miller and Bertoud,: *An Anthology of British Teapots*, London, 1985

Sandon, H.: *Flight & Barr Worcester Porcelain*: Woodbridge, 1978

Sandon, H.: *Royal Worcester Porcelain*: London, 1973

Sandon, H.: *Sandon Guide to Royal Worcester Figures 1900–1965*, Reference Works (Publishing & Distribution) Ltd

Twitchett, John: *Royal Crown Derby*, London, 1976

Whiter, L.: *Spode*, London, 1970

FAKES AND FORGERIES

Atterbury, Paul, ed.: *History of Porcelain*, 1982

Battie, David and Turner, Michael: *The Price Guide to 19th and 20th Century British Porcelain*, Woodbridge, 1980

Battie, David: *The Black Arts. The A.J.B. Kiddell Museum of Fakes and Forgeries at Sotheby's*, Ceramics Magazine II, February/March, 1986

Kurz, O.: *Fakes — A Handbook for Collectors*, London, 1948

Litchfield, Frederick: *Antiques, Genuine and Spurious*, London, 1921

GLOSSARY

acid gilding Process invented at Minton, c.1873, which involved etching patterns with hydrofluoric acid and then **gilding** and burnishing them, to create low-relief gold patterns on **porcelain**.

a galletto Italian, pattern of cocks, painted in red and gold in the Chinese style, at Doccia.

anhua Chinese term meaning 'secret decoration'; faint incised or painted designs in white slip on a white **body**, produced from the Ming period.

ao-Kutani Japanese, seventeenth-century ware, in which green predominates.

Arita Japanese porcelain produced at Arita, which includes **Imari** wares. The polychrome wares in **Kakiemon** style were also produced here.

armorial porcelain Porcelain decorated with the coat-of-arms of the owner, painted or **transfer-printed** onto the ware.

Art Deco Style that emerged at the beginning of the twentieth century and lasted until World War II. Characterized by generally simpler, more geometric, shapes and designs than the preceding **Art Nouveau**.

artificial porcelain See **soft-paste porcelain**.

Art Nouveau Movement evolving around 1880 in England, but with stronger roots on the Continent and in America, distinguished by its organic patterns, particularly floral motifs with sinuous tendrils.

a tulipano Italian, Doccia pattern of a peony spray painted in formal Oriental style.

basketweave pattern See **osier pattern**.

bat-printing Short-lived variation of **transfer-printing**, developed in the mid-1770s, and most common in Staffordshire c.1800, in which slabs of glue or gelatin (bats) were used to transfer a design from an engraved plate onto a glazed surface.

Batavian ware Relates to the name of the Dutch staging post (now Jakarta) in Java from which Chinese **porcelain** was exported in the eighteenth century. Specifically applied to wares with a coffee-coloured ground.

Bérainesque Designs after Jean Bérain (1639–1711), usually of architectural fantasies. Most common on mid-eighteenth century Moustiers **faience**.

bianco sopra bianco Technique developed in the Yongzheng period in China, in which white enamel patterns are used on glazed white porcelain.

biscuit Unglazed **porcelain** or **earthenware** fired only once; also a class of unglazed ware produced at Sèvres in the mid-eighteenth century and at Derby for figures.

bisque Incorrect term for **biscuit**; usually applied to unglazed **porcelain** dolls' heads and figures.

blanc de Chine Cream-coloured Chinese **porcelain**, made at Dehua in Fujian province from the Ming dynasty onwards and imitated in Europe.

blanks Undecorated pieces of **porcelain**. Also 'in the white'.

bleu céleste Sèvres **ground** colour, a cerulean blue, developed in 1752 by Jean Hellot and introduced at Vincennes the following year.

bleu lapis Bright copper-blue **ground** used by Vincennes in the 1750s; streaked like lapis lazuli, hence its name.

bleu soufflé See **powder blue**.

blue scale Pattern of blue overlapping scales, usually **underglaze**.

bocage Literally 'thicket' or 'woodland'; **porcelain** foliage, often used as a support or background for figures.

body Mixture of materials that forms **earthenware**, **porcelain**, and **stoneware**. In porcelain it is often called 'paste'. See **hard paste**, **soft paste**.

bonbonnière Small, covered box made to contain sweets, often in fanciful shapes.

bone ash Burned animal bone added in small quantities to a ceramic **body** to fuse the ingredients and stabilize them, introduced in England c.1750. In larger quantities – up to 50 percent – it formed English **artificial porcelain**. In about 1755 it was added to **true porcelain** to produce **bone china**.

bone china Often shortened to 'china', a mixture of clay and **kaolin** to which **bone ash** is added, producing a modified **true porcelain**. Introduced in England c.1794.

cachepot Flower pot or pot on a stand, made of **porcelain** or **earthenware**, to contain or hide an ordinary flower pot.

campana vase Inverted-bell shaped vase, with a handle on each shoulder.

Canton porcelain In Europe: a Chinese export design of flower and figure panels, on a gilt, green-scrolled ground, called **Rose Medallion** in America. In America: late eighteenth- and early nineteenth-century style of **underglaze** blue landscapes within a stylized border.

cartouche A scroll-edged panel.

cartouche

cash pattern Chinese design, also known as coin pattern. Repeated motif of coins with a square central hole.

cavetto Depression in the centre of the plate; also called the well of the plate.

celadon Commonly, Chinese **stoneware** with a grey-green **glaze** whose colour derives from a small percentage of iron oxides. Also, any glaze of this colour.

china Term derived from 'China ware', ie. exported from China, in the eighteenth century, and now loosely applied to any **porcelain**.

china clay Another term for **kaolin**, a white clay which, with **petuntse**, forms **true porcelain**. Chemically it is a form of aluminium silicate.

Chinamen English, eighteenth-century porcelain dealers.

chinoiserie Fanciful European designs evoking China.

ciselé gilding Gilding which is thickly applied and then tooled in patterns to catch the light and heighten the effect.

Cizhou Chinese **stoneware** produced in north China in the Song dynasty.

clair de lune Literally 'moonlight'; pale purplish-blue **glaze** used on eighteenth-century Chinese **porcelain**, made by adding **cobalt blue** to a clear feldspathic glaze. Usually **crackled**.

clobbering Overglaze enamelling and **gilding** added in Europe to existing **underglaze** blue decoration on Chinese export **porcelain**.

cloisonné Technique in which wires separate colours, used in Japan on porcelain in the latter half of the nineteenth century.

cloud pattern Design of spiral scrolls, often in square form, painted or incised into Chinese **porcelain**.

cobalt blue Pigment made from the mineral cobalt aluminate, used in blue-and-white decoration, particularly **underglaze**.

colloidal gold Gold dispersed in a liquid so that it remains in suspension, and used in **gilding**.

comb pattern Nabeshima pattern also found on **Arita** and **Kutani** wares in the form of a toothed-comb design, often painted in **underglaze** blue.

Compagnie-des-Indes Porcelain shipped from China to France by the French East India Company.

cong Chinese Neolithic vessel said to be a symbol of the earth.

crackle Intentional pattern of fine **glaze** cracks that result when the glaze shrinks more than the **body** after **firing**. Chinese technique developed during the Song dynasty.

craze Unintentional network of cracks that appears in the **glaze** when it shrinks. Caused by poor correlation between **body** and glaze, or temperature extremes.

creamware Yellowish, lead-glazed **earthenware** developed by Wedgwood, among others, in the mid-eighteenth century.

déjeuner A breakfast service.

delftware See **tin-glazed earthenware**.

diaper Repeated pattern of diamonds or other geometrical forms; common on Chinese **porcelain**.

Ding Yao Chinese **porcelain** made in China from the tenth century, with an ivory-white body but an orange translucency.

doucai Chinese term meaning literally, 'dove-tailed colours', or 'contrasting' or 'contending' colours. Identified by **underglaze** blue outlines around the contrasting **overglaze enamels**. First produced during the reign of Chenghua (1465–87).

dry edge Unglazed area around the base of figures.

earthenware All pottery except **stoneware**, ie. pottery that is not vitrified. See **creamware**, **tin-glazed earthenware**.

Eclecticism Movement prevalent in the mid-nineteenth century in which styles from a variety of periods were imitated and mixed.

enamels Colours used **overglaze**, made from glass paste pigmented with metallic oxides.

encre de Chine Decoration of Chinese **porcelain** almost entirely in black and grey and usually derived from prints, commonly known as **Jesuitware**.

en grisaille See *encre de Chine*.

étui Small box containing small implements such as needles, scissors, pencils, etc.

fahua Chinese **stoneware** or porcelain produced in the Ming period, decorated with **glazes** of different colours, separated by raised lines of clay.

faience See **tin-glazed earthenware**.

famille noire Meaning 'black family', a category of Chinese *famille-verte* **porcelain** with a black ground.

famille rose Literally, 'pink family', a class of Chinese eighteenth-century **porcelain** in which the predominant colours are opaque **enamel** pinks and carmines.

famille verte Meaning 'green family', Chinese **porcelain** which is characterized by a brilliant green **enamel**, although also includes iron-red, blue, yellow and aubergine.

feldspar Chinese **petuntse**; essential ingredient of most **true porcelain**, which fuses at a high temperature (1450°C/2642°F) and vitrifies. It can also be used as a **glaze**.

firing Baking process of pottery or **porcelain** in a kiln. The temperatures range from 800°C (1472°F) for **earthenware** to 1450°C (2642°F) for a **hard-paste**, or **true porcelain**.

FitzHugh pattern Broad border on Chinese blue-and-white ware of flowers, fruit and butterflies over a background of latticework, produced in the last quarter of the eighteenth century. Believed to have been named after an English family who ordered an exportware service.

flambé glaze Richly coloured **glaze** made from reduced copper which produced a deep crimson and rich red, streaked with purple or turquoise and often lightly **crackled**. First produced in the Song period, but also occurs on eighteenth-century Chinese **porcelain**, and was imitated later in Europe, mainly at Copenhagen and in Staffordshire. See **sang de boeuf**.

flatware Plates, saucers and dishes, as opposed to cups, tureens, etc.

fluting Repeated pattern of parallel concave vertical grooves.

fluting

flux Substance, such as **bone ash**, added to a **glaze** or **body** to lower the point of fusion during the **firing** process.

foot-rim Projecting ring around the base of a plate, bowl, etc.

former See **repairer**.

frit Powdered glass, fused and then ground and added to clay to make **soft-paste porcelain**.

frit porcelain Artificial or **soft-paste porcelain**.

gadroon Border pattern, usually a series of convex, vertical or spiralling curves, or **reeding**.

gadroon

garniture de cheminée Set of three, five or seven cylindrical and baluster-shaped jars and vases made to decorate a mantelpiece, and produced from the late seventeenth century.

gilding Application of gold to ceramic **body**. The gold was used either as leaf or mixed with honey or mercury. From 1855 liquid gold was used, resulting in a strong colour when fired. Seen on **Imari** and also on Baroque and **Rococo porcelain**. See **acid-gilding**, **cis<U+200B>elé gilding**, and **gloss-gilding**.

glaze Form of glass, coated, dusted or sprayed over the **body**, which becomes smooth, hard and translucent after **firing**, and renders the surface impermeable. A range of colours and effects can be produced.

gloss-gilding Gold in solution and hand-painted or mechanically applied onto **porcelain**. Perfected by M.G. Kühn at Meissen in the late 1820s.

'goat and bee' jug Jug in the form of two seated goats supporting a vase-shaped body with a bee, and a twig handle. Produced by Chelsea in the mid-eighteenth century.

green Term for unfired ware.

grisaille See *encre de Chine*.

gros bleu Dark-blue **ground** colour applied by sponging, developed at Sèvres in 1749.

ground Base or background colour, usually monochrome.

guan Chinese jars High-shouldered, truncated jars.

guanyao Chinese official ware of the Song dynasty. Fine **stoneware** with a **crackled glaze**, ranging from grey to blue-green in colour.

guilloche Neoclassical design of twisting bands, spirals, double spirals, linked chains, etc.

guilloche

hard-paste or **true porcelain**. A mixture of **kaolin** or **china clay** and **petuntse** or china rock, discovered in China in the Tang dynasty and in Europe by Böttger at Meissen in 1788. Fired at 1400°C (2552°F).

Hausmalerei Wares enamelled by Hausmaler, or 'home painters' who worked on bought-in, undecorated **blanks**. Chiefly produced in Germany during the early eighteenth century.

heaping and piling Accidental effect on fourteenth- and fifteenth-century Chinese blue-and-white porcelain, resulting in concentrations of cobalt in spots on the painting. Intentionally achieved on reproductions made in the eighteenth century.

Historismus German term for the excessive regard for past styles prevalent in the nineteenth century. See **Eclecticism**.

Hob in the Well Japanese **Kakiemon** design copied by European factories, based on the childhood of a Song dynasty sage whose playmate fell into a fishbowl and was about to drown when the sage smashed the bowl and saved him.

hongs European 'factories' or warehouses on the Chinese mainland, used to receive and store goods, including porcelain.

hookah Middle Eastern smoking pipe designed so that the smoke is drawn through water to cool it.

huashi Chinese term, literally 'slippery stone', used to describe a **soft-paste** Chinese **porcelain** used for small, delicately decorated pieces; made from the early eighteenth century.

Imari Japanese **porcelain** made at **Arita** and shipped from **Imari** to Europe in the late seventeenth and eighteenth centuries. Characterized by an **underglaze** blue, iron-red, and gilding.

Indianische Blumen German term for Meissen flowers painted between 1720–1740, combining **Kakiemon** and *famille verte* styles. The name derives from the East India Companies.

'in the white' See **blanks**.

Japonaise Also Japanesque; European decoration influenced by Japan, c.1862–1900.

jasperware Red **stoneware** made by Böttger, at Meissen, in the early eighteenth century.

Jesuitware See **encre de Chine**.

'jewelled' Decoration of **enamels** over gold foil simulating inset precious stones.

Jugendstil German form of **Art Nouveau**.

Kakiemon Arita Porcelain decorated from the late seventeenth century, in **enamels**, by the **Kakiemon** family and others, much copied in Europe.

kaolin Essential component of **true porcelain**; fine white **china clay**.

kendi Drinking vessel of globular form with vertical neck and short spout.

kinrande Japanese term for gilt designs on a red ground used in China from the mid-sixteenth century, and copied in Japan.

kintledge Porcelain intended for use as ballast.

ko-Kutani Japanese term, meaning 'old **Kutani**', as opposed to **ao-Kutani**, which is 'green **Kutani**'.

ko-sometsuke Japanese term for imported Chinese 'old blue and white' **porcelain** made from the late sixteenth to the mid-seventeenth centuries.

kraak-porselein Dutch term for late Ming Chinese blue-and-white porcelain shipped to Europe in a merchant vessel called a carrack.

Kutani Japanese **porcelain** made at Kutani in Kaga province from the early seventeenth century. See also **ko-Kutani**.

kylin Chinese dragon-headed mythical beast.

lambrequins French term for a Baroque design of lacework, scrolls and drapery.

Laub-und-Bandelwerk German term, meaning, literally, 'leaf- and strapwork'; Baroque lacy or leafy **cartouches**, usually framing a painting.

Laub-und-Bandelwerk

leys jars From the Chinese word *lei*, which refers to a large wine-jar of rounded shape, sometimes with handles on the shoulders. An early **porcelain** form.

libation cup Boat-shaped ceremonial cup.

lingzhi Chinese fungus used as a decorative motif; it is a symbol of longevity.

lithophanes Thin, low-relief plaques that, when held to the light, produce a chiaroscuro picture. Also known as 'Berlin transparencies'.

long Elizas Corruption from Dutch of 'Lange Lijsen', elongated Chinese figures imitated on English and Dutch wares.

luted joints Joints sealed with fluid clay **slip**.

maiolica See **tin-glazed earthenware**.

Mandarin pattern Decoration found on Chinese export **porcelain**, of figures, within complex **diaper** borders and with a pronounced purple/red colour bias. Late eighteenth to early nineteenth centuries.

manganese Mineral used as a pigment, producing a purple-brown colour.

Manier Blumen German term meaning 'mannered flowers'; describes sharply defined flower painting produced at Meissen in the eighteenth century.

marchand mercier French term which describes a general dealer in works of art in France.

masso bastardo Italian term for hybrid **hard-paste** made in the eighteenth century at Doccia; grey, with a rough, sticky, smeared surface which is prone to fire cracks.

mazarine blue English version of **gros bleu**, developed at Chelsea in the 1750s.

meiping Chinese baluster vase with high shoulders and a short flared neck, designed to hold a single spray of prunus.

millefleurs French term for floral decoration that first appeared in the Kangxi reign (1662–1722) and later evolved into a dense, overall pattern.

monteith Large circular or oval bowl for iced water, with a scalloped rim to hold glasses by the foot so that they can be cooled in the water.

monteith

moon-flask Disc-shaped vase, usually with a pair of handles flanking a short, straight neck.

moons Spots in fired paste, which are translucent when held up to the light.

mordant Substance used as a fixative during the **gilding** or painting process.

muffle Chamber inside a kiln that protects objects being fired from smoke and flames; muffle colours, or **enamels**, are fired at temperatures between 700–900°C (1292–1652°F).

Nabeshima Japanese **porcelain** made near **Arita**, at Okawachi, from the mid-seventeenth century. Palette includes pale **underglaze** blue and red, blue and **celadon**.

Nankin porcelain Blue-and-white export **porcelain** decorated with landscapes with complex borders, late eighteenth to early nineteenth centuries.

nigoshide Japanese term for milky-white **Kakiemon porcelain** with an almost colourless **glaze**.

noborigama Japanese, stepped, chambered, climbing kiln which allowed a close control of the atmosphere and temperature gradient during **firing**.

Ombrierte Deutsche Blumen German term for botanical style of flower painting with shading; introduced in 1731 by J.G. Klinger at Meissen, and copied at Chelsea c.1755.

on-glaze See **overglaze**.

osier pattern Relief basketwork pattern of woven willow twigs (osiers) used on borders at Meissen, from the 1730s.

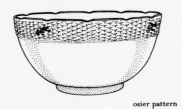

osier pattern

overglaze Painted or **transfer-printed** decoration on a fired **glaze**, which is then **fired** at a lower temperature.

pap-warmer Cup which contains food, set on a stand which holds a candle or lamp that warms the food. Made from the eighteenth century. Also called a food-warmer.

parian Marble-like **biscuit porcelain**, made from **feldspar** and **china clay**, introduced in England in 1845. Used mainly for figures and copies of classical sculptures.

pâte-sur-pâte Literally, 'paste on paste'; technique of building up a design with successive layers of liquid slip.

peach-bloom Glaze first used on Kangxi wares, based on copper. During **firing** the glaze took on a range of hues, from a velvety peach-red to sage-green.

petuntse Chinese feldspathic rock, essential component of **hard-paste porcelain**.

pilgrim flask Gourd-shaped flattened flask, with ring handles at the shoulders.

porcelain See **artificial porcelain**, **true porcelain**, and **bone china**.

powder-blue Speckled blue ground achieved by blowing dry colour through a gauze; originally used in China, but copied at Sèvres, as **bleu soufflé.**

press-moulding Technique of pressing clay into a mould, used to make small figures or **sprigged** decoration.

puce Purple-red colour derived from **manganese** oxide.

punch'ong Korean variation of **celadon stoneware** made in south Korea from the early fifteenth to late sixteenth centuries. Greyish with a coarse texture, usually covered with **slip**.

Qingbai See **Yingqing**.

reeding Converse of **fluting**; parallel, vertical pattern in the form of reeds.

repairer Craftsman who assembles the separately moulded parts of a figure or object.

robin's egg glaze Speckled, pale-blue **glaze** introduced during the reign of Kangxi.

Rococo Style of decoration developed in France in the reign of Louis XV (1715–74), distinguished by asymmetrical ornament, scrollwork, rockwork, shells and foliage.

rolwagen Dutch, term for a Chinese transitional tall, cylindrical vase with a short, constricted neck.

rose du Barry See *rose Pompadour.*

Rose Medallion See **Canton.**

rose Pompadour Deep-pink **glaze** used as a **ground** colour, developed at Sèvres in 1757, probably by Hellot, and discontinued after the death of Mme de Pompadour in 1764. Also known in England as **rose du Barry.**

ruyao Chinese, imperial Song ware, with buff **body** and pale lavender **crackled glaze.**

ruyi Heart-shaped design used as a border.

saggar Refractory clay box that protects objects during **firing.**

saltglaze stoneware **Stoneware** which has ordinary salt thrown into the kiln where it fuses with the clay, forming a clear, impermeable **glaze.**

sang de boeuf Literally, 'ox-blood'; a brilliant-red **glaze** with darker patches developed in China during the Qing dynasty.

Schwarzlot German linear painting in black, usually after engraving.

Secession Movement Group of Austrian artists and designers, whose style ran parallel with **Art Nouveau** in France.

seladon fond Sea-green **ground** which was used during the 1730s at Meissen.

sgraffito Designs which are engraved through the slip to reveal the differently coloured **body** beneath.

sherds Also potsherds; fragments of **porcelain**, frequently found in excavated kiln sites, enabling wares to be attributed.

shoki-Imari Japanese, early **Imari** porcelain, made at **Arita.**

shou Chinese symbol or ideogram for longevity.

Shu-fu Chinese white **porcelain** produced during the Yuan period, marked with the characters 'shu-fu', meaning 'Privy Council'.

slip Liquid or diluted clay.

slip-casting Liquid clay poured into a porous plaster mould. The water is absorbed by the mould and the surplus is poured off. The mould is then removed and the clay fired.

soapstone Also soaprock, a form of steatite; added to a **porcelain body** instead of **kaolin** to strengthen it and enable it to withstand sudden changes in temperature. Introduced in Bristol in 1750.

soft-paste porcelain Also **artificial porcelain**; made from white clay and ground glass, or frit, mixed together, and fired at 1100°C (2012°F). Medici and Sèvres (*pâte tendre*) used the **body**, as did Chelsea.

sprigging Application of small low-relief, mould-case ornaments onto the **body** and attached by thin **slip.**

spur marks Rough marks or faults in the **glaze**, usually on the base of a piece, made by the support called a cockspur on which the piece rested in the kiln; common on Chelsea and **Imari porcelain.**

stampino Italian, method of decorating **porcelain** in blue and white with a stencil.

stilt marks Marks on the **foot-rim** of plates, created by the points of conical stilts which supported the pieces in the kiln.

stoneware Opaque ceramic between **earthenware** and **porcelain**. Fired at a higher temperature than earthenware, which vitrifies it, making it watertight without having to be glazed. Introduced into England from Germany in the late seventeenth century.

Supra-Cargoes Also called Super-Cargoes; men employed by the East India Company to sell the outward cargo in China and buy Chinese goods for sale in England.

swag Decorative device such as a loop of foliage, festoon or garland of flowers.

tazza Italian, shallow bowl on a stem, sometimes with handles. Synonymous with comport, in England, and used in a dessert service to hold fruit.

tea-dust glaze Speckled dark-brown **glaze** of greenish hue, used by Qing potters, and produced by separately blowing lead-silicate and iron-oxide glazes through a fine gauze onto a brown **ground**, the effect resembling ground tea leaves.

temmoku Japanese, dark, treacle-coloured **glaze** with a high content of iron-oxide, used in China in Henan, from the Song period.

throwing The shaping of ceramics on a wheel to produce hollow objects.

tin-glazed earthenware **Earthenware** glazed with a tin-oxide **glaze**, which is glassy and white, resembling the surface of Chinese **porcelain**. Also known as **delftware** in England, **faience** in France and Germany, and **maiolica** in Italy.

transfer-printing Method of mass-producing designs. An engraved copper plate is inked with ceramic pigment which is transferred to paper in a press. While the ceramic colour is still wet, the design is placed on the **porcelain** surface.

Transitional Porcelain Produced in Jingdezhen between the end of the Ming dynasty and the start of the Manchu period of the Qing dynasty.

trophies A composition, painted or in relief, emblematic of war, gardening, love, etc., incorporating appropriate articles such as arms, watering cans or bows and arrows respectively.

true porcelain See **hard-paste porcelain.**

tureen Deep covered soup or vegetable dish.

underglaze Coloured coating or decoration applied to the **biscuit**. This is then **glazed** and **fired.**

vitrifiable colours Enamels that become glassy and permanent when **fired** in the kiln.

well Also **cavetto**; depressed central part of a plate.

wucai Chinese term meaning, literally, 'five colours'; a palette introduced during the Ming dynasty in which part of the design is rendered in **cobalt blue** beneath the **glaze** and the remainder added in **enamels** of four other colours – iron red, turquoise, yellow and green.

yingqing Chinese term meaning literally, 'cloudy', 'misty' or 'shadow blue', one of the earliest forms of Chinese **porcelain**, made in the Song period. Translucent off-white **body** with a blue-tinged **glaze**, usually decorated with carved or moulded floral designs.

Yueh Chinese **stoneware** with a green or **celadon glaze.**

SUMMARY OF FACTORIES AND BIOGRAPHIES

Aaron, Michel (d.1856): manufacturer in Limoges 1832–45 at Michel & Valin.

Acier, Michel-Victor (1736–9): principal modeller at Meissen 1764–81.

Acora, Portugal: attempts to make porcelain here during the second half of the 18thc.

Alcock, Samuel & Co., Cobridge, Staffordshire: c.1826–59. Operated as The Hill Pottery, Burslem, from 1830.

Alluaud, François (1739–99) and son François (1788–1866): manufacturers in Limoges, late 18thc–1876; taken over by Haviland.

Altwasser, Silesia: C. Tielsch & Co., 1845–1918; 1918–present C.M. Hutchenreuter.

Amstel, France, 1771–78: factory which produced mainly tableware.

Annam, northern Vietnam: semi-porcelain, Song dynasty onwards.

Anreiter, J.C.W. (c.1702–1747): hausmaler from Vienna; worked at Doccia, Italy with son Anton (d.1801) until 1746.

Ansbach, Bavaria, Germany: c.1758–62; moved to Castle of Bruckberg; sold 1806 and closed 1860.

Arita: main site of kilns in Japan, 1620–present.

Arras, France: 1770–90; also decoration of Sèvres blanks.

Auffenwerth, Johann (d.1726): Augsburg hausmaler succeeded by his daughters.

Aulikzek, Dominikus (1734–1804): modellmeister at Nymphenburg 1765–97.

Aynsley, John & Sons (Ltd), Longton, Staffordshire: 1864–present.

Bachelier, Jean-Jacques (1724–1806): joined Vincennes as flower painter 1751, variously modeller, sculptor, art director, salesman at Sèvres. Dismissed 1793.

Baldock, Edward Holmes: 19thc. London dealer in china and furniture. Redecorated Sèvres porcelain.

Ball, William: see Vauxhall.

Batavia, Java: Dutch East India trading port.

Bauer, Adam: chief modeller at Frankenthal 1775–78.

Beijing (Peking): capital of China, seat of the Emperors and site of enamel-decoration on porcelain for Imperial use.

Belleek, County Fermanagh, N. Ireland: parian, 1863–present.

Benckgraff, Johann (d.1753): painter at Höchst 1751–53.

Bérain, Jean (1637–1711): Belgian-born painter and designer; son Jean continued his work (1674–1728).

Berlin, 1751–present:
Wilhelm Kaspar Wegely (1751–57) Johann Ernst Gotzkowsky (1761–63) Bought by Frederick the Great in 1763 becoming the Königliche Porzellan Manufaktur (KPM); name changed to Staatliche Porzellan Manufaktur (SPM) in 1918.

Billingsley, William (1730–1823): flower painter at Derby, left 1795 for Pinxton, left 1799 for Mansfield until 1801, at Worcester 1808–13. See also Nantgarw.

Boch, William: eldest in family of porcelain makers who ran several factories in Green Point, New York, during 1850s and 1860s.

Boizot, Louis-Simon (1743–1809): sculptor and master modeller at Sèvres 1773–1800, continued working until death.

Bonnin and Morris, Philadelphia, Pennsylvania, USA, 1770–73.

Böttengruber, Ignaz: hausmaler in Breslau c.1720–c.1735.

Böttger, Johann Friedrich (1682–1719): alchemist, discoverer of true porcelain in Europe, 1708, with Tschirnhausen; manager at Meissen from 1710.

Boullemier, Anton (c.1840–1900): Sèvres designer and painter, worked at Minton from 1872.

Bourne, Charles, Fenton, Staffordshire: bone china 1817–30.

Bow, London, 1744–75: managed by Edward Heylyn and Thomas Frye who patented first porcelain body in England in 1744.

Bristol:
(i) 1750–52 Benjamin Lund and William Miller. Factory taken over by Worcester 1752.
(ii) hard-paste porcelain factory transferred from Plymouth 1770 by William Cookworthy. Bought 1774 by Richard Champion; closed 1781.

Broome, Isaac (1836–1922): sculptor responsible for modelling some of America's finest parian busts and ornamental wares while working for Ott and Brewer in the late 1870s.

Buen Retiro: see Capo di Monte.

Bustelli, Franz Anton (1723–63): modeller at Nymphenburg 1754–63.

Canton, China: port in southern China from which porcelain was exported; also a centre for export enamelling.

Capo di Monte 1743–59: soft-paste porcelain, founded by Charles III, King of Naples and Sicily. Factory moved to Buen Retiro, Spain, 1759–1808. Hard paste from 1803.

Cartlidge, Charles (d.1860): Staffordshire-born potter who set up a factory at Greenpoint, New York, see Charles Cartlidge and Co.

Cassel, Germany, 1766–88.

Caughley, Shropshire, 1772–99: soapstone body, Thomas Turner; 1795–99 hybrid hard-paste. Taken over by Coalport in 1799 and closed 1814.

Ceramic Art Co., Trenton, New Jersey, 1889–present. Reorganized as Lenox, Incorporated in 1906. Only major porcelain manufactory in the USA today.

Chaffers, Richard (1731–65): potter in Liverpool 1754–65.

Chamberlain, Robert: painter at Worcester, set up as an independent decorator 1786; porcelain from c.1791.

Champion, Richard (1743–91): experiments with hard-paste porcelain, took over Cookworthy's Bristol factory 1774.

Chantilly, France, 1725–c.1800: soft-paste porcelain, founded by Louis-Henri, Duc de Condé (1692–1740), managed by Ciquaire Cirou until 1751.

Charles Cartlidge and Co., Greenpoint, New York, USA: 1848–56.

Chelsea, c.1745–84: Charles Gouyn (c.1745–49), succeeded by Nicholas Sprimont, as manager (1749–58) and proprietor (c.1758–69). Sold to William Duesbury I 1770; closed 1784; moulds to Derby.

Chicaneau, Pierre: see Saint-Cloud.

Christian, Philip: see Shaw's Brow.

Coalport, Shropshire, mid-1790s–1926: John Rose; Anstice, Horton and Thomas Rose 1803–14.

Cookworthy, William (1705–80): Devon pharmacist who discovered Cornish china clay porcelain by 1758. Experiments resulted in hard-paste porcelain 1768 in Plymouth; transferred to Bristol 1770.

Copenhagen, Denmark, 1759–present:
(i) L. Fournier (1759–65), soft paste.
(ii) F.H. Müller 1774, hard paste; Royal Copenhagen Manufactory from 1779.
(iii) Bing and Grondahl 1854–present.

Dagoty & Honoré, Paris, until 1822.

Daniel, H. & R.: originally decorators of Spode, 1805–22, manufacturers 1826–46.

Darte Frères, Paris, c.1795–1840.

Davenport, Longport, Staffordshire: 1794, hard paste (until c.1812) and bone china c.1808–87.

Décasse & Chanou: porcelain makers, successors to Dr. Henry Mead, New York City, USA, 1825–27.

Dehua: see Fujian province.

d'Entrecolles, Père (died 1741): Jesuit missionary living in Jingdezhen who wrote letters on porcelain manufacture in 1712 and 1722.

Derby 1750–1848 and c.1878–present: (i) Andrew Planché c.1750–56; William Duesbury I, 1756–86; Chelsea-Derby 1770–84; William Duesbury II 1786, with Michael Kean 1795–97; Michael Kean 1797–1811; Robert Bloor 1811–28; closed 1848.
(ii) New factory King Street 1848–1935.
(iii) Derby Crown Porcelain Company 1876; Royal Crown Derby Porcelain Co. Ltd, 1890 to present.

Dihl & Guérhard: Paris, patron duc d'Angoulême, 1781–1829.

Doccia, Italy, 1735–present: hybrid hard paste, Carlo Ginori and family.

Doulton & Co., c.1858–1956: earthenware and stoneware Burslem works, earthenware and porcelain 1882, Doulton Fine China Ltd from 1955.

Duplessis, Jean-Claude-Chambellan, (c.1695–1744): goldsmith, designer of models at Sèvres 1748–74.

Duvivier, H.-J.: painter at Tournay 1763–71; known for exotic birds.

Eberlein, Johann Friedrich (1696–1749): modeller at Meissen 1735–49.

Ellwangen, Germany: unidentified c.1758.

Falconet, Etienne-Maurice (1716–91): sculptor and director of modelling at Sèvres 1757–66 when he left for St. Petersburg.

Feilner, Simon (d.1798): painter and modeller at Höchst c.1750–53; modellmeister at Fürstenberg 1753–68; Frankenthal in 1770; director from 1775.

Fontainebleau: hard-paste porcelain from 1795, Jacob Petit 1836–62.

Fournier, Louis: modeller at Vincennes 1747–49; Chantilly 1752-56 and Copenhagen 1759–65.

Frankenthal, 1755–94: J.J. Ringler and Charles-François Hannong and Carl and Joseph-Adam Hannong, managers; bought by Elector Karl Theodor in 1762, managed by Simon Feilner, 1775–94. When closed, moulds removed to Nymphenburg.

Fujian province, China: blanc-de-Chine ware from late 16thc.

Fukagawa, Eizaiemon: founder of factory in Arita, c.1879.

Fulda, Germany, 1764–89.

Fürstenberg, Germany, 1753–present.

Gardner, Francis: Englishman who opened factory at Verbilki near Moscow in 1765.

Gilbody, Samuel, Liverpool, 1754–61.

Giles, James: decorator in Soho, London, mainly of Worcester 1760s–76.

Girl-in-a-swing Factory, Chelsea, c.1752–54.

Gotha, Germany, 1756–1834.

Grainger, Thomas and family, Worcester, c.1805: hybrid paste; bone china 1812; various titles until 1902.

Gricci, Giuseppe (d.1770): modeller at Capo di Monte 1745–59; Buen Retiro 1750–70 where he became art director. Succeeded by sons Carlos (d.1795) and·Felipe (d.1803).

Groszbeitenbach, Thuringia, Germany, 1777–present.

Hadley, James (1837–1903): designer and modeller at Worcester from 1860s. Set up as freelance in 1875 and own factory 1896; amalgamated with Royal Worcester 1902.

The Hague, Holland, 1776–90.

Hancock, Robert (1730–1817): engraver for transfer-printing, Worcester c.1757; partner 1772–74; Caughley 1775 and elsewhere.

Hannong, Joseph-Adam (1734–c.1800): ran Frankenthal factory from 1757, owner from 1759; sold to Karl Theodor in 1762. Porcelain at Strasburg and Haguenau from 1768; closed 1781.

Hannong, Paul-Antoine (1700–60): porcelain at Haguenau 1752–55; moved to Frankenthal.

Hellot, Jean (1685–1766): chemist at Vincennes and Sèvres.

Herend, Hungary: established Moritz Fischer, 1839–present, hard-paste porcelain, particularly copies after Chinese.

Herold, Christian Friedrich (1700–79): painter at Meissen 1725–77.

Herold, Johann-Gregor (also Höroldt) (1696–1775): chemist and painter of chinoiseries at Meissen 1720–56 and 1763–76.

Heubach: see Kloster Veilsdorf.

Hirado: island off Kyushu, factory from 1770; taken over by Fukugawa c.1910.

Höchst, Germany, 1743–96: first managed by A.F. von Löwenfinck.

Hunger, Christoph Conrad: arcanist and gilder at Meissen c.1715; Vienna 1717–19; Vezzi 1720–24; Copenhagen 1730s; St. Petersburg 1744–present, and elsewhere.

Hürten, Charles Ferdinand (1818–97): German flower painter working at Sèvres 1846–59 and at Copeland 1859–97.

Imari: port in Japan through which Arita porcelain was shipped.

Jingdezhen: main production area of porcelain in China Yuan dynasty–present.

Jones, George, Stoke-on-Trent, c.1864–1957: earthenware, bone china and parian.

Jüchtzer, Christoph Gottfried (1752–1812): modeller under Kändler, art director 1781.

Kändler, Johann Joachim (1706–75): modeller at Meissen 1731–75, modellmeister from 1733.

Kakiemon, Sakaida: quasi-legendary figure of the 17thc, giving name to family of enamelled wares from Arita, Japan.

Kauffmann, Angelica (1741–1807): Swiss painter and decorator working in England 1760–81. Much copied on ceramics, particularly by transfer.

Kelsterbach, Germany: 1761–68 and 1789–1802.

Kirchmayer, J. (1773–1845): modeller at Nymphenburg 1802–19.

Kirchner, Johann Gottlob (b.1706): modeller at Meissen 1727–28 and 1730–33.

Kirschner, Friedrich (1748–89): painter at Ludwigsburg 1770–83.

Klinger, Johann Gottfried: flower painter at Meissen 1731–46; Vienna until death in 1781.

Kloster-Veilsdorf, Thuringia: 1760–present; established by Friedrich Wilhelm Eugen. Bought by Eduard Albert Heubach 1863, thereafter specializing in doll heads.

Koryu, Korea: manufacturing centre from 12thc.

Kothgasser, Anton (1769–1851): glass-enameller and painter on Vienna porcelain.

Knowles, Taylor and Knowles, Ohio, USA, 1854.

Kozan, Makuzu (Miyakawa) (fl. 1868–1912): innovative potter in Ota, near Yokohama, Japan, late 19th and early 20thc.

Krog, Arnold (1856–1931): art director and chemist at Royal Copenhagen from 1885.

Kutani: kilns in Kaga, Japan, mid 17thc–present.

Kyushu: southern island of Japan; site of numerous kilns

Le Nove, Italy: hard-paste porcelain 1762–c.1773 and 1781–1835.

Lessore, Emile (1805–76): painter (mainly on earthenware) at Minton 1858, and Wedgwood until 1863 when he returned to France.

Limbach, Thuringia, Germany 1772–c.1800.

Lille: soft-paste porcelain c.1711–c.1730; hard paste c.1784–1817.

Limehouse, London: c.1745–48; wares formerly attributed to William Reid of Liverpool.

Limoges: porcelain manufacturing centre in France. Factories include: Grallet, Massie et Fourneirs 1771–84 directed by Louis XVI (1784–96); Baignol 1797–1854; Joubert et Monnerie 1795–1808; Alluard and family 1808–76; Michel & Valin 1832-45; David Haviland 1842, (& Co from 1892).

Linck, Franz Konrad (1732–93): modellmeister at Frankenthal 1762–66.

Littler, William (1725–84): potter at Longton Hall 1750–60 and West Pans, Scotland 1764–77.

Liverpool: see Richard Chaffers; Philip Christian; Shaw's Brow; James, John and Seth Pennington; Samuel Gilbody; Vauxhall and Limehouse.

Longton Hall, Staffordshire: Littler, William 1750–60.

Löwenfinck, Adam Friedrich von (1714–54): painter at Meissen 1726–36, Höchst 1743–49; later at various faience factories.

Lowestoft, Suffolk, 1757–c.1799.

Lück, Johann Christoph Ludwig (d.1780): modellmeister at Meissen 1728–29 and Vienna c.1750.

Lück, Johann Friedrich (d.1797): repairer at Meissen 1741–57; modeller at Höchst c.1757; Frankenthal 1758–64; Meissen thereafter.

Lück, Karl Gottlieb (d.1775): modeller at Frankenthal 1756–75, modellmeister from 1766.

Ludwigsburg 1759–1824: founded by Duke Karl Eugen of Württenburg, managed by J.J. Ringler, 1759–99.

Lunéville, France: hard-paste porcelain 1766–77, stock sold to Niderviller in 1780.

Luplau, Anton Carl (d.1795): modeller at Fürstenberg 1765–76 and at Royal Copenhagen.

Marieberg, Sweden, 1759–82: faience, soft- and very little hard-paste porcelain.

Marseilles, France: various factories; faience from 1677, hard-paste porcelain 1773–93 under Joseph-Gaspurd Robert.

Mason, Miles: Liverpool, 1792–1800, Staffordshire c.1802–16; hybrid hard-paste porcelain, bone china c.1806; developed ironstone.

Mayer, Franz Ferdinand: hausmaler in Pressnitz c.1745–c.1770.

Mead, Dr. Henry (1775–1843): involved sporadically in manufacturing porcelain in New York City, USA from 1816–24.

Medici, Florence, Italy: soft-paste porcelain 1575–87 under patronage of Francesco de Medici, Grand Duke of Tuscany (1541–87).

Meissen, 1710–present: Augustus II of Saxony patron 1670–1733. Experimental work to discover secret of true porcelain by von Tschirnhausen and Böttger. Managed by Count Heinrich von Bruhl until 1763. Academic (or dot) period 1763-c.1780. Count Camillo Marcolini 1780–1814.

Melchior, Johann Peter (1742–1825): modeller at Höchst 1767–79; Frankenthal 1779–93 and Nymphenburg 1797–1822.

Mennecy, France: started by François Barbin (1689–1765), patron Duc de Villeroy; decorating from 1734 (Paris); removed 1748 to Mennecy, 1773 (Bourg-la-Reine), closed 1806.

Meyer, Friedrich Elias (1723–85): modeller at Meissen 1748–61, modellmeister at Berlin 1762–85.

Minton, Stoke-on-Trent, 1793–present: founded Thomas Minton (1766–1836), bone china c.1800–16 and 1824–present. Mintons from 1873.

Moscow:
(i) Francis Gardner, Englishman, founded factory c.1765.
(ii) Popoff 1806–72.
(iii) Kusnetsoff 19thc.

Muller, Karl: sculptor at Union Porcelain Works, Brooklyn, USA in 1870s.

Nabeshima, Okawachi, Japan, late 17thc onwards.

Nanking, China: port from which blue-and-white Jingdezhen porcelain was exported.

Nantgarw, Glamorgan, Wales: founded by William Billingsley 1813, transferred to Swansea 1814. Billingsley returned to Nantgarw 1817; closed production (although decoration continued) 1820; went to Coalport.

Naples, Italy: founded by King Ferdinand of Naples 1771; sold 1807; removed to site near Capo di Monte hill, closed 1834.

Neu, Wenzel (c.1708–74): repairer and modeller at Fulda 1765–74.

New Hall, Shelton, Staffordshire: hard paste or bone china 1781–1835.

Niderviller, Lorraine, France: faience (from 1754) and porcelain (1768–1827).

Niedermayer, Johann Joseph (d.1784): modellmeister at Vienna 1747–84; his son Matthias director 1805–27.

Nigg, Joseph (fl. 1800–43): flower painter at Vienna.

Noritake, Japan: mass-produced export wares from c.1900–present.

Nymphenburg, Bavaria, Germany, 1753–present: founded by J.J. Ringler.

Nyon, Switzerland: founded by F. Müller and Jacob Dortu c.1780–late 19thc; hard paste.

O'Neale, Jeffryes Hamett: painter at Chelsea c.1753–5 and Worcester 1768–1770.

Ott and Brewer, Trenton, New Jersey, USA, 1863–92.

Ottweiller, Germany, 1764–94.

Paquier, Claudius Innocentius du (d.1751): founder of Vienna factory.

Pennington, James, John and Seth: Liverpool, various sites c.1765–late 18thc.

Pennington, Seth: Liverpool 1778–1805.

Petit, Jacob: Belleville, France, c.1830; Fontainebleau 1843–66.

Pfalz-Zweibrücken, Germany, 1767–75.

Philadelphia, USA 1770–1838: several factories including Bonnin and Morris 1770–73, William Ellis Tucker 1827–38.

Pillement, Jean, French (1728–1808): painter and designer of chinoiseries, particularly popular in England.

Pillivuyt et Cie: retailers in Paris 1817, factories at Foescy, Mehum and Noirlac; 1851 Charles Pillivuyt at Mahun-sur-Yèvre.

Pinxton, Derbyshire 1796–1813: John Coke and William Billingsley (until 1799); John Cutts *c.*1803–13.

Plymouth, Devonshire: first English hard-paste factory; established by William Cookworthy, 1768. Moved to Bristol 1770.

Poterat, Louis: see Rouen.

Potschappel: see Thieme, Carl.

Preissler, Daniel (1636–1733), and son Ignaz (b.1676): hausmalers in Bohemia *c.*1720–39.

Priestman, James: modeller in USA in 1880s.

Pronk, Cornelis, Dutch (1691–1759): designs used as source material on Japanese and Chinese porcelain from 1734.

Reid, William: see Limehouse.

Reinicke, Peter (1715–68): modeller at Meissen from 1743 until death.

Ridgway, Staffordshire: various partnerships, most important of which was John and William making bone china from 1814–30.

Riedel, Gottlieb Friedrich (1724–84): painter at Meissen 1743–54, Höchst *c.*1756; painting director at Frankenthal 1757–59 and Ludwigsburg 1759–79.

Riese, Johann Carl Friedrich: modellmeister at Berlin 1789–1834.

Ringler, Joseph Jakob (1730–1804): painter and arcanist at Vienna from 1744; at Höchst 1750–52; Strasbourg 1752–54; Nymphenburg 1754–57; Ludwigsburg 1759–99.

Rockingham, nr. Swinton, Yorkshire, *c.*1745–1842: porcelain from *c.*1826.

Rose, John: see Coalport.

Rouen, France: patent to open factory 1673 to Louis Poterat (1612–96), soft-paste porcelain late 17thc.

Rozenburg, Hague, Holland: established 1883 by William Wolff Freiherr von Gudenburg, eggshell porcelain from 1889.

Rue Clignancourt, Paris 1771–89: Pierre Dernelle, patron M. le comte de Provence.

Rue Thiroux, Paris 1775–1870: André-Marie Leboeuf, patron Marie-Antoinette.

Russinger, Laurentius: modeller at Höchst 1759–67, modellmeister 1762; 1768 at Fulda; manager at La Courtille, Paris 1771–95.

Saint-Cloud, France: soft-paste porcelain from, possibly, 1678 but more likely 1702–1800, founded by Pierre Chicaneau.

Samson, Edmé, Saint-Maurice: reproductions of Eastern and Western ceramics and glass 1845–1978.

St. Petersburg, Russia, 1744–present: Imperial factory run by C.K. Hunger and Dimitri Vinogradoff.

Schönheit, Johann Carl (1730–1805): modeller at Meissen 1745–1805.

Seixas, David: potter in Trenton, USA, *c.*1812–16 and Philadelphia 1817–22.

Seuter, Bartholomäus and Abraham (1678–1754): Augsburg hausmalers.

Sèvres, 1740–present: established at Vincennes, soft-paste porcelain from 1748; moved to Sèvres 1759; controlled by Louis XV from 1759.

Shaw's Brow, Liverpool: Richard Chaffers 1754–65, Philip Christian, Pennington 1776–99, soapstone porcelain 1765–76.

Sitzendorf, Thuringia, 1850–present: mostly copies of 18thc porcelain, particularly Meissen.

Solon, Marc Louis (1835–1913): ceramist at Sèvres and Minton (1870–1904) specializing in *pâte-sur-pâte*.

Spode, Stoke-on-Trent, Staffordshire: 1770 pottery; porcelain and bone china from *c.*1797. Taken over by Copeland and Garrett 1833; continued under various titles, becoming Spode Ltd in 1970.

Sprimont, Nicholas (1716–71): silversmith, managed Chelsea 1749–58 and took over 1758.

Stephan, Pierre: French modeller working at Chelsea and Derby 1770–95.

Strasbourg, France: C.F. Hannong 1752–54, transferred to Frankenthal.

Swansea, Glamorgan, Wales 1814–22: see Nantgarw.

Teichert, C.: established 1863 at Meissen, products include copies of Meissen underglaze-blue wares.

Thieme, Carl, Potschappel, 19thc: mostly copies of 18thc porcelain, particularly Meissen.

Tournay, Flanders: founded 1751 by F.J. Peterinck, closed mid-19thc.

Tucker, William Ellis (d.1832), Philadelphia, USA: began a whiteware factory in Philadelphia in 1826; succeeded by brother who continued until 1838.

Union Porcelain Works, Greenpoint, New York, USA:
(i) 1863–1901 managed by Thomas C. Smith.
(ii) continued until financial failure in 1924.

Union States Pottery Co., Bennington, Vermont, USA 1849–58.

Vauxhall, London, 1751–64: Nicholas Crisp, wares formerly attributed to William Ball, Liverpool.

Venice, Italy:
(i) 1720–35 Francesco Vezzi (1651–1740) and C.K. Hunger.
(ii) 1758–63 N.F. Hewelki.
(iii) Geminiano Cozzi 1764–1812.

Vienna, 1719–1866: founded by C.I. du Paquier; state factory from 1744; directed by Konrad von Sorgenthal 1784–1805.

Vincennes: see Sèvres.

Vinovo, Italy: P.A. Hannong 1776–80; revived by Dr. Vittorio Amedeo Gioanetti (1729–1815) 1780–96; re-opened 1815–20 by Giovanni Lomello.

Vogelmann, Carl: modeller at Kelsterbach 1761–64.

Volkstedt, Thuringia, Germany, *c.*1760–present.

von Tschirnhausen, Count Ehrenfried Walter (1651–1708): experiments to discover true porcelain from 1675; with Böttger succeeds 1708.

Wallendorf, Thuringia, Germany 1764–1833.

Wedgwood, *c.*1759–present: pottery, various locations in Staffordshire; bone china from 1813–1829.

Weesp, Holland, 1757–71: relocated at Oude Loosdrecht, Holland 1771–82 and to Amstel, France 1784–1820.

Worcester, various factories:
(i) 1751 founded Dr. Wall (retired 1774, d.1776) various ownerships–present; now Royal Worcester Spode Ltd.
(ii) Chamberlain.
(iii) Grainger.
(iv) Hadley.

Würzburg, Germany, 1775–88.

Zürich, Switzerland: soft paste 1763 and then hard paste, 1765–late 19thc.

Neolithic	**8th or 7th millennium BC– 18th/16th century BC**
Shang	**18th/16th century BC–1028 BC**
Western Zhou	**1027–771**
Eastern Zhou	**771–256**
Spring and Autumn Era	**722–481**
Warring Era	**481–221**
Qin	**221–206**
Western Han	**206–12 BC**
Hsin	**12–23 AD**
Eastern Han	**25–221**
Three Kingdoms and Western Chin	**219–316**
Eastern Jin and Five Principalities	**317–419**
Nan-Pei-Ch'ao I	**420–500**
Nan-Pei-Ch'ao II	**501–580**
Sui	**581–617**
Tang	**618–906**
Five Dynasties	**907–960**
Liao	**907–1125**
Song	**960–1279**
Northern Song 960–1127	
Southern Song 1128–1279	
Jin	**1115–1234**
Yuan (Mongols)	**1280–1368**
Ming	**1368–1644**
Hongwu 1368–1398	
Jianwen 1399–1402	
Yongle 1403–1425	
Xuande 1426–1435	
Zhengtong 1436–1449	
Jingtai 1450–1457	
Tianshun 1457–1464	
Chenghua 1465–1487	
Hongzhi 1488–1505	
Zhengde 1506–1521	
Jiajing 1522–1566	
Longqing 1567–1572	
Wanli 1573–1619	
Taichang 1620	
Tianqi 1621–1627	
Chongzhen 1628–1643	
Qing	**1644–1912**
Shunzhi 1644–1661	
Kangxi 1662–1722	
Yongzheng 1723–1735	
Qianlong 1735–1795	
Jiaqing 1796–1820	
Daoguang 1821–1850	
Xianfeng 1851–1861	
Tongzhi 1862–1874	
Guangxu 1875–1908	
Xuantong 1909–1912	
Republic of China	**1912 to present**

INDEX

ACKNOWLEDGMENTS

The publisher thanks the following photographers and organizations for their kind permission to reproduce the photographs in this book:

1 By courtesy of the Trustees of the Victoria and Albert Museum; 2 National Trust Photo Library/Horst Kolo; 4 The Minton Museum, Royal Doulton; 4–5 Edimedia; 9 Mary Evans Picture Library; 10 The Antique Collector/Ronald W. Raven Collection; 16 above Ann Ronan Picture Library; 20 below Percival David Foundation of Chinese Art; 21 below National Museum of Ireland; 23 below Percival David Foundation of Chinese Art; 26 left Courtesy of the Trustees of the British Museum; 28 above Percival David Foundation of Chinese Art; 31 left Asian Art Museum of San Francisco, The Avery Brundage Collection (D81 P8); 32 right Courtesy of the Trustees of the British Museum; 33 right Asian Art Museum of San Francisco, The Avery Brundage Collection (B69 P95L); 34 By courtesy of the Trustees of the Victoria and Albert Museum; 35–39 By courtesy of the Trustees of the Victoria and Albert Museum; 50 Geoffrey Godden; 51 above The Mansell Collection; 53 above left Bernheimer Fine Arts; 53 below National Trust Photo Library/Horst Kolo; 56 below Geoffrey Godden; 58 Edimedia/J. Guillot/Connaissance Des Arts; 61 below Geoffrey Godden; 62 above Geoffrey Godden; 65 above left Geoffrey Godden; 66 Geoffrey Godden; 70 Museum het Princessehof; 71 Ashmolean Museum, Oxford; 72 left By courtesy of the Trustees of the Victoria and Albert Museum; 72 right Ashmolean Museum, Oxford; 73 left and centre Ashmolean Museum, Oxford; 73 right Courtesy of the Trustees of the British Museum; 74 left By courtesy of the Trustees of the Victoria and Albert Museum; 74 right Courtesy of the Trustees of the British Museum; 75 left By courtesy of the Trustees of the Victoria and Albert Museum; 75 above right The Burghley House Collection; 76 above left Ashmolean Museum, Oxford; 76 above right By courtesy of the Trustees of the Victoria and Albert Museum; 76 below Ashmolean Museum, Oxford; 78 The Seattle Museum, Eugene Fuller Memorial Collection, 52.102; 79 left Collections Baur, Geneva/Photographer Pierre-Alain Ferrazini; 79 right Ashmolean Museum, Oxford; 80 Ashmolean Museum, Oxford; 81 below The Mansell Collection; 86 left Réunion des Musées Nationaux; 86 right By courtesy of the Trustees of the Victoria and Albert Museum; 87 Réunion des Musées Nationaux; 88 above Eileen Tweedy/Grassi-Museum, Leipzig; 90 below left The Trustees, The Cecil Higgins Art Gallery, Bedford; 90 below right The National Trust Photo Library/Jonathan Gibson; 92 above Angelo Hornak (from Goodwood House by courtesy of the Trustees); 93 above VEB Staatliche Porzellan-Manufaktur Meissen; 93 below left VEB Staatliche Porzellan-Manufaktur Meissen; 93 below right Angelo Hornak; 95 Kunsthistorisches Museum, Vienna; 96 The National Trust Photo Library/Jonathan Gibson; 98 above The Trustees, The Cecil Higgins Art Gallery, Bedford; 100 The National Trust Photo Library/Angelo Hornak; 101 above The Trustees, The Cecil Higgins Art Gallery, Bedford; 102 below The J. Paul Getty Museum; 103 The National Trust Photo Library/M. Fiennes; 104 A y R MAS; 105 left Christie's Colour Library; 105 right Courtesy of the Trustees of the British Museum; 106 left The Trustees, The Cecil Higgins Art Gallery, Bedford; 107 left By courtesy of the Trustees of the Victoria and Albert Museum; 109 below left The National Trust, Waddesdon Manor; 110 above left Guy Bouchet/Conran Octopus; 110 below

Manufacture Nationale de Sèvres; 111 By courtesy of the Trustees of the Victoria and Albert Museum; 113 Christie's Colour Library; 116 above Mary Evans Picture Library; 116 below Fitzwilliam Museum, Cambridge; 117 By courtesy of the Trustees of the Victoria and Albert Museum; 118 Courtesy City of Bristol Museum & Art Gallery; 119 above The Trustees, The Cecil Higgins Art Gallery, Bedford; 119 below Simon Spero; 120 above Fitzwilliam Museum, Cambridge; 120 below By courtesy of the Trustees of the Victoria and Albert Museum; 121 above left National Trust Photo Library/Jonathan Gibson; 121 above right By courtesy of the Trustees of the Victoria and Albert Museum; 121 below Bridgeman Art Library/Victoria and Albert Museum; 122 above Fitzwilliam Museum, Cambridge; 123 left Fitzwilliam Museum, Cambridge; 123 right By courtesy of the Trustees of the Victoria and Albert Museum; 124 By courtesy of the Trustees of the Victoria and Albert Museum; 125 above By courtesy of the Trustees of the Victoria and Albert Museum; 125 below Simon Spero; 126 above left City of Bristol Museum & Art Gallery; 126 above right The Dyson Perrins Museum Trust; 128 City of Derby Museums and Art Gallery; 129 above Lincolnshire County Council, Recreational Services: Usher Gallery, Lincoln; 129 below The Trustees, The Cecil Higgins Art Gallery, Bedford; 130 The Trustees, The Cecil Higgins Art Gallery, Bedford; 131 Royal Institution of Cornwall County Museum and Art Gallery (From the Edgar Rees Collection); 132 above By courtesy of the Trustees of the Victoria and Albert Museum; 133 above By courtesy of the Trustees of the Victoria and Albert Museum; 133 below Royal Institution of Cornwall County Museum and Art Gallery (From the Edgar Rees Collection); 135 above right City of Bristol Museum & Art Gallery; 135 below left City of Bristol Museum & Art Gallery; 135 below right National Trust Photo Library/Jonathan Gibson; 138 Norfolk Museums Service (Norwich Castle Museum); 139 above Fitzwilliam Museum, Cambridge; 141 above left Lincolnshire County Council, Recreational Services: Usher Gallery, Lincoln; 141 below Lincolnshire County Council, Recreational Services: Usher Gallery, Lincoln; 142 National Museum & Galleries on Merseyside, Liverpool Museum; 143 above left Fitzwilliam Museum, Cambridge; 145 below The Minton Museum, Royal Doulton; 146 above Christie's Colour Library; 147 Jimmy Jones; 148 above Jimmy Jones; 148 below National Museum of Wales; 149 below By Courtesy of the Wedgwood Museum Trustees, Barlaston, Stoke-on-Trent, Staffordshire; 154 right Kölnisches Stadt Museum; 155 centre Réunion des Musées Nationaux; 155 right Macdonald/Aldus Archive; 156 above Musée Nationale Adrien-Dubouche, Limoges; 157 above Musée Nationale Adrien-Dubouche, Limoges; 162 By courtesy of the Trustees of the Victoria and Albert Museum; 163 below Edimedia; 164 above Museum für Angewandte Kunst; 164 below Bauhaus-Archiv; 165 below By courtesy of the Trustees of the Victoria and Albert Museum; 168 The Minton Museum, Royal Doulton; 169 above The Minton Museum, Royal Doulton; 170–171 The Minton Museum, Royal Doulton; 172 Phillips, London; 173 above The Dyson Perrins Museum Trust; 174 right The Dyson Perrins Museum Trust; 176 The Royal Crown Derby Museum; 177 left Susannah Price/Conran Octopus (Private Collection); 178 above Royal Pavilion, Art Gallery and Museums, Brighton; 179 right By Courtesy of the Wedgwood Museum Trustees, Barlaston, Stoke-on-Trent, Staffordshire; 180 above By courtesy of the Trustees of the Victoria and Albert Museum;

181 left Royal Doulton; 183 above Collection of the Newark Museum (Gift of Sara Carr 1924); 183 below left Collection of Mr. & Mrs. George M. Kaufman, courtesy of The Metropolitan Museum of New York; 183 below right William Doyle Galleries.

The following photographs were taken especially for Conran Octopus by:

SUSANNAH PRICE
City Museum and Art Gallery, Stoke-on-Trent
132 below (4213), 135 above left (260), 143 above right (169158), 143 below (courtesy Geoffrey Godden), 144 (courtesy Geoffrey Godden), 146 below (234P1982), 149 above (52P1975), 180 below (Gift of Mary Pratt and Rachel Lorking in memory of Mrs M. Stewart)

The Ironbridge Gorge Museum Trust
140, 178 below (collection A31), 179 left (collection 1989 3393)

Spode Museum Trust
145 above, 177 centre and right

SIMON LEE
Design Museum
165 above

The following photographs were provided by Sotheby's:

Sotheby's London/photography Ken Adler; 40, 48, 68, 84, 114, 136, 150, 166

Sotheby's Billingshurst 32 left, 82–83, 173 below, 175

Sotheby's Geneva 11, 90 above, 112, 152 below

Sotheby's Hong Kong 22, 25 below, 42, 43 right, 45 above, 47, 99

Sotheby's London 6, 14, 16 below, 17–19, 20 above, 21 above, 23 above, 23 centre, 24, 25 above, 26 right, 26 below, 27, 28 below left, 28 below right, 29, 30, 31 right, 33 left, 44, 45 below, 46, 51 below, 53 above right, 54, 55, 56 above, 57, 59 above, 61 above and centre, 64, 65 above right, 65 below, 67, 75 below right, 77, 81 above, 88 below, 89 right, 91, 94, 97 right, 102 above, 106 right, 107 right, 108, 109 above, 109 below right, 110 above right, 122 below, 126 below, 127, 139 below, 141 above right, 152 above, 153, 154 left, 155 left, 156 below, 157 above, 158, 159 above, 160, 161, 163 above, 169 below, 174 left and centre, 181 right, 185–191

Sotheby's Monaco 59 below, 60, 62 below, 63 left

Sotheby's New York 63 right, 89 left, 92 below, 96 above, 97 left, 98 below, 101 below, 159 below, 182